COLLABORATIVE GOVERNANCE REGIMES

Public Management and Change Series

Beryl A. Radin, *Series Editor*

Editorial Board

Selected Titles in the Series

COLLABORATIVE GOVERNANCE REGIMES

Kirk Emerson and Tina Nabatchi

Georgetown University Press
Washington, DC

Library of Congress Cataloging-in-Publication Data

Emerson, Kirk, author.
    Collaborative governance regimes / Kirk Emerson and Tina Nabatchi.
        pages cm —   (Public management and change series)
    Includes bibliographical references and index.
    Summary: Collaboration among public agencies, across different governmental levels, and/or with the private and civic sectors and the public is increasingly called on to handle the complex, multi-jurisdictional challenges we face in the 21st century. Experiments in collaborative public management, multi-partner governance, joined-up or network government, hybrid sectoral arrangements, co-management regimes, participatory governance, and civic engagement have evolved, and, in some cases, transformed the way the public's business is getting done. The growth of these innovative collaborative governance systems has outpaced scholarship. While the academic literature has spawned numerous case studies and context- or policy-specific models for collaboration, there have been few efforts to integrate extant knowledge into a framework that is broadly applicable for both research and practice and across sectors, settings, and scales. This book seeks to fill that gap.
    ISBN 978-1-62616-252-5 (hc : alk. paper) — ISBN 978-1-62616-253-2 (pb : alk. paper) — ISBN 978-1-62616-254-9 (eb)
    1. Public administration—North America. 2. Intergovernmental cooperation—North America. 3. Interagency coordination—North America. 4. Public–private sector cooperation—North America. I. Nabatchi, Tina, author. II. Title. III. Series: Public management and change.
    JJ1010.E45 2015
    352.3—dc23   2015007454

16 15   9 8 7 6 5 4 3 2 First printing

Printed in the United States of America

Cover design by N. Putens

For all those who study and practice collaboration across the challenging divides of institutions, sectors, disciplines, and interpersonal difference.

Contents

Part IV: Collaborative Governance Regimes

List of Illustrations

Preface

This book has been years in the making. Almost everyone in the fields of public administration, public policy, political science, conflict resolution, and public participation has at least a passing acquaintance with the term "collaborative governance," but few would claim close familiarity. Practitioners are still experimenting with different ways of working across institutional and sectoral divides, and researchers are still exploring how best to conceptualize and study collaborative governance.

As "pracademics" in conflict management, consensus building, and public participation, we began our research on collaborative governance in 2009, wanting to expand our knowledge by drawing on a vast array of multidisciplinary scholarship, the professional and applied literature, and our own experiences in practice. Early in our efforts, we became intrigued with the sheer diversity of ways in which one can think about collaborative governance—is it a process, an institution, or a network? We grappled with fundamental questions of structure, context, and agency, and we were forced to think about our own normative and instrumental assumptions. This book is the result of these efforts.

We hope, and expect, that this book will be useful for a wide variety of readers—scholars and researchers who want a framework for their theory building and empirical studies, graduate students from multiple disciplines who are trying to make sense of collaborative governance and its diverse literatures, public managers who want (or need) to work across institutional boundaries to address problems, practitioners who are trying to improve their collaborative work, and advocates for governance reforms and innovations.

Acknowledgments

We are deeply indebted to the scholars, practitioners, conveners, public managers, and others who care about public governance and who have worked tirelessly to lead, study, organize, and promote collaboration across boundaries. This book would not have been possible without their insightful research and discoveries during the past several decades.

We are grateful to the many people who provided invaluable comments on our work, including the editors and anonymous reviewers of this book, as well as the reviewers of our first article on this topic, which appeared in the *Journal of Public Administration and Theory and Research* in 2012. We are also grateful to Michael McGuire, Rosemary O'Leary, and Jos Raadschelders, who offered excellent feedback on our draft proposal for this book. We are particularly appreciative of Craig Thomas for his encouragement and critical insights on both our original article and this book.

We also want to acknowledge the support provided by the Program for the Advancement of Research on Conflict and Collaboration at Syracuse University's Maxwell School of Citizenship and Public Affairs, as well as by the University of Arizona's School of Government and Public Policy. Their financial support helped to provide honoraria for our case authors and to underwrite the graphic designs of our framework by Raquel Goodrich—who did a stellar job. In addition, we want to thank Emma Ertinger, a candidate for a master's in public administration degree at the Maxwell School, who helped with editing and reference checking.

Finally, we would like to thank our case authors—Allison Bramwell, Robin Bronen, Andrea K. Gerlak, Tanya Heikkila, and Chantelise Pells—for contributing their own research to this book. Their case illustrations and studies enriched our understanding of collaborative governance regimes and, we trust, that of our readers. We are also grateful to Patrick Callan and Noreen Savelle, both of the National Center for Public Policy and Higher Education, for their review of the case illustration on the National Collaborative for Higher Education.

Part I

An Overview of Collaborative Governance

Introduction
Stepping In: The Context for Collaborative Governance

Gettin' good players is easy. Gettin' 'em to play together
is the hard part.
—Casey Stengel, "The Old Perfessor"

People have been working together to address shared problems since the beginning of civilization, and, over time, they have devised many ingenious ways of organizing to accomplish collective endeavors. One of the most successful organizational approaches has been the creation of the state as separate from society, and, with that, the development of bureaucracy and hierarchy (Fukuyama 2011; Raadschelders, Vigoda-Gadot, and Kisner 2015). The nature of that separation has ebbed and flowed over centuries of experimentation. By the mid–twentieth century, the structural divide between the public and private sectors in the United States was probably at its peak, as the New Deal and federal initiatives in the aftermath of World War II expanded and solidified governmental functions (Fukuyama 2014).

By the turn of the twenty-first century, however, the public/private divide had softened, if not crumbled, as the state hollowed out, the private contracting of public work expanded, and myriad nongovernmental organizations emerged to fill the gaps (Goldsmith and Eggers 2004; Kettl 2002; Light 2002). By necessity, people in various organizations started working directly together across institutional and sectoral boundaries. Today, distinctions between the public, private, and nonprofit sectors are far less clear or rigid, and the hierarchies within the sectors are far more permeable (Kettl 2006). Although structural, political, and cultural impediments to crossing these divides still endure, an increasing demand for cross-boundary collaboration continues to fuel the growth and experimentation with collaborative governance arrangements.

Along with this experimentation has come an explosion of research- and practice-based interest. Scholars and students are seeking to understand these new collaborative arrangements, while practitioners are seeking to improve their collaborative efforts. Elected and professional government officials are searching for more effective and efficient ways of collaborating to get public work done, while civic reformers and activists are looking to increase responsiveness and equity through collaborative governance. Yet despite this broad and growing interest, and the consequent wealth of academic- and practitioner-oriented research, many questions remain. How do collaborative efforts actually work? What do they have in common, and how are they different? Are they successful? How can they be improved? These were among the many questions that prompted us to begin research on collaborative governance in 2009. We continue to explore these questions in this book.

Our research led us not to an overarching theory of collaborative governance but rather to a framework that integrates the different pieces of the collaborative governance puzzle into a dynamic system—what we call a "collaborative governance regime" (CGR). We first presented our integrative framework for collaborative governance in a 2012 article in the *Journal of Public Administration Research and Theory* (Emerson, Nabatchi, and Balogh 2012). Since then, we have received feedback from practitioners and academics at conferences and workshops around the world. On the basis of their comments, innumerable conversations with colleagues, and our continuing research, we have refined our framework and deepened our understanding of CGRs. This book is the result of these efforts.

When we started writing this book, we knew that in addition to our own experiences with and research on collaborative governance, we also wanted to include others' perspectives on and applications of the integrative framework for collaborative governance. To facilitate this, we issued a call for case studies and illustrations that use our integrative framework as an analytic device. From nearly a dozen proposals, we selected four cases written by contributors, and we added two of our own. In selecting these cases, we wanted a diverse range of examples that included what we (and others) had observed were important distinguishing characteristics of collaborative governance arrangements—the scale of the issue and locus of participants (i.e., local, regional, national), the size of the collaborating body (i.e., the number of participants engaged), and the specific policy arena (e.g., place-based or policy-oriented). For broader appeal, we were also interested in a geographic range of cases. That the cases turned out to be located in the United States, Mexico, and Canada was frankly serendipitous. As a result, the shorter case illustrations and more in-depth case studies throughout this book provide excellent examples of the breadth and complexity of CGRs across America. Consider the following brief case overviews:

- In light of ongoing concerns about higher education in the United States, but despite heavy competition for a finite supply of students, several state governments opted to work with public and private colleges and universities and with national educational groups to set priorities for improving higher education policies.

- After years of conflict and concern over the degradation of the Everglades, the US Congress mandated that federal, state, local, and tribal governments work together to restore this culturally and environmentally significant ecosystem in South Florida.

- As Tucson grappled with concerns about potentially hazardous levels of noise from military jets during training sorties from a nearby air force base, an independent convener was employed to help the community and the base move from contentious debate to collaborative negotiations and decisions.

- After decades of struggling with complex governance challenges and policy gaps in the greater Toronto metropolitan region, a wide array of political, administrative, and civic leaders coalesced to better address political, social, environmental, and other social needs.

- When a remote Alaska Native village began collapsing into the Bering Sea as eroding coastal storms and melting permafrost made it uninhabitable, federal, state, and tribal governments began working together to relocate the community—despite the fact that no single government or agency had the specific responsibility or resources to solve the problem.

- When Mexico reorganized its national water law in 1992 and decentralized local groundwater management, community actors were given the opportunity to collaborate and change long-standing economic and cultural power imbalances.

Before we can examine the integrative framework and cases, however, we must first set the stage for this book. With this introductory chapter, we invite readers to step in and explore the context of collaborative governance. We begin by briefly discussing the growing demand for collaborative governance, focusing particularly on "wicked" problems (defined below) and the changing nature of governance, and exploring how those trends have contributed to experimentation with collaborative governance arrangements. Next, we explain the purposes behind this book and the specific contributions we seek to make to the field of collaborative governance. We conclude with a brief review of the book's content and organization.

The Demand for Collaborative Governance

The rise of collaborative governance can be attributed to many factors, but two long-standing trends are particularly salient. First, "wicked problems"—a term coined by Rittel and Weber (1973) that refers to problems that are difficult or impossible to solve because of incomplete or contradictory information, rapidly shifting environments, and complex interdependencies—are increasing (Head 2008). Examples of wicked problems abound, ranging from domestic issues—such as the impoverishment of education, health care, and justice systems; the crumbling of transportation, utility, energy, and other infrastructure systems; and recurring crises in housing, financial, and industrial markets—to international and global issues, such as climate change, food and water shortages, infectious disease, human trafficking, and the illegal arms trade.

Second, just as the number and complexity of public problems are growing, so, too, is the context in which these problems must be solved becoming more complex: "Sustainable resources for public agencies and programs are diminishing on a daily basis. . . . Public coffers are strained, and in some cases, completely drained; . . . public sector labor markets are largely broken and in distress; and . . . fungible supplies of political support for policies and programs are declining at break-neck pace across all levels of government and throughout the world" (Nabatchi, Goerdel, and Peffer 2011, i29). In the following discussion, we briefly unpack these two trends, explaining how the rise of wicked problems and the changing context of governance are contributing to the demand for cross-boundary collaboration.

The Rise of Wicked Problems

There are tame problems, and there are wicked problems. Tame problems are well defined and easily addressed. For example, nearly 58 million Americans are eligible to receive Social Security benefits from the federal government; the Social Security Administration issues and mails monthly checks to recipients across the nation. During the winter, ice forms and expands beneath the surface of the state roads, creating frost heaves; in the spring, state and local departments of transportation send crews and equipment to make the needed repairs. Storms sometimes cause flooding, leading to sewerage overages that affect municipal water quality; the local utility provider regularly tests water safety and informs the public about problems. These tame problems are well defined and have obvious solutions that can be objectively evaluated. Of course, implementation of their solutions—issuing checks, scheduling road maintenance, or reporting test results—is sometimes complicated; but, in general, the responsible organization uses its expertise and management systems to address tame problems with relative ease.

Increasingly, however, twenty-first-century problems are wicked—they are not tame, and their solutions are not simple. Income inequality—measured as the share of total income going to different sections of the population—is now at or near the highest levels on record in the United States, threatening economic growth, people's quality of life, and the stability of political and financial systems. Climate change is warming the atmosphere and oceans, resulting in (among other issues) rising sea levels that threaten island nations and coastal communities, extreme and prolonged weather events that harm and displace large, vulnerable populations around the world, and shifting patterns of agricultural production that cause food and water shortages. Human trafficking is exploding; every year, between 600,000 and 800,000 people—the majority of whom are women and children—are trafficked across international borders in a global industry that annually generates about $32 billion in profits.

These wicked problems are dynamic and complex, with no clear definition and no obvious solution. They involve multiple stakeholders in multiple organizations across multiple jurisdictions who may see and understand the problem and solution differently. Because wicked problems ignore the boundaries that shape our public sphere, the responses to these problems must transcend these boundaries, including governmental, sectoral, jurisdictional, geographic, and even conceptual demarcations. In short, the fact that wicked problems cannot be addressed by a single organization acting alone is encouraging collaborative governance.

The Changing Context of Governance

More than forty years ago, Harlan Cleveland (1972, 13) observed that people want "less government and more governance." His vision of government was one where the "organizations that get things done" serve as "systems . . . in which control is loose, power diffused, and centers of decision plural"; where "decision making" is an "intricate process of multilateral brokerage both inside and outside the [responsible] organization"; where organizations are "horizontal" and "more collegial, consensual, and consultative"; and where "the bigger the problems to be tackled, the more real power is diffused and the larger the number of persons who can exercise it—if they work at it." Some aspects of Cleveland's vision have not materialized; many organizations remain hierarchical, with few vestiges of collegial, consensual, and consultative behavior. However, other aspects of his vision have emerged; we now live in a networked world filled with multilateral decision making and big problems that involve many people and diffuse sources of power. In any case, the context of governance has changed considerably since Cleveland's observation, and it continues to evolve.

Government used to do the public's work directly. This is no longer always true. Devolution, decentralization, and other related forces have shifted the provision of public goods and services from the federal government to state and local governments. In turn, the rise of market-based tools—such as contracting, commercialization, partnerships, grants, outsourcing, concession arrangements, and privatization—has enabled government to further extend previously public responsibilities beyond its boundaries to the private and nonprofit sectors (Kettl 2006). Together, these forces have given rise to the "hollow state"—a metaphor for the shrinking of government and loss of direct public services (Milward and Provan 2000)—and also to the "fragmented and disarticulated state" (Frederickson 1999, 702)—where "jurisdictions of all types—nation-states, states, provinces, cities, counties, and special districts—are losing their borders." As a result of these changes, public goods and services are now being provided by elaborate networks of indirect administrative approaches conducted by myriad organizations in the public, private, and nonprofit sectors (Goldsmith and Eggers 2004; Kettl 2006; Light 2002; Salamon 2002). The work needed to organize, direct, and manage these networks greatly enhances the opportunities and incentives for collaborative governance.

This shift to complex, networked arrangements is not the only change in the governance context. We also are seeing extraordinary, and regularly occurring, fiscal upheavals and policy crises. Government is plagued by gridlock, highly polarized policy debates, and an inability to agree on seemingly commonsense measures. The result has been not only a decline in political and budgetary support for policies and programs but also a reduction in problem-solving capacities. In turn, this has helped produce the highest levels of citizen distrust and frustration—indeed, disgust—with government that we have ever seen (Steinhauser 2014). However, citizens are now equipped with technological tools that enable them to connect with each other—and with government agencies, private institutions, and civil society organizations—in ways unimagined just a few decades ago. They are increasingly using these tools to demand government responsiveness and effective solutions (Nabatchi and Leighninger 2015).

In sum, we now live in a world that is increasingly beset by wicked problems that must be addressed in a continually evolving, complex governance context. Governments at all levels in the United States, and in nations around the world, have been trying to adapt to these new conditions. "Collaborative governance," an umbrella term for myriad cross-boundary, multi-institutional arrangements, is not only a significant adaptive response to these conditions but is also spurring tremendous innovation.

Experiments with Collaborative Governance Arrangements

There is considerable diversity in the forms, functions, and scales of collaborative governance arrangements. Several decades of experimentation and innovation have led to numerous variations—ranging from intergovernmental and interstate arrangements, interagency work, and "joined up" government to public service contracting, public–private partnerships, co-management and adaptive management systems, and local multistakeholder collaboratives. During the last few decades, emerging systems of collaborative governance have attracted the attention of scholars and practitioners around the world working in multiple disciplines, including public administration, public policy, political science, conflict resolution, planning, and environmental studies (Ansell and Gash 2008; Bingham and O'Leary 2008).

Scholars are working to catch up with the advances in the practice of collaborative governance, and new knowledge is being produced rapidly—ranging from case studies of particular instances or forms of collaborative governance to research on the structures for and processes of collaboration to empirical analyses of leadership skills for collaboration. Some scholars connect these new arrangements to the historic study of intergovernmental cooperation in the 1960s (e.g., Agranoff and McGuire 2003; Wright 1988; Elazar 1962, 1984), whereas others trace their roots back to the birth of American federalism itself—"the most enduring model of collaborative problem resolution" (McGuire 2006, 34). Some examine collaborative governance through theoretical lenses, such as group theory (Bentley 1949), collective action (Olsen 1965), and institutional analysis (Ostrom 1990). Other scholars connect it to broader concepts of public administration and democracy (e.g., Frederickson 1991; Jun 2002; Kettl 2002) or to citizen participation (e.g., Fung and Wright 2001; Nabatchi 2010; Sirianni 2009; Torres 2003), whereas still others focus more specifically on public management (e.g., Agranoff and McGuire 2001a; Kettl 2006; McGuire 2006).

This diversity of research approaches is mirrored in the work of practitioners who have advanced best practices. Some of this work focuses on collaborative governance writ large (e.g., Bardach 1998; Carlson 2007; Donahue and Zechauser 2011; Emerson and Smutko 2011; Henton et al. 2005), but often it is situated within the context of alternative dispute resolution, which is not surprising, given collaboration's historic roots in that field (Koontz and Thomas 2006). For example, some practitioners have focused on methods for convening groups and ensuring diverse participation (e.g., Margerum 2011). Others have looked at how to foster principled engagement, for example, through ground rules (e.g., Schwarz 1995), consensus building (e.g., Carlson and Arthur 1999), and interest-based negotiation (e.g., O'Leary and Bingham 2007). Our search for the commonalities across these variations in applications and disciplines led us to develop our integrative framework for collaborative governance (Emerson, Nabatchi, and Balogh 2012), which we further explore and advance in this book.

The Purposes of This Book

In this book, we seek to improve the study and practice of collaborative governance. We do so by focusing on four major goals. First, we try to make sense of the numerous terms and concepts associated with collaborative governance. Scholars and practitioners have defined collaborative governance in myriad ways, and have introduced numerous terms for describing various collaborative governance arrangements. This accumulation of terms and definitions is not only confusing but also has led to imprecision, which is hindering the study and practice of collaborative governance. To address this issue, we offer a broader, integrative definition of collaborative governance: the processes and structures of public policy decision making and management that enable people to engage across boundaries. We also introduce and develop the concept of a collaborative governance regime: a system for public decision making in which cross-boundary collaboration represents the prevailing pattern of behavior and activity (Emerson, Nabatchi, and Balogh 2012).

Second, we encourage more systematic study of collaborative governance and CGRs. Many scholars and practitioners have explored and introduced very useful frameworks for collaborative governance (e.g., Ansell and Gash 2008; Bryson, Crosby, and Stone 2006; Margerum 2011; Thomson and Perry 2006). We build on these efforts and integrate them into a multidimensional framework that is generalizable, or more broadly applicable across settings, scales, and other variations in collaborative governance arrangements.

Third, we try to make sense of the considerable variations in collaborative arrangements and to identify the different basic types of CGRs. Scholars and practitioners have long recognized that collaborative arrangements are neither alike nor equal, and many have developed typologies to capture and explain variations (e.g., Cheng and Daniels 2005; Cheng, Kruger, and Daniels 2003; Gray 1989; Henton et al. 2005; Moore and Koontz 2003; Margerum 2011). After studying a range of CGRs, some of which are presented in this book, we introduce a typology organized around how CGRs form and subsequently develop.

Fourth and finally, we seek to contribute to the empirical study of CGRs' performance. Most scholars and practitioners recognize that collaboration is hard work, and that sometimes, despite the best efforts of participants, CGRs fail to live up to their potential. Assessing the performance of collaborative governance systems is conceptually and methodologically challenging. We introduce an approach to CGR performance assessment that provides more clarity in addressing some of these challenges. We emphasize the performance of both the CGR's collaborative process (or its collaboration dynamics, as we call it) and its productivity (the actions, outcomes, and adaptation generated by its collaboration dynamics).

An Overview of This Book

This book is organized into four parts. Although each chapter draws from and builds upon earlier ones, the parts of the book may be read either in sequence or independently. Part I, in which we broadly explore the study of collaborative governance and CGRs, will be helpful for all readers. In addition to this introduction, chapter 1 provides a bird's-eye view of our topic. Specifically, we introduce the concept of collaborative governance, explore its genesis and definitions, and discuss its historical and theoretical perspectives. We also summarize the integrative framework for collaborative governance and explain how it applies to a variety of contexts and applications.

Part II moves from the bird's-eye view of collaborative governance to a more detailed exploration of how collaborative governance works. We do this by taking readers step-by-step through our integrative framework in a series of chapters. Each chapter presents a specific set of dimensions, components, and elements of the framework, and provides brief case illustrations. Given the in-depth focus on the integrative framework for collaborative governance, part II may be of particular interest to scholars.

In chapter 2 we focus on the surrounding system context—that is, the broader set of conditions—that influences the formation and performance of CGRs. We also explore the four drivers that are essential to the formation of a CGR. The system context, the drivers, and regime formation are illustrated with a short case on the National Collaborative for Higher Education Policy.

In chapter 3 we concentrate on the central components of collaboration dynamics, including principled engagement, which focuses on behavioral elements; shared motivation, which focuses on interpersonal elements; and the capacity for joint action, which focuses on functional elements. Collaboration dynamics are illustrated with a detailed case about the Everglades Restoration Task Force, by Tanya Heikkila and Andrea Gerlak.

In chapter 4 we explore the CGR production chain: the actions that emerge from collaboration dynamics, the outcomes that result from these actions, and the internal and external adaptation that can occur as a consequence. We illustrate this production chain with a short case about the Military Community Compatibility Committee.

Part III moves from considering the framework's components to illustrating it as a whole through three in-depth case studies of CGRs. The contributing authors use the integrative framework to provide accounts of specific CGRs in Canada, the United States, and Mexico. Given the illustrative nature of these cases, part III should be particularly useful for graduate students and practitioners.

In chapter 5 Allison Bramwell describes the Greater Toronto Civic Action Alliance which was initiated by regional leaders to address complex governance challenges and policy gaps in Canada's largest urban region. Through this CGR, political and administrative officials from the federal, provincial, and municipal governments, along with business and community leaders, were engaged to promote community-based civic action in the politically fragmented and socially diverse Toronto metropolitan region. As a CGR, the Civic Action Alliance evolved over time to address several critical, crosscutting challenges.

In chapter 6 Robin Bronen describes the Newtok Planning Group, an ad hoc CGR of twenty-five tribal, state, federal, and nongovernmental agencies and organizations that are dedicated to relocating the Yup'ik Eskimo community in Newtok, Alaska, to higher ground. The acute environmental conditions affecting the community's public health and safety that necessitate this relocation, along with the absence of any one responsible public agency, required collaboration and led to the creation of this CGR. Newtok's tribal government continues to lead this effort, in partnership with Alaska's Department of Commerce, Community, and Economic Development.

In chapter 7 Chantelise Pells describes the Comité Técnicas de Aguas Subterraneas (COTAS) Guadalupe, a local CGR involving groundwater users. After the decentralization of water use mandated by Mexico's 1992 Water Law, COTAS Guadalupe was created to improve groundwater management at the subbasin level through the broader participation of water users in coordination with watershed councils and government representatives. Though this CGR has had limited autonomy and guidance, and has faced many initial challenges, it continues to evolve.

Part IV builds on the integrative framework to provide a foundation for further theorizing and empirical research. Specifically, we present our typology of CGRs, approach to performance assessment, and recommendations for designing and managing CGRs. Given the focus on theory, research, and practice, part IV should be useful for all readers.

In chapter 8 we begin with an exploration of other relevant typologies and then present our CGR typology, which is based on how CGRs are formed and takes a path-dependent approach to their continued development and performance. We identify and describe three specific formative types of CGRs—self-initiated, independently convened, and externally directed—each of which is distinguished by a set of prevailing conditions and characteristics, as well as by initial patterns of collaboration dynamics. Throughout the chapter, we return to the cases to illustrate our typology.

In chapter 9 we review some of the key challenges for evaluating CGRs' performance and lay out our approach to performance assessment. We address issues of performance measurement, and provide potential indicators, data sources, and methods for assessing the antecedents and formation of CGRs, as well as for assessing their process and productivity.

Finally, in the conclusion we offer summary observations on and recommendations for collaborative governance and CGRs. On the basis of our framework, the CGR typology, and the cases described in the book, we also provide recommendations for practitioners on how to improve the design and management of CGRs, as well as suggestions for scholars on future research topics.

With this overview in mind, we invite readers to step in to the world of collaborative governance and collaborative governance regimes.

CHAPTER 1

Collaborative Governance and Collaborative Governance Regimes

The world is a thing of utter inordinate complexity and richness and
strangeness that is absolutely awesome.
—Douglas Adams

"Collaborative governance" has become quite a buzzword in the world of
twenty-first-century public administration and management. It is used both
intentionally and casually to refer to all sorts of endeavors that involve working on public policy issues beyond the confines of governmental bureaucracies. We would like to clarify the meaning of "collaborative governance,"
but doing so first requires definitional work and an exploration of associated
terms and concepts.

There are, however, several challenges for such an exploration. First, "collaborative governance," as a concept and a term, has a complex provenance.
The first use of the term dates back several decades, and it has since been
splashed across the headlines in both the academic and professional worlds.
Second, the term is used in practice and scholarship in many different ways,
which makes it difficult to synthesize, define, and evaluate. Practice and research on collaborative governance, collaborative public management, public–private partnerships, local watershed associations, community-based
collaborations, and myriad other applications have been growing since the
1980s (e.g., Goldsmith and Eggers 2004; Gray 1989; Kettl 2006; McGuire 2006;
Sabatier et al. 2005). Third, collaborative governance is "an idea that resonates
with many," which has led to both a great diversity of views and ideas and
"101 definitions" of the term (O'Leary and Vij 2012, 508).

To begin our exploration, we open this chapter by presenting some definitions and explaining how we understand and use terms associated with the
concept of collaborative governance. Next, we discuss some of the many
approaches that have been used to study cross-boundary collaboration and
that have influenced our thinking about collaborative governance regimes

(CGRs). We then present our integrative framework for collaborative governance. Finally, we discuss some of the most salient variations among CGRs and conclude with a chapter summary.

Defining Our Terms

We begin with *governance*, a seemingly simple term with many complex meanings. "Governance" (a gerund or noun derived from a verb) can be applied to the public, private, or non-profit sector. In general, governance refers to the act of governing, or how actors use processes and make decisions to exercise authority and control, grant power, take action, and ensure performance—all of which are guided by sets of principles, norms, roles, and procedures around which actors converge (see Frederickson 2007). However, and as we suggested in the introduction, the nature of governance is changing, and so too is the notion of public governance.

Public governance has become something different and more encompassing than just government; it also describes processes and institutions for public decision making and action that include actors from both government and other sectors (cf. Kettl 2002; Morse and Stephens 2012). Specifically, we view *public governance* as systems of (1) "laws, administrative rules, judicial rulings, and practices that constrain, prescribe, and enable . . . the production and delivery of publicly supported goods and services" (Lynn, Heinrich, and Hill 2000, 235) and that (2) "guide collective decision making . . . [by the] groups of individuals or organisations or systems of organisations making decisions" (Stoker 2004, 3).

As the meaning of public governance has expanded, so too has its scholarly and practical use. In his Gaus Lecture, George Frederickson (1999) declared that the study and practice of public administration have become the study and practice of governance, and that the new cross-boundary forms of governance have extended well beyond traditional approaches to government service. Similarly, Goldsmith and Eggers (2004, 7) wrote, "The traditional, hierarchical model of government simply does not meet the demands of this complex, rapidly changing age. Rigid bureaucratic systems that operate with command-and-control procedures, narrow work restrictions, and inward-looking cultures and operational models are particularly ill suited to addressing problems that often transcend organizational boundaries." This has led some scholars to assert that the "new governance" (Salamon 2002) is made up of horizontal networks involving public, private, and nonprofit organizations rather than simply hierarchical organizations (Bingham, Nabatchi, and

O'Leary 2005). In short, modern governance is understood to be more horizontal in nature, more cross-boundary, and more collaborative.

The collaborative nature of modern governance has inspired numerous explorations of the term *collaboration*. On its face, the word "collaboration" is relatively easy to understand, being derived from Latin and literally meaning to co-labor or work together. Early and eloquently, Barbara Gray (1985, 912) defined the act of collaborating in a multiparty setting as "the pooling of appreciations and/or tangible resources (e.g., information, money, labor) by two or more stakeholders to solve a set of problems which neither can solve individually." Implicit in this definition is the impetus for collaboration (shared problems that cannot be solved alone), as well as the multifaceted attitudes, behaviors, and resources of people working together toward this shared goal.

More recently and more specifically, Richard Margerum (2011, 6) defined collaboration as "an approach to solving complex problems in which a diverse group of autonomous stakeholders deliberates to build consensus and develop networks for translating consensus to results." He adds to the characterization of collaboration the individual, diverse, and independent actors who, on and with their own authority, develop internal agreements that are implemented through external networks. Both of these definitions shape our understanding of collaborative governance.

In this book we sometimes refer to *cross-boundary collaboration* when we speak generically about the need for or the activity of collaboration among people from different organizations, sectors, or jurisdictions (Agranoff and Rinkle 1986; Bardach 1998; Thomas 2003). Cross-boundary collaboration, however, is not synonymous or interchangeable with collaborative governance, which we view as an interactive system that evolves over time. However, cross-boundary collaboration may be considered a precursor to collaborative governance, and ultimately to the creation of a CGR.

Although the merging of the words "collaborative" and "governance" is a relatively new phenomenon, the combined term is used frequently, in many different settings, by many different scholars and practitioners, and with many different meanings. The earliest published use of "collaborative governance" we found was in two 1978 articles in the education journal *Theory into Practice*, where the term was used to refer to new structures for facilitating in-service teaching and teaching centers (Howey and Joyce 1978; Yarger and Yarger 1978). Almost two decades later, the term resurfaced in the education field, where it was used to refer to community-based education models (Chaskin and Richman 1992; Finn-Stevenson and Stern 1997).

In practice, one of the earliest formal uses of the term was in 1997, when the Institute for Patient Care Services at Massachusetts General Hospital established its Collaborative Governance Program. The Institute defined collaborative governance as "the decision-making process that places the authority, responsibility and accountability for patient care with practicing clinicians. Collaborative governance is based on the beliefs that a shared vision and common goals lead to a highly committed and productive workforce, that participation is empowering, and that people will make appropriate decisions when sufficient knowledge is known and communicated" (Institute for Patient Care Services and Massachusetts General Hospital 2002).

In academia, the first institution to incorporate the moniker in its name was the Weil Program on Collaborative Governance, which was established in 2002 at the John F. Kennedy School of Government at Harvard University. Early working papers for the Weil Program by Mark Moore (2002) and John Donahue (2004) placed an emphasis on the added value of private-sector expertise and knowledge that could be brought to bear on public-sector problems. Subsequent associated scholarship explored cases of *distributed* collaborative governance in Europe in the 1990s, focusing on classes of subnational approaches to public–private partnerships and governing arrangements that drew on corporate and community stakeholders (e.g., Culpepper 2004).

Other institutions, building on the practice of conflict resolution and the nascent deliberative democracy movement, emphasized the collaborative dimension of the term. In 2005, the William and Flora Hewlett Foundation issued a *Guide for Grantmakers* on collaborative governance (Henton et al. 2005), and the Policy Consensus Initiative at Portland State University initiated the University Network for Collaborative Governance in 2008. In both instances, their definitions of collaborative governance encompassed forums for public deliberation, community problem solving, and multistakeholder dispute resolution.

In 2006, a policy-oriented research Consortium on Collaborative Governance was organized jointly by the Bedrosian Center at the University of Southern California's Sol Price School of Public Policy (at the time, called the School of Policy, Planning, and Development); the School of Government and Public Policy (previously, the School of Public Administration and Policy) at the University of Arizona; and the Evans School of Public Affairs at the University of Washington. These universities' orientation toward collaborative governance derived from their shared research interest in networks and new institutions for public service and management.

The term *collaborative governance* was given more specific definition by Ansell and Gash (2008) in their widely cited article in the *Journal of Policy Administration Research and Theory*, which analyzed 137 documented cases from a broadly ranging literature. They defined collaborative governance as "a governing arrangement where one or more public agencies directly engage nonstate stakeholders in a collective decision-making process that is formal, consensus oriented, and deliberative and that aims to make or implement public policy or manage public programs or assets" (Ansell and Gash 2008, 544).

We build on Ansell and Gash's definition but expand it to cover a broader suite of agents, structures, processes, and actions that enable collaboration across organizations, jurisdictions, and sectors. We emphasize the cross-boundary nature of what Kettl (2006) described as "the collaborative imperative," and we do not limit collaborative governance to government-initiated efforts. Rather, we view collaborative governance as including institutional forms that extend beyond the conventional focus on the public manager or public sector (cf. McGuire 2006). We also recognize that collaborative governance may, to varying degrees, involve public participation and civic engagement when associated with some kind of longer-term system.

Specifically, we define *collaborative governance* as the processes and structures of public policy decision making and management that engage people across the boundaries of public agencies, levels of government, and/or the public, private, and civic spheres to carry out a public purpose that could not otherwise be accomplished (see also Emerson, Nabatchi, and Balogh 2012, 3). This broad definition of collaborative governance provides the basis for developing an integrative framework for comparative and aggregate empirical analyses across diverse theoretical, normative, and applied perspectives.

The concept of a *collaborative governance regime* is central to our framework and to this book, and is inspired, in part, by George Frederickson's (1999, 2007) calls for the study of governance regimes. A CGR is a type of public governance system in which cross-boundary collaboration represents the predominant mode for conduct, decision making, and activity between autonomous participants who have come together to achieve some collective purpose defined by one or more target goals. Specifically, we define a CGR as a "particular mode of, or system for, public decision making in which cross-boundary collaboration represents the prevailing pattern of behavior and activity" (Emerson, Nabatchi, and Balogh 2012, 6).

Some might object to our use of the word "regime," given that its traditional uses connote an authoritarian and hard-wired system of governing (e.g., the Ancien Régime in France or a communist regime) or refer to the specific political party or governing coalition in power (e.g., the social democrat regime). However, we borrow the term from international political theory, where "regime" refers to sustained cooperation between state and nonstate actors. Specifically, we draw on Stephen Krasner's (1983, 2) definition of regime as a governing arrangement that is imbued with a set of explicit and implicit "principles, norms, rules, and decision-making procedures around which actor expectations converge in a given issue area." The Bretton Woods International Monetary System, the International Monetary Fund, the United Nations, the Kyoto Protocol, the International Atomic Energy Agency, and the Nuclear Non-Proliferation Treaty are all examples of cooperative international regimes. We chose this derivation of "regime" because of its integrative reference to cross-boundary institutional cooperation, its inclusion of both state and nonstate actors, and the implied potential for lateral collaboration within a multiplicity of vertical and horizontal authorities. In closely related and complementary scholarship, Jochim and May (2010) draw from the literature on political science and public policy to theorize about boundary-spanning policy regimes that are used to address policy problems.

Our definition of CGRs is intentionally broad, covering a wide range of collaborative systems; however, it is also specific enough to allow CGRs to be distinguished from other collaborative activities, in four main ways. First, CGRs have broad public policy or public service orientations (as opposed to narrower private or organizational orientations). Second, they are cross-organizational systems involving a range of autonomous organizations representing different interests and/or jurisdictions (as opposed to like-minded coalitions). Third, CGRs develop intentional institutional and procedural norms and rules that foster collaboration (as opposed to simple ground rules for guiding behavior in a short-term endeavor). Fourth and finally, CGRs experience repeated interactions between their participants and are active over some period of time, usually greater than one year (as opposed to short-term cooperation or one-time participatory forums). Thus, though collaborative governance is a generic and generalized term, the concept of CGRs connotes a specific and particular application that allows for the identification and differentiation of various types of collaborative systems. We identify three specific formative types of CGRs—self-initiated, independently convened, and externally directed—which we further develop in chapters 2 and 8. Each CGR type is not only set apart by the way it is formed but is also distinguished by a set of prevailing conditions and characteristics.

Before we move on, it is useful to make one additional point: Like cross-boundary collaboration and collaborative governance, CGRs are not static phenomena; they change, develop, and adapt over time. Given their dynamic and evolutionary nature, CGRs may well have a "life cycle," from birth through development and ultimately to death or disbandment. It is important to keep this point in mind, although we do not address it in detail until later in the book.

Perspectives on Collaborative Governance

Before describing our integrative framework for collaborative governance, it is important to discuss some of the key perspectives and approaches that have shaped our thinking and influenced our work. The study and practice of collaborative governance have built on the shoulders of many professional fields, academic disciplines, and intellectual traditions. As many observers have stated, practice has led theory, and researchers are still trying to catch up with what has become a de facto way of governing across organizational, jurisdictional, and sectoral boundaries. As now studied, collaborative governance is truly an interdisciplinary concept that is viewed through many different lenses. It is the proverbial elephant, conceived as multiple different species by blind people who touch only its legs or trunk or tail. But each perspective has contributed to our multifaceted understanding, providing valuable insights and multiple frames through which to think about cross-boundary collaboration, collaborative governance, and CGRs. In this section, we briefly discuss the frames that have most informed our thinking and our efforts to provide a more integrated multidimensional framework for understanding collaborative governance.

Collaborative Governance as Institutional Arrangements

One approach to collaborative governance is viewed through the lens of new institutionalism (Powell and DiMaggio 2012; March and Olsen 1983; North 1991; Ostrom 1990). For example, the late Elinor Ostrom and her colleagues constructed the Institutional Analysis and Development (IAD) framework to better explain self-governing institutions and behavior within and across organizations (e.g., Ostrom 2011). For multiple individuals or organizations to collaborate across boundaries, they must establish, monitor, and enforce new rules of engagement, develop informal norms and build trust, and create joint theories and strategies for action (Schlager 1995). Although the general focus of collective action research has been on how nongovernmental groups with shared interests can organize themselves to solve problems (and particularly those concerning well-bounded commons, or common-pool resources), the IAD framework offers much that can be applied to more diverse settings where cooperation is needed between heterogeneous organizations with very different missions, interests, and values. It is from this theoretical lens that notions of nested systems of governance and polycentrism—where overlapping formal and informal jurisdictions or authorities coordinate and clarify institutional rules—have arisen (McGinnis 2011).

More recent work on the Socio-Ecological Systems (SES) framework also informs our thinking, particularly about the surrounding system context within which collaborative governance arises (Ostrom 2009; see also Berkes, Colding, and Folke 2002). The SES framework emphasizes the dynamic complexities of the ongoing interactions and adaptations between the physical and spatial environment and the human and institutional environment.

Collaborative Governance as Structural Relations

The study of social networks has advanced scholars' understanding of the structure of relationships between individuals, groups, and organizations (Brass et al. 2004; Knoke and Yang 2008). Here, the emphasis is on patterns of interactions and connections, rather than on institutional arrangements. Network theory looks at the formal and informal links among people and organizations, which are based on an assumption of some kind of interdependence. Social network theory examines the personal connections and connectedness among individuals. The underlying idea is that people are influenced by the recurring social interactions they encounter in networks of relationships. Participation in interpersonal networks influences behavior, and, in the aggregate, can build social capital and power within communities.

Extending from social network theory, public network theory focuses on the structure of connections among organizations within and across sectors. In this context, networks are often juxtaposed with hierarchies and markets, as three different systems of social organization or forms of governance (Powell 1990). The unit of analysis is the relationship among two or more organizations, and these relationships are measured by factors such as the centrality, frequency, and quality of relational linkages or ties. Network analysis can chart the direction and intensity of ties within networks by documenting patterns of communication and information exchange.

Public service networks and their administration have a direct bearing on the effectiveness of CGRs (Brass et al. 2004; Milward and Provan 2000; Provan and Milward 1995). For example, the characteristics of the multiorganizational network within which a CGR operates are important dimensions of the system context for collaborative governance. Likewise, the value of assessing performance from the perspective of clients, participants, and the network itself has influenced our approach to measuring the performance of CGRs (Provan and Milward 2001). Heterogeneous public goal-directed networks, as described by Provan, Fish, and Sydow (2007), come closest to our definition of collaborative governance.

Collaborative Governance as an Advocacy Coalition

The Advocacy Coalition Framework, which was initially developed by Sabatier (1988) and was later refined by Sabatier and Jenkins-Smith (1993), provides an approach to policy formation through competing coalitions within policy subsystems (see also Weible et al. 2011). These coalitions arise by attracting people with sufficiently similar policy belief systems to coordinate their actions across many different public and private institutions at multiple levels. Although collaborative governance is not limited to policy formation per se, one can think about collaborative governance as an across-coalition engagement among diverse groups with a range of belief systems where some kind of power sharing is needed to change a status quo situation that all actors recognize as unacceptable. Sabatier and Jenkins-Smith (1999, 150) suggest that in such settings, a "grand coalition" may lead to consensus-forming processes, but they caution that such cross coalitions may be "quite unstable unless (1) the arrangement produces a continuously 'fair' distribution of benefits to all coalitions and (2) new leaders committed to consensus replace old warriors within the coalitions." Within our framework, fairness and leadership are incorporated as key features of principled engagement in effective CGRs.

Collaborative Governance as a Developmental Process

Still other scholars and practitioners focus on the process of collaboration—the dynamics of the interpersonal and group interactions among actors representing different institutions or constituencies. Chief among these interactions is the negotiation process itself. The study of negotiation builds on a rich intellectual heritage of game theory, communication theory, behavioral economics, social psychology, family systems, and conflict management, among many other lenses. Lessons learned from two-party and multiparty negotiations in the personal sphere, corporate world, political arena, and internationally have direct relevance to the process dynamics of collaborative governance, particularly regarding the development of trust in ongoing deliberation and consensus building (Fisher and Ury 1981; Lax and Sebenius 1986; Raiffa 1982).

Of particular note is the development of principled or interest-based negotiation by the Harvard Law School Program on Negotiation, which has had a significant influence on the education and training of professional negotiators, mediators, and facilitators, as well as public and corporate managers. The essence of this approach is a process whereby parties move from competitive zero-sum bargaining to more cooperative negotiations that optimize mutual gains and minimize aggregate losses (Fisher and Ury 1981). The negotiation process itself involves a sequence of interactive steps and requires specific cognitive and behavioral skills that can be learned.

Collaborative Governance as a Functional Performance Sequence

Many researchers are interested in the instrumental performance of collaborative governance and the functional or causal sequence of conditions, attributes, activities, and accomplishments. Wood and Gray (1991) offer one of the earliest performance frameworks for cross-boundary collaboration, specifying a causal relationship over time that flows directionally from initial or antecedent conditions to an intervention or process that then yields outcomes.

Drawing on this framework, Thomson and Perry (2006) note several antecedents, including high levels of interdependence between parties, the need for resources and risk sharing, a previous history of efforts to collaborate, and complex issues where resource pooling is necessary. They also enumerate several preferred outcomes, such as goal achievement, social capital formation, leveraging of new resources, and a capacity for self-governance. Moreover, through their empirical work, Thomson and Perry (2006) identify five process elements as essential for effective collaboration: governance, administration, organizational autonomy, mutuality, and norms of trust and reciprocity.

In their critical review of a broad range of studies, Ansell and Gash (2008) provide a Contingency Model for Collaborative Governance that identifies and clusters a variety of factors that are useful for organizing the practice of collaborative governance and predicting its outcomes. By contingency, they mean that the nature and quality of the collaboration outcomes are dependent on the process, and that the process itself is affected by or dependent on three major contributing elements: the starting conditions, the institutional design, and facilitative leadership.

Our Perspective on Collaborative Governance and Collaborative Governance Regimes

Although each of the approaches discussed above is useful for understanding collaborative governance, none adequately captures our thinking about CGRs. To deepen our understanding, we reviewed and synthesized a broad array of literature across numerous fields, and then began to cross-walk and integrate several of the conceptual approaches and empirical frameworks for multiparty, cross-boundary collaboration. Included among the empirical frameworks we studied are those for cross-sector collaboration (Bryson, Crosby, and Stone 2006); collaborative planning (Bentrup 2001; Innes and Booher 1999; Selin and Chavez 1995); collaboration processes (Daniels and

Walker 2001; Ring and Van de Ven 1994; Thomson and Perry 2006; Wood and Gray 1991); network management (Koppenjan and Klijn 2004; Milward and Provan 2000); collaborative public management (Agranoff and McGuire 2001b; Cooper, Bryer, and Meek 2006; Leach 2006a); environmental governance and conflict resolution (Agrawal and Lemos 2007; Emerson et al. 2009); and collaborative governance (Ansell and Gash 2008).

In comparing others' frameworks, we found expected overlap and considerable variation, stemming, in part, from the different research traditions, policy arenas, and scales in which scholars work. However, we also encountered a larger, more significant challenge: The extant frameworks lack generalizability, and, consequently, they are often inapplicable across different settings, sectors, geographic and temporal scales, policy arenas, and process mechanisms. For example, Selin and Chavez (1995) focus on environmental planning and management generally, whereas Bentrup (2001) focuses specifically on watershed planning. Koppenjan and Klijn (2004) study problem-solving and decision-making in networks, whereas Ring and Van de Ven (1994) examine business transactions. Moreover, the frameworks vary by the nature of the conceptual problem addressed. For example, Thomson and Perry (2006) focus on the processes of interorganizational partnerships, whereas Cooper, Bryer, and Meek (2006) examine the dynamics of engaging stakeholders and the public in community planning.

These issues led us to develop the integrative framework for collaborative governance, which first formally appeared as the lead article in a 2012 issue of the *Journal of Public Administration Research and Theory* (Emerson, Nabatchi, and Balogh 2012). We had four main objectives in that article. First, we wanted to develop an organizing framework that could speak to different research traditions and be generalizable across variations in collaborative arrangements. Second, we wanted to design an empirically and theoretically grounded framework to help explain and assess CGRs and their variations. Third, we wanted to create a framework that was neither overly simplistic nor overly specified and thus burdened with long lists of variables and exacting conditions to meet and test (cf. Ostrom 2007). Fourth and finally, we wanted a framework that would lend itself well to future theory development and model testing (cf. Ostrom 2005; for more on the differences among frameworks, theories, and models, see box 1.1).

To achieve these objectives, we integrated the theoretical, empirical, and practice-oriented literature on how collaborative systems work along with our own professional experience, to identify the general components and elements of collaborative governance and to build our framework. Our framework is not meant to correspond to all the characteristics of any one particular case of collaborative governance, but rather to identify what is common to most cases of collaborative governance. Thus, it is useful for examining and comparing not only common or expected cases of collaborative governance but also unique and unexpected cases. It is useful for examining and comparing cases where collaborative governance worked as intended, and also cases where collaborative governance went awry and failed to achieve its objectives. Finally, as becomes evident in chapters 8 and 9, the framework provides the

---

Box 1.1 A Note about Frameworks, Theories, and Models

The political scientist and Nobel laureate Elinor Ostrom (2005) encouraged scholars to distinguish among theories, frameworks, and models, especially when studying institutions and the way people make decisions and work together (see also Schlager 1999). These distinctions are also helpful in exploring cross-boundary collaboration, collaborative governance, and collaborative governance regimes.

Frameworks specify general sets of variables (and the relationships among the variables) that are of interest to a researcher. In essence, frameworks identify the pieces of the puzzle about which one is curious, and organize those puzzle pieces, or concepts, in a general way that can then guide further inquiry. Frameworks attempt to include all the major concepts that would be needed to understand any number of configurations of the full puzzle.

Theories are more specific and provide an interpretive structure for frameworks. They provide explanations, predictions, or diagnoses about how the puzzle pieces in a framework interact, fit together, and perform over time. Theories might focus on one certain area of a framework or address the workings of an entire framework. A framework can provoke or lend itself to many different theories.

Models, which are even more specific than theories, allow researchers to develop and test hypotheses about a limited set of variables and their relationships within a framework. They are the basis for specific experiments and empirical research. Enough empirical testing of models and consistent findings over several cases might lead to support for or disproof of particular theories.

In this book we present our integrative framework for collaborative governance, which attempts to identify and arrange the concepts needed to study and understand collaborative governance regimes. We also point to a variety of theories that may inform improvements in the effectiveness of CGRs. For example, we argue that interest-based problem-solving and conflict resolution techniques can strengthen certain elements within collaboration dynamics under certain conditions. We hope this book sets the stage for the further development and testing of theories and models for collaborative governance and collaborative governance regimes.

foundations for a typology of CGRs and an approach to assessing collaborative performance.

Moreover, although the integrative framework identifies the general features of collaborative governance, it does not assume a one-size-fits-all approach to CGRs. Rather, the framework brings together and recognizes behavioral, relational, and structural elements and uses performance logic. Accordingly, the framework can be used to further the science of collaborative governance—for example, by helping scholars systematically and empirically describe collaborative governance and its many forms. It can be used to further the craft of collaborative governance—for example, by helping practitioners identify the right tools for designing and managing the various CGR types or instruments to use in a particular situation. And it can be used to further the art of collaborative governance—for example, by elucidating various ways of getting things done and raising the profile of skills such as facilitation, negotiation, and conflict resolution.

Finally, it is important to note that the framework (and our discussion of it) is not meant to champion or advocate collaborative governance. Indeed, collaborative governance cannot (and often should not) be used in all circumstances. That said, the framework can help us better understand when, where, why, how, and to what effect collaborative governance and CGRs can be used. With this in mind, we now provide an overview of our integrative framework for collaborative governance.

Overview of the Integrative Framework for Collaborative Governance

Our integrative framework for collaborative governance, depicted in figure 1.1, specifies a set of nested dimensions, within which various components and elements are posited to work together in a dynamic, nonlinear, iterative fashion. Specifically, the nested dimensions, shown as ovals in the figure (intended to illustrate multidimensional spheres), represent the general system context, the CGR, and its internal collaboration dynamics and actions.[1] The outermost oval, depicted by solid lines and darkly shaded, represents the surrounding *system context*, which includes the host of political, legal, socioeconomic, environmental, and other influences that affect and are affected by the CGR. From this system context emerge four essential *drivers*, drawn as the triangular wedge on the left, including perceived uncertainty, interdependence, consequential incentives, and initiating leadership. These drivers help initiate the CGR, which is represented by the second oval with the dashed outline, and set its preliminary direction.

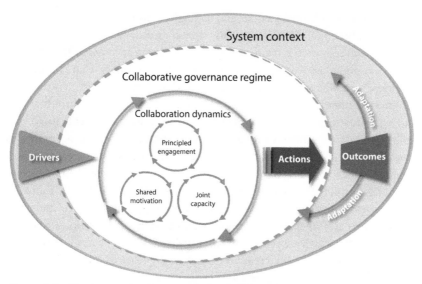

Figure 1.1   The Integrative Framework for Collaborative Governance

During and after the formation of the CGR, its participants engage in *collaboration dynamics*, represented by three dynamic and interacting components: principled engagement, shared motivation, and the capacity for joint action. Through the progressive cycling of collaboration dynamics, participants develop a collective purpose, a set of target goals, and a shared theory of change to accomplish those goals, which guide the collaborative *actions* of the CGR. These actions lead to *outcomes*, which in turn may lead to *adaptation* within the system context or the CGR itself. In chapters 2 through 4 we discuss the CGR's dimensions, components, and elements in detail and provide specific case illustrations. Here, we briefly summarize the framework and explore several recognized variations among CGRs.

The System Context and Drivers

Collaborative governance is initiated and evolves within a multilayered system context. Major elements of the system context include resource or service conditions, policy and legal frameworks, socioeconomic and cultural characteristics, network characteristics, political dynamics and power relations, and the history of conflict. This external system context creates opportunities and constraints, and influences the general parameters within which a CGR unfolds and operates. Moreover, although the CGR is affected by the system context at both the outset and throughout its life cycle, most CGRs are formed in hopes of also affecting this context through its actions.

Four drivers emerge from this system context and provide the impetus for cross-boundary collaboration. Uncertainty, a primary characteristic of "wicked" problems, can drive groups to collaborate to reduce, diffuse, and share risk. Interdependence refers to the perceived necessity of mutual reliance in situations where individuals and organizations are unable to accomplish goals on their own. Consequential incentives refer to internal pressures (issues, resource needs, interests, or opportunities) or external pressures (situational or institutional crises, threats, or opportunities) that must be addressed to mitigate risk for key stakeholders and the broader public. Finally, initiating leadership is necessary to drive preliminary engagement among potential participants and to create the conditions to launch collaboration dynamics. These drivers, which are present to varying degrees and in various reinforcing combinations, initiate the creation of CGRs. We discuss the system context and drivers in detail in chapter 2.

CGRs and Collaboration Dynamics

As defined above, the term *collaborative governance regime* denotes a system in which cross-boundary collaboration represents the predominant mode for conduct, decision making, and activity among autonomous participants who have come together to achieve some collective purpose defined by one or more target goals. Although the specific formation of a CGR varies (see chapters 2 and 8), we conceptualize all CGRs as being constituted by their collaboration dynamics and the specific actions taken as a consequence of those dynamics.

Collaboration dynamics, which are on the process side of the collaborative governance equation, consists of three interacting components, each of which contains four elements: (1) principled engagement, which contains discovery, definition, deliberation, and determination; (2) shared motivation, which contains trust, mutual understanding, internal legitimacy, and commitment; and (3) the capacity for joint action, which contains procedural and institutional arrangements, leadership, knowledge, and resources. These elements work together dynamically to reinforce their individual components, and the three components work together in an interactive and iterative way to reinforce one another. The quality and extent of principled engagement, shared motivation, and the capacity for joint action depend on the productive and self-reinforcing interactions among their elements, and the overall quality and extent of collaboration dynamics depend on the productive and self-reinforcing interactions among its three components. Through collaboration dynamics, participants develop a shared theory of change that specifies the direction and actions of the CGR over the longer term. We discuss CGR formation in chapter 2 and collaboration dynamics in chapter 3. In chapter 8 we construct a typology of CGRs based on formative type and demonstrate how collaboration dynamics vary among CGR types. In chapter 9 we discuss assessing the performance of collaboration dynamics.

Collaborative Actions, Outcomes, and Adaptation

Collaborative actions, outcomes, and adaptation are on the production side of the collaborative governance equation; these are the products of the process of collaboration dynamics. Collaborative actions are the output of collaboration dynamics; they are the steps taken by the CGR to attain its target goals and achieve its common purpose, and should be derived from the shared theory of change. Collaborative actions will vary depending on the context of the CGR and whether its collective purpose is broad (e.g., addressing strategic development or a particular policy issue or area), or narrow (e.g., tackling a particular project or gathering and analyzing specific information) (Huxham et al. 2000). Actions may be carried out by all the CGR participants or the organizations they represent, by individual CGR participants, or by external entities. Examples of collaborative actions range from intermediate outputs—such as securing endorsements; providing information or training to constituents or the public; enacting policy measures, laws, or regulations; and marshalling external resources—to end outputs—such as deploying staff; siting or building facilities; issuing permits; cleaning or restoring environments; carrying out new management practices; monitoring implementation; and enforcing compliance.

Outcomes are the consequences of collaborative actions.[2] They can be physical, environmental, social, economic, political, and/or cultural. They can be specific, discrete, and short term; or they can be broad, cumulative, and long term. Most often, outcomes are assessed in terms of whether the CGR achieved its collective purpose and attained its target goals—that is, whether the CGR produced the intended changes of state for the issue, problem, or service that it was formed to address. However, in addition to altering the target goal, outcomes may also affect the CGR as a whole and/or its participant organizations.

Collaborative governance is frequently advocated because of its potential to transform the context of a complex situation or issue. We refer to such potential transformative change as adaptation, which occurs in response to the outcomes of collaborative actions. Just as outcomes can be related to the target goal, CGR, or participant organizations, so too can adaptation occur at each of these levels. We discuss actions, outcomes, and adaptation in chapter 4, and in chapter 9, we discuss productivity performance, or how to assess the production chain of actions, outcomes, and adaptation.

By unpacking, yet still connecting, the various components and elements of collaborative governance, our integrative framework offers practitioners and scholars a way to think about the general concept of working across boundaries, to describe and assess CGRs, and to delve into specific variations and their implications. We next turn to a brief examination of some potential variations among CGRs.

Variations in CGRs: Thinking about Species and Genus

CGRs can vary across several salient features. Some have suggested that scholars of collaborative governance have been more focused on the species than on the genus—they have looked at individual case examples of collaborative governance or specific types of collaborative governance rather than at its overall practice (Ansell and Gash 2008, 544). We agree with this assessment, but only in part. On one hand, there is a tremendous volume of site-specific case studies on individual collaborative initiatives; research on policy-specific issues such as on public health, watersheds, and natural resources management; and research on specific types of collaborative arrangements, such as in regulatory negotiation, joined-up government, and public–private partnerships (Ansell and Gash 2008). However, there have been few attempts to aggregate this *species*-based knowledge about collaborative governance in a way that allows us to cumulatively assess the *genus* of collaborative governance. On the other hand, the research on individual sites, policies, and forms of collaborative governance has not gone far enough to enable distinctions to be made among species of CGRs. In other words, research has not sufficiently focused on identifying the relevant variations among CGRs. In chapter 8, we offer a CGR typology that is based on the way CGRs are formed and assumes a path-dependent approach to their development and performance. For our current purposes, we wish to say only a few words about the most obvious variations in the form and function of CGRs, with some foreshadowing of how these variations play out in our typology.

Sponsors and Conveners

CGRs can have a variety of sponsors (i.e., those who fund all or part of a collaborative endeavor) and conveners (i.e., those who plan and lead a collaborative endeavor) (Carlson 2007; Leach 2006b; Koontz et al. 2004). Typical sponsors of a CGR include elected officials, public managers, planners, and

other administrative officials; executives of private businesses or corpora-
tions; directors of community groups or informal networks of stakeholders;
and leaders of bridging institutions such as foundations, nonprofit organizations, and colleges and universities. Sometimes a sponsor will also serve as a
convener; however, other times, sponsors will contract with an expert convener, such as a facilitator or conflict resolution specialist working as a solo
practitioner, a consultant in a nonprofit or for-profit organization, or even in
academia. Moreover, sometimes the sponsors and conveners emerge from the
initiating leadership, whereas other times the initiating leadership will seek
out and gain the buy-in of sponsors and conveners.

The organizational locus of the sponsors and conveners influences the formation and evolution of CGRs, particularly in terms of whether participation
is voluntary or mandatory. Some efforts arise organically at the grassroots
level, others emerge from the "grasstop" efforts of governmental decision
makers, and still others are instigated by independent convening or boundary-
spanning organizations. These variations in how individuals come together
to form and direct a CGR provide the foundation for our typology of CGRs.
Specifically, we assert that there are three formative types of CGRs—self-
initiated, independently convened, and externally directed. In addition to influencing their composition and collaboration dynamics, the way in which
CGRs are formed and the differences among sponsors and conveners influence and shape many of the other dimensions by which CGRs vary.

Collective Purpose

Although the collective purpose, or broad intent, of a CGR can vary tremendously, most purposes can be categorized as either policy-oriented or site-
specific (Emerson et al. 2003). A policy-oriented CGR works on specific issues
within a general policy domain, such as education, the environment, energy,
transportation, or health care. In such cases, the CGR is focused on a class of
resources, services, situations, or locations. In contrast, a site-specific CGR at-
tends to a specific issue related to a particular place, such as a neighborhood,
city, state, or region. In such cases, the CGR is likely to focus more on planning and implementation vis-à-vis a specific and discrete resource, service,
situation, or location.

Other variations in purpose also shape the extent and nature of the CGR.
For example, whether the issue at hand is driven by a perceived problem or
conflict, or by the promise of an opportunity, molds the shared theory of
change and the nature and spirit of collaboration dynamics, among many
other dimensions of the CGR. Likewise, whether the problem or opportunity
is pressing and acute or chronic and long term influences the urgency and

time frame of the CGR's form and function, as well as the speed with which participants are mobilized.

Locus of Action and Geographic Scale

CGRs may engage in work with intended actions and outcomes at the local, state, regional, national, or international levels, though actions often also result in outcomes for the participant organizations and even the CGR itself. The locus of action is directly related to the collective purpose of the CGR— that is, the nature of the focal public problem or opportunity and its effects determines whether the CGR effort originates at a community, local, state, regional, or even national or cross-national level. Moreover, the locus of action has a direct bearing on the CGR's geographic scale, which concerns the number of intergovernmental jurisdictions involved in a collaborative effort. Because they deal with a class of resources, services, situations, or locations, policy-oriented CGRs generally cover multiple intergovernmental jurisdictions, and thus have a larger geographic scale. In contrast, because they deal with a particular and discrete resource, service, situation, or location, site-specific CGRs generally cover fewer intergovernmental jurisdictions, and thus have a smaller geographic scale.

Participant Selection and Recruitment

The participants in a CGR (sometimes called stakeholders, parties, partners, members, or collaborators[3]) are typically individuals who represent an autonomous client, constituency, decision maker, public agency, nongovernmental organization, business or corporation, or community—though they may also sometimes represent themselves as individual citizens or stakeholders or the public at large. As representatives of others, these participants bring to the table the cultures, missions, and mandates of the organizations or constituents they represent, as well as their own individual sets of attitudes, values, interests, and knowledge. The selection and recruitment of participants, who may range from 3 to 10,000 or more, may vary considerably from state-based participants (e.g., expert administrators and elected representatives) to mini-publics (e.g., professional or lay stakeholders, or randomly selected, self-selected, or recruited individuals) to diffuse members of the public (Fung 2006).

Who the participants are and whom they represent are central issues in public engagement (cf. Bryson et al. 2013; Fung 2003, 2006; Fung and Wright 2001; Nabatchi and Leighninger 2015; Thomas 1995, 2012), and also in CGRs. Although most agree that getting the right people to the table is important, the level of inclusion and diversity perceived to be necessary depends on the

CGR's normative organizing principles and intended outcomes. Decisions about participants are greatly influenced by the system context and the drivers for collaboration, as well as by the nature of the CGR's formative type. For example, self-initiated CGRs are more likely to have voluntary participation, whereas independently convened CGRs are more likely to have induced participation, and externally directed CGRs are more likely to have incentivized or mandated participation.

The Nature and Locus of Shared Decision-Making Authority

Decision making in a multiparticipant collaborative endeavor is usually done by working toward some form of consensus, which means that all participants either agree to a group decision or at least can live with the decision if it is not their first choice. Although CGRs typically strive to achieve a consensus among all participants, this may not always be possible. In such cases, decisions can be made with a supermajority agreement or some other kind of decision rule. Sometimes, public agencies or government representatives may have the ultimate authority to make a decision; other times, decision-making authority will be shared by some or all of the member organizations.

The success of collaborative decision making may be influenced by several factors, including whether the participants are respected by the people affected by the decision, the participants' expertise, and the group's authority to make decisions (for a discussion of deliberation and decision making in collaborative governance, see Choi and Robertson 2013). Furthermore, the nature and extent of group authority or autonomy are influenced by the CGR formative type. Group autonomy is greatest in self-initiated CGRs, is negotiated or facilitated in independently convened CGRs, and is most constrained in externally directed CGRs.

Degree of Formalization

All CGRs have a certain degree of formalization. Indeed, formalization is a requisite because collaborative governance requires structured arrangements for the development and implementation of joint activities using shared resources (cf. Ansell and Gash 2008). Some CGRs will be more formal than others, and the level of formality is often determined by its formative type and evolves through collaboration dynamics. At least initially, externally directed CGRs tend to have high levels of formalization, independently convened CGRs tend to have moderate levels, and self-initiated CGRs tend to have low levels. That said, all CGRs need to develop formal and informal rules, protocols, and structures to manage their interactions over time. The formalized elements of a CGR may range from simple verbal agreements about ground rules for meetings and general agreement on a shared purpose to specific decision-making rules and operating protocols to more official institutional instruments such as charters, by-laws, and representational requirements.

Each of these dimensions of CGR variation—sponsors and conveners, collective purpose, locus of action and geographic scale, participant selection and recruitment, nature and locus of shared decision-making authority, and degree of formalization—are interrelated and shape the form and function of the CGR at the outset and over time. For example, although sponsors and conveners may have a particular purpose in mind, that purpose needs to become collectively shared and translated over time into target goals and a theory of change. This collective ownership and translation occurs through the process of collaboration dynamics, which evolves as more participants join the effort or as the locus of action and geographic scale of the CGR change. Similarly, the locus of action and geographic scale may require the addition or subtraction of potential participants, perhaps in response to the need for a particular locus for shared decision-making authority. Alternatively, a CGR may need to become more or less formalized depending on the nature of decision-making authority. These and other variations among CGRs are discussed in detail in chapter 8.

Summary

In this chapter, we first clarified the derivation and use of the terms "governance," "public governance," "cross-boundary collaboration," "collaborative governance," and "collaborative governance regimes," and we described several conceptual perspectives that contribute to our framework, typology, and views of performance. We also summarized our integrative framework for collaborative governance, which provides a broad conceptual map for situating and exploring the components of a wide variety of CGRs. The framework integrates theory, practice, and knowledge from a wide variety of fields, and can be applied to analyses at different scales, in different policy arenas, and at varying levels of complexity. Finally, as a prelude to later discussions on CGRs and how they vary, we offered some of the more observable differences among the many species of collaborative governance, including sponsors and conveners, collective purpose, locus of action and geographic scale, participant selection and recruitment, locus of decision-making authority, and degree of formalization. In part II of the book, we unpack the integrative framework for collaborative governance, focusing specifically on system context, drivers, and regime formation in chapter 2; on collaboration dynamics in chapter 3; and on collaborative actions, outcomes, and adaptation in chapter 4.

Notes

1. In our 2012 article (Emerson, Nabatchi, and Balogh 2012), we depicted the system context, CGR, and collaboration dynamics as nested boxes. However, because those boxes did not adequately illustrate the dynamic nature of collaborative governance, we revised the figure and now use ovals. Likewise, we no longer use interlocking gears for the three components of collaboration dynamics, because the gears were too mechanistic in their portrayal of what are more fluid and iterative interactions.

2. In our 2012 article (Emerson, Nabatchi, and Balogh 2012), we refer to the results of collaborative action as "impacts"; but in this book, we refer to these results as "outcomes." This change reflects a stronger adherence to the terminology in the performance measurement and management literature (e.g., see Heinrich 2002; Koontz and Thomas 2006). Specifically, the term "impacts" has a very specific meaning in the performance literature; use of the term requires the experimental methods that verify the added value of the program above and beyond what would have happened otherwise in a comparable setting. Here, we are more interested in the outcomes of collaborative actions as they relate to the CGR's target goals and shared theory of change, although we believe that assessment of impacts is also important.

3. We recognize that the word "collaborator" has a negative and derogatory connotation, given its historic use to refer to someone who works traitorously with an enemy. This pejorative connotation is particularly strong when the term is used in reference to those who provided intelligence or assistance to the Nazi regime during World War II. In this book we try to reclaim this term by going back to its literal origins describing those who co-labor, or work with others, particularly in the context of collaborative governance and CGRs.

Part II

The Integrative Framework for Collaborative Governance

CHAPTER 2

Initiating Collaborative Governance

The System Context, Drivers, and Regime Formation

> The secret of getting ahead is getting started.
> —Mark Twain

Getting started can be the most difficult challenge for collaborative governance. As with all collective action problems, it is difficult to stimulate individuals to act beyond their immediate self-interest and work together on shared problems. It is particularly difficult to stimulate heterogeneous groups of people to work in concert across organizational and sectoral divides (Thomas 2003; Ostrom 1998; Schlager 1995). Given this challenging context, how do collaborative governance regimes (CGRs) emerge and form? What conditions and factors influence their creation and development?

In this chapter we discuss the surrounding system context—that is, the broader set of conditions that influence the formation and performance of CGRs—as well as the essential drivers that work together to initiate this collaboration. We then offer a short case illustration of the National Collaborative for Higher Education Policy, which demonstrates the role of the system context and drivers in CGR formation. We conclude with a brief chapter summary.

The System Context

Cross-boundary collaboration does not occur in a vacuum. Like nearly everything in the organizational world, CGRs emerge and evolve within a complex system context (shown in figure 2.1) that consists of numerous, layered, and interrelated conditions—political, legal, economic, social, cultural, and environmental (Borrini-Feyerabend 1996). This broad and dynamic context creates opportunities and constraints that directly affect CGRs at the outset and shape their contours as they evolve. Specifically, the context not only influences the initiation of CGRs but also affects the dynamics and performance of CGRs over time. For example, once collaboration has been started, expected events (e.g., an election, the passage of legislation, or the enactment of a regulation) and unexpected events (e.g., an extreme weather event or the resignation of a significant leader) can open up new possibilities or pose unanticipated challenges. This ongoing temporal nature led us to depict the system context in the integrative framework as a three-dimensional space surrounding the CGR and its outcomes and adaptation, rather than as a separate set of starting conditions.

It is important to analyze this dynamic system context to develop a fuller understanding of the practicality, viability, and sustainability of CGRs. Some conditions pose risks that may discourage an emergent CGR early in the process, whereas other conditions, if unidentified, may derail the CGR down the line. For example, without a robust understanding of the system context, potential participants may take certain conditions as "givens"—as things that cannot be changed—and consequently may determine that collaboration is undesirable or infeasible. Alternatively, participants may accept the conditions at the outset and proceed accordingly, allowing those givens to shape their collective purpose, target goals, and shared theory of change—only to discover that the conditions change, greatly affecting their work. In either case, a comprehensive understanding of the system context could have better informed the participants about the opportunities for and constraints on cross-boundary collaboration.

Not only does the system context shape the overall nature of the CGR; the CGR's collaborative actions and the consequent outcomes of those actions can also affect the system context (see chapter 4). Indeed, one of the core rationales for embarking on collaborative governance is to influence the surrounding set of conditions that create, aggravate, or sustain a problem. Efforts to foster changes in these surrounding conditions are inherently long term and complex, and no effort will be successful unless the participants are clear about the conditions targeted for change.

In short, CGR initiators and participants should have a robust understanding of the many conditions in the surrounding system context, and they should move from ignoring or treating these conditions as "givens" to treating them as issues that can and should be monitored and addressed over time. Researchers have identified several external conditions that may influence the nature and prospects of CGRs (e.g., Ansell and Gash 2008; Bryson, Crosby, and Stone 2006; Thomson and Perry 2006; Wood and Gray 1991). Here, we present six of the most salient conditions, but we recognize that this is not an exhaustive enumeration.

First, *public resource or service conditions* are particularly central, providing the baseline problem or opportunity around which CGRs form. Public

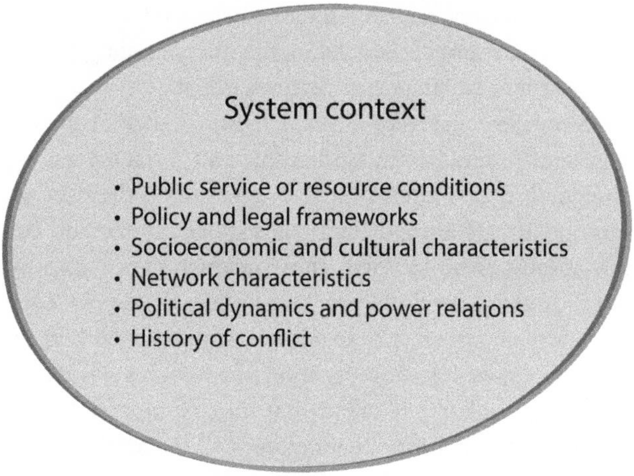

System context

- Public service or resource conditions
- Policy and legal frameworks
- Socioeconomic and cultural characteristics
- Network characteristics
- Political dynamics and power relations
- History of conflict

Figure 2.1   The System Context

resource conditions include the state of depletion, pollution, or extraction potential of environmental and natural resources. Human-made resource conditions refer to the inadequacy, deterioration, or risk to public health or safety of physical infrastructure, such as potable water supplies, transportation systems, and public housing. Public service conditions encompass the quality, extent, and distribution of public health and human services, public education, welfare assistance, the public regulation of financial services, and so forth. The breadth and variety of these resource and service conditions are considerable, and CGRs generally emerge in response to concerns about them. In particular, these and other related conditions might be targeted for improvement, expansion, or limitation through collaborative action (e.g., Ostrom 1990; Provan, Fish, and Sydow 2007).

Second, *policy and legal frameworks* emerging from legislative, administrative, regulatory, and judicial systems enable and constrain not only public decision making and private action but also the work of CGRs (Bryson, Crosby, and Stone 2006; Scott and Meyer 1991; DiMaggio and Powell 1983). These institutional frameworks include the substantive laws, rules, regulations, mandates, executive orders, policy guidance memorandums, and other legal requirements that relate to the management of public resources and services, as well as to the procedural provisions that affect opportunities for cross-boundary collaboration. For example, collaborative endeavors can be facilitated and/or hindered by state open meeting laws, state administrative procedures acts, the Federal Advisory Committee Act, and the federal Administrative Procedure Act, among other local ordinances and state and federal laws and regulations (see Bingham 2008, 2010; Bingham, Nabatchi, and

O'Leary 2005). Moreover, and as discussed below, effective collaborative action is connected to, if not embedded in, the many existing public policy and legal frameworks that facilitate and circumscribe it.

Third, *socioeconomic and cultural characteristics*—such as income and education levels, community health, and ethnic and racial diversity—create the fabric of the public that is interested in, or affected by, the issue at hand (e.g., Sabatier et al. 2005). The importance of socioeconomic and cultural characteristics is at least twofold. First, these characteristics may contribute to the quality of, or problems with, public resource and service conditions. For example, high levels of poverty or low levels of public health in a community might require the expansion or integration of resources and services. Second, they reflect the pool of public talent that may be tapped, the financial and information resources that may be accessed, and the level of complexity that must be addressed in collaborative problem solving. For example, a community with limited internal expertise or financial resources may need to connect with a larger network of better-resourced communities to access assistance, or a well-endowed state may not choose to draw on federal incentives to address a public service issue in a particular manner.

Fourth, *network characteristics* can help or hinder CGR efforts. Networks have been defined as "structures of interdependence involving multiple organizations or parts thereof, where one unit is not merely the formal subordinate of the others in some larger hierarchical arrangement" (O'Toole 1997, 45). In the context of CGRs, networks can be thought of in two ways: (1) as the preexisting complex of overlapping social and organizational networks of which individual collaborators are already a part; and (2) as the existing network that connects collaborators, or what scholars refer to as the degree of structural embeddedness (Bryson, Crosby, and Stone 2006; Jones, Hesterly, and Borgatti 1997; Ring and Van de Ven 1994).

Particular network characteristics of interest include their density and strength of relationships or ties. Networks are dense when there are more direct links between a greater number of organizations, and they are sparse when there are fewer direct links between organizations. The strength of ties within networks is operationalized by the frequency of interactions between members. Ties are weak when there are few interactions, and they are strong when there are many interactions (e.g., Granovetter 1973). The denser the network and stronger the ties, the more likely networked organizations are to have the social capital needed to effectively communicate and share information and other resources. Moreover, groups and organizations that already communicate and share information are more likely to collaborate in the future (Selin and Chavez 1995).

Fifth, *political dynamics and power relations* exist both formally and informally within and across all sectors and will affect the formation, continuation, and performance of CGRs. Power is rarely distributed evenly, and the patterns of influence and control create conditions that not only shape public perceptions but also shape the individual perceptions and inclinations of potential collaboration participants as they decide whether to pursue their goals through a CGR. Political dynamics and power relations have many sources, such as specific organizational control mechanisms, financial resources and responsibilities, funding processes, and organizational standard operating procedures. These political and power conditions are critical in providing or limiting access to and support from public decision makers. Moreover, extreme imbalances in power between stakeholders can make collaboration particularly difficult (e.g., Ansell and Gash 2008; Bryson, Crosby, and Stone 2006; Huxham and Vangen 2005).

Sixth and finally, *the history of conflict* between key actors and organizations is another important condition in the system context. Conflict affects the levels of trust between salient organizations (which are potential CGR participants); and trust, another dimension of social capital, affects the potential for bringing people together to collaborate (e.g., Ansell and Gash 2008; Radin 1996; Thomson and Perry 2006). Past conflicts can pose challenges for building future working relationships and may inhibit a CGR's start-up or, at a minimum, may require attention, if not repair, before moving forward.

Together, public resource or service conditions, policy and legal frameworks, socioeconomic and cultural characteristics, network characteristics, political dynamics and power relations, and the history of conflict, among other factors in the broad system context, shape the prospects for and challenges of initiating and sustaining CGRs. They also affect the evolution of CGRs over time. However, despite their importance, the conditions in the surrounding system context do not in and of themselves lead to the formation of a CGR. These conditions are merely influences, not causal factors. They provide the context from which the drivers of CGRs emerge.

The Drivers

Researchers broadly recognize that the "conditions present at the outset of collaboration can either facilitate or discourage cooperation between stakeholders and between agencies and stakeholders" (Ansell and Gash 2008, 550). But what propels the initiation of CGRs? We have identified four important drivers without which, we posit, the call for collaboration would likely go unheeded and collaborative governance would not unfold: (1) uncertainty, (2) interdependence, (3) consequential incentives, and (4) initiating leadership (see figure 2.2). We explore each of these in turn.

Uncertainty

For many public policy issues, the underlying challenges and possible solutions are known, clear, and agreed upon; however, for other policy concerns, claims about what is true and what is false are unknown, ambiguous, or disputed (Lindley 2006). These unknowns are captured in the first driver, uncertainty, which refers to situations of doubt, ambiguity, limited information, and instability related to current and future conditions, events, resource availability, or decisions by other actors. Drawing on work by Emery and Trist (1965), Bryson, Crosby, and Stone (2006, 45) refer to this condition as "turbulence," noting that such complex situations necessitate—or, as we would say, "drive"—organizations "to decrease uncertainty and increase organizational stability."

The potential sources of uncertainty are numerous. Uncertainty is a main feature of "wicked" societal problems (Koppenjan and Klijn 2004; Rittel and Webber 1973). As we discussed in the introduction, wicked problems create uncertainty, in large part because there is no agreement on what the problem is. Indeed, how to formulate the problem *is* the problem. It is more than just the lack of one simple solution; rather, there are competing and unknown solutions that further heighten the uncertainty about the problem. Uncertainty can also arise from partially observable and/or stochastic environments, along with ignorance and/or apathy. Regardless of its source, uncertainty can drive groups to reduce, diffuse, and share risk through collaboration. It can also foster creativity and innovation.

Uncertainty, of course, can also drive groups to compete. Collective uncertainty about societal problems can generate controversy and adversarialism—as, for example, with climate change or immigration policy. A polarizing political environment merely fans the flames of uncertainty, as with the debate over national policies such as health care reform and reproductive rights. If the public and those representing its diverse interests were endowed with perfect information about a problem and its solution, they would be able to act independently to pursue their interests or respond to risk (Bentrup 2001). One key to turning the response to uncertainty from competition to cooperation is the acknowledgment of the second driver: interdependence.

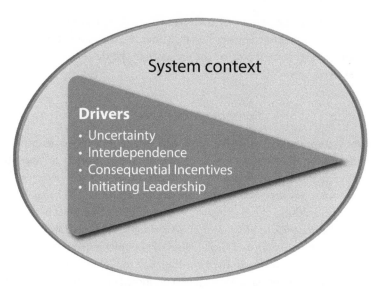

Figure 2.2   Drivers for the Formation of a Collaborative Governance Regime

Interdependence

Collaboration often occurs because individuals and organizations cannot accomplish an important objective alone (Gray 1989; Thomson and Perry 2006). In a world of shrinking resources and growing interconnected problems, interdependence—the necessity of mutual reliance for accomplishing goals— is an almost constant state. Interdependence becomes an essential driver for CGRs after previous attempts to go it alone prove unsuccessful. Simply put, we often "fail into collaboration" (Bryson, Crosby, and Stone 2006).

When a public authority, jurisdiction, service / resource provider, community group, or nongovernmental organization does not succeed in addressing a key public issue or need through its internal organization and with its own resources, then reaching out to other agencies or sectors (or responding to others' overtures) may become necessary. And necessity, as we are told, is the mother of invention. Necessity can lead to innovation, risk taking, and sometimes strange bedfellows, when it requires working with previous competitors and others outside one's organization, sector, or network.

Game theory suggests that when players have shared information and repeated opportunities to exchange or interact, they will recognize their interdependence and seek ways out of the cooperators' dilemma (Lichbach 1996). Thus, the mere existence of interdependence is not enough to drive collaboration. Rather, people are motivated to collaborate only when interdependencies are recognized by key actors. Moreover, the motivation to address interdependencies is enhanced by the presence of the third driver: consequential incentives.

Consequential Incentives

People need enticements to collaborate, and when these enticements are seen as being connected to important outcomes, the motivation to collaborate increases. Hence the importance of consequential incentives—which refer to internal issues, resource needs, interests, or opportunities, or to external situational or institutional crises, threats, or opportunities that must be addressed to mitigate salient risk or advance desired conditions for key stakeholders and the broader public. Ansell and Gash (2008) incorporate incentives to participation as a starting condition in their contingency model for collaborative governance, and several other scholars have conducted research that informs our understanding of incentives (e.g., Gray 1989; Gunton and Day 2003; Imperial 2005; Susskind and Cruikshank 1987). Not all incentives will be sufficiently prominent to drive the formation of a CGR. To promote collaboration across boundaries, potential participants must be aware of the incentive and understand that giving it attention and working together may have positive effects, whereas inattention and failure to work together may have negative effects. Ultimately, this broad awareness helps create the motivating pressure that induces individuals to come together to act.

Consequential incentives can take many forms. An incentive may be a matter of mandate. For example, a new law or regulation requiring collaboration between diverse stakeholder groups might be enacted. An incentive may be of a temporal nature. For example, a policy window may open or an administrative or judicial deadline may require a timely response. An incentive may emerge from a dramatic triggering event or a new set of indisputable facts that makes clear the scope or intensity of the negative consequences of inaction (Selin and Chavez 1995). For example, an extreme weather event or other natural disaster may heighten emergency responders' awareness of the need for more collaboration on the ground.

Not all consequential incentives are negative. For example, a grant or other funding opportunity may emerge that requires the development of a collaborative initiative. The positive rewards of collaboration can themselves be consequential. The enticement of monetary compensation or reputational gains from participation in a CGR may be an important inducement, as might be the potential revenues or indirect benefits of a problem solved through collaboration. Garnering more negotiating power at the table may be enough incentive to join a collaborative endeavor. Finally, the consequences of *not* participating in a CGR initiative can also matter. For example, exclusion from sharing joint gains, the lost opportunity to influence a public decision, or the potential negative perceptions of others may incentivize collaboration.

More important than the particular form of the incentive is its consequential nature. The incentive must have the properties that make people want to capture ensuing benefits or avoid ensuing losses. However, even with important and significant consequential incentives, a fourth driver, initiating leadership, must also be present before a CGR can be launched.

Initiating Leadership

The importance of leadership to cross-boundary collaboration is widely appreciated by both practitioners and academics (e.g., Ansell and Gash 2008; Bingham and O'Leary 2008; Susskind and Cruikshank 1987). Collaboration both demands and cultivates opportunities for multiple kinds of leadership over the course of an endeavor (Carlson 2007). Thus, leadership is an essential driver and can be a significant outgrowth of collaboration (see chapter 3).

Here we focus on one specific type of leadership—initiating leadership—which is the final and perhaps most essential driver for the formation of CGRs. Initiating leadership refers to the presence and actions of a person or core group that stimulates interest in and instigates preliminary discussions about creating a collaborative endeavor. Initiating leaders appreciate the challenges of the system context and recognize the presence and pressure of the other three drivers: the uncertainty of future conditions, the interdependencies between actors, and the consequences of (in)action. Perhaps most important, initiating leaders must then generate and supply the "motivational force" for participants to come together. In essence, initiating leaders act much like a conductor who assembles and directs musicians who may have never played together before.

Initiating leaders may emerge from a variety of organizations or groups (Koontz et al. 2004). For example, they may come from one or more government agencies, elected or political offices, or nongovernmental organizations or civic groups. They may also come from the private sector or be an influential member of the public. Regardless of their organizational home, initiating leaders, by virtue of their personal stature and reputation, attract key stakeholders either directly or indirectly through others. Thus, in pursuing a collaborative effort, initiating leaders tend to have dense professional and social networks, tend to be known by key individuals, and tend to be seen as sufficiently credible and trustworthy. They are able to exercise their formal or informal authority and strategic vision to create the climate and opportunity for cooperation and to frame the central issue(s) in a sufficiently broad and inclusive manner (Gray 1989). Effective initiating leaders are viewed as committed to collaborative problem solving, as willing to not advocate for one particular solution, and as reliably impartial with respect to other participants' preferences (Bryson, Crosby, and Stone 2006; Selin and Chavez 1995). In addition, access to sufficient upfront resources (e.g., staff or meeting location) and the ability to absorb the initial transaction costs of convening or sponsoring a CGR can strengthen the work of initiating leaders (Schneider et al. 2003).

These four drivers—uncertainty, interdependence, consequential incentives, and initiating leadership—work to various degrees and in various combinations to propel the creation of CGRs. In earlier work, we proposed that the presence of one or more of these drivers was necessary for a CGR to begin, and that the more drivers that were present and recognized by participants, the more likely it was that a CGR would be initiated (Emerson, Nabatchi, and Balogh 2012). We also now see these drivers as being strongly interconnected. For example, the idea of collaborating with others typically emerges in response to incomplete information (uncertainty) concerning a problem or issue that cannot be addressed by actors working alone (interdependence). But uncertainty and interdependence may not be enough to drive collaboration without some pressure to act to avoid accruing losses or forgoing benefits (consequential incentives). Even in light of these consequential incentives, CGRs may not take off unless someone can bring together the relevant parties (initiating leadership). The inverse also holds: Initiating leaders will not be able to convene others unless they have some level of appreciation for (and can convince the potential collaborators about) the realities of uncertainty, interdependence, and consequential incentives and how these issues affect participants' interests. In short, we have extended our proposition about drivers beyond the notion that only one might suffice toward a more complex understanding about how they work in different combinations in relation to the formative type of CGR, an idea we discuss further in chapter 8.

Finally, it is important to recognize the changing nature of CGR drivers. In some cases, all four drivers will be present and visible simultaneously. In other cases, the drivers may not be present at the same moment or to the same extent. They may emerge, recede, or evolve over time and in response to each other, as well as to changing conditions in the system context. For example, initiating leaders may recognize the need for consequential incentives and take action to develop them. Or interdependencies may grow and gain attention as uncertainty increases about conditions in the system context. Or uncertainty may motivate a person to take a leadership role in trying to convene others. Viewed this way, all four drivers are likely to be present to some degree at the outset and may well evolve and reinforce one another to create the impetus necessary to bring key collaborators together.

Initiating Collaborative Governance Regimes

Once the essential drivers emerge out of the system context, how do CGRs actually get started? There are many avenues by which CGRs form, depending in large part on the assessments and actions of the initiating leaders and their organizational setting and the relationships that are relevant to the issue at hand.

The organizational setting of the initiating leadership plays a significant role in the formation of CGRs and forms the basis for our CGR typology presented in chapter 8. In some cases, CGRs will arise organically at the grass-roots level, where the initiating leaders form the nucleus of participants directly affected by the situation and organize to address a shared problem. In our typology, we call these self-initiated CGRs. Over time, this nucleus may grow to become more inclusive of diverse interests or integrated with other sources of official or informal authority and influence. Examples of self-initiated CGRs include Western rangeland cooperatives, like the Malpai Borderlands Group (www.malpaiborderlandsgroup.org) and the Altar Valley Conservation Alliance (www.altarvalleyconservation.org), as well as many local watershed associations (e.g., see Margerum 2011; Weber 2003).

In other cases, CGRs are encouraged from above, at the "grasstops" level, where initiating leaders draw on inducements (or, in some cases, mandates) to incentivize collaboration at another level (Donahue and Zeckhauser 2011). We call these externally directed CGRs. For example, since 2001, the Collaborative Forest Restoration program of the US Forest Service has provided grants to groups in New Mexico to foster the collaborative, science-based restoration of critical forests. The eligibility requirement for these grants stipulates that applicants must "include a diverse and balanced group of stakeholders as well as appropriate Federal, Tribal, State, County, and Municipal government representatives" (CFRP 2014).

In still other cases, initiating leaders may work through boundary-spanning organizations to convene and incentivize voluntary collaboration between participants by brokering initial gatherings and managing early rounds of collaboration dynamics. We call these independently convened CGRs. These boundary-spanning organizations are often activated by the standing and commitment of the initiating leaders, as well as by funding opportunities. They may assist the leaders in assessing the system context and in recommending appropriate first steps to engaging participants in prospective collaborative efforts. For example, the William D. Ruckelshaus Center at the University of Washington often serves in this boundary-spanning role by convening multiple parties in voluntary collaborative approaches for policy development and dispute resolution (http://ruckelshauscenter.wsu.edu). In chapter 8 we further develop these three formative types of CGRs (self-initiated, independently convened, and externally directed) and explore how the types vary in their path-dependent development.

Regardless of the organizational setting for collaboration, CGR formation starts with the assembling of participants by the initiating leaders. In some cases, participants are required to participate in the CGR. Mandated participation is especially common in grasstop, externally directed CGRs because the initiating leaders have the formal power to command and instruct parties to work together. In other cases, however, participants come to the table voluntarily—by choice—as is typically the case in self-initiated CGRs. Independently convened CGRs may have both voluntary and mandated participation. Gaining voluntary participation is challenging and often dependent on the informal power and relationship capital of the initiating leaders.

In any case, the task of assembling participants can be made easier if the initiating leaders do the homework necessary to create an attractive forum for collaboration. Specifically, the initiating leaders need to think about who the "right" participants are, and why they will want to come together. To do so, leaders should determine who will view collaboration as a means to influence decision making and who is likely to share a vision of what could be accomplished collectively. Moreover, the leaders should assess the costs and benefits for participants in terms of transaction costs, power sharing, resources, time, and effort. In addition, the leaders should address issues of participant representation not only to assure balanced voices, public buy-in, and legitimacy but also to generate a useful diversity of perspectives and ideas, which can lead to a deeper and more thoughtful and comprehensive consideration of issues and potential solutions. In many ways, these appraisals return the initiating leaders to the assessment of drivers for collaboration, particularly in terms of incentivizing collaboration.

Such incentives can be enhanced through the invitation process. Getting the involvement of those with credibility and legitimacy, those who bring the needed talents and resources, and those who are team players can help encourage others to come to the table. Direct and personal invitations that speak to shared concerns or values and the importance of collaboration can be critical to such efforts. Building the norms of trust and reciprocity up front as participants come to the table can help with collaboration dynamics, the processes through which participants engage, build motivation, and develop the capacity for joint action (see chapter 3). In turn, this is likely to improve both process and productivity performance (see chapter 9). In the next section we show the importance of the surrounding system context and the essential drivers with a short case illustration concerning the formation of a CGR to address higher education policy.

Case Illustration: The National Collaborative for Higher Education Policy

The National Collaborative for Higher Education Policy was launched in 2003 by the Education Commission of the States, the National Center for Higher Education Management Systems, and the National Center for Public Policy and Higher Education (NCPPHE). The goal of the National Collaborative was to help states improve their higher education performance by assisting with the examination of state higher education policies and the development of broad agreement about statewide priorities for improvement. This case provides an excellent illustration of the multifaceted and complex nature of the conditions in the surrounding system context, as well as the drivers needed for the initiation of a CGR.

The NCPPHE, an independent policy research organization, was established in 1998 to promote public policies that enhance Americans' opportunities to pursue and achieve high-quality education and training beyond high school (www.highereducation.org/about/about.shtml). Recognizing the lack of a common national framework for evaluating and comparing the fifty US states' higher education performance, the NCPPHE decided to launch a long-term evaluation project, Measuring Up, to assess and evaluate systems of higher education in each of the states. Specifically, the evaluation project sought to grade each state on how well it prepared students to participate in an accessible and affordable system of higher education that meets their educational needs and prepares them to contribute to the larger society. Data were compiled and analyzed for five categories of performance: preparation, participation, affordability, completion, and benefits. These five categories were selected because they have a crucial impact on opportunity and are highly susceptible to being influenced by state policy (Callan, Doyle, and Finney 2001).

The project's first report, *Measuring Up 2000: The State-by-State Report Card for Higher Education*, asserted that "higher education's benefits are unevenly and often unfairly distributed; they simply do not reflect the distribution of talent across our country. Despite the major accomplishments of higher education in America, geography, wealth, income, and ethnicity still play far too great a role in determining the opportunities that Americans have to prepare for, enroll in, afford, and complete college" (Callan, Doyle, and Finney 2001, 12).

The second report, *Measuring Up 2002*, updated each state's performance and compared the 2000 and 2002 results. The report concluded that opportunities for higher education were at a standstill for the nation as a whole. Together, these reports provided the background data that led to the formation of the National Collaborative for Higher Education Policy.

The System Context for Higher Education

As noted earlier in the chapter, CGRs emerge and evolve within a complex system context that consists of numerous, layered, and interrelated conditions. Here, we briefly analyze the system context affecting higher education in the fifty US states.

In terms of public resource or service conditions, the 2000 and 2002 Measuring Up reports demonstrated a wide variety of problems with higher education in the United States. Although those reports give specific data for specific states, it is useful to highlight summary results. The 2000 report concluded: "The state where one lives makes a big difference in one's opportunity for education and, ultimately, in one's life chances. And it isn't simply a matter of how prosperous the state is: only about 25 percent of the variations in state performance on the indicators used for grading are attributable to state wealth. This means that 75 percent of the difference in performance is related to other factors, such as state policy and leadership. Improvement is clearly possible for every state" (Callan, Doyle, and Finney 2001, 16).

The 2002 Measuring Up report compared states' results on five performance areas. The report found that states made the most progress in preparing students for college-level education; however, only four states improved on all measures of preparation, and students in many states still did not have the opportunity to take challenging high school courses that could prepare them for college. The report also found that only seven states improved their performance on all measures of participation, and that only eleven states improved their performance on all measures of affordability. Moreover, though five states improved their performance on all measures of the timely completion of certificates and degrees, the completion of degrees at four-year colleges and universities remained low, even among the top-performing states. In sum, these findings suggested that despite modest improvements in some states, the benefits of higher education were not accessible to all Americans.

These findings were especially troubling in light of research showing that the United States is falling behind other countries in terms of developing a skilled and knowledgeable workforce. For example, a 2003 Organization for Economic Cooperation and Development comparison of thirty nations found that the United States (1) ranked behind the top five countries in the percentage of twenty- to twenty-four-year-olds with a high school credential; (2) slipped to fifth in the percentage of eighteen- to twenty-four-year-olds enrolled in college; (3) ranked in the bottom half of countries on the proportion of students who complete college certificate or degree programs; (4) ranked among the top nations in the educational attainment of older adults (age thirty-five to sixty-four); but (5) dropped to a tie for seventh in the educational attainment of younger adults (age twenty-five to thirty-four) (Davies 2006). Additional data analysis by the National Center for Higher Education Management Systems revealed:

> The educational pipeline that runs from the start of high school through the completion of college leaks considerably in every state and large numbers of students drop out at key transition points along the way. On average across the nation, for every 100 students who are in the ninth grade, less than half will enroll in college within four years and only about one-fifth will earn a two-year degree (within three years of enrolling in college) or a four-year degree (within six years of enrolling in college). In some states, the losses are more significant in high school; in other states, college going rates are low; and in still others, college students do not persist to earn certificates or degrees (Davies 2006, 3–4).

These and other data led some to suggest that "educational achievement in the United States has stagnated over the last two decades" and that if the issue is not addressed soon, "the educational advancement of other nations compared with the United States may change both the way we live and the freedoms we enjoy" (Davies 2006, 1).

Although these data reveal declines in and real challenges for higher education as a public resource and service, the policy and legal frameworks are also problematic: "States are the primary public policy units for all education within our federal system, from public school systems to colleges and universities" (Callan, Doyle, and Finney 2001, 12). States control public schools, shape the organizational structures of public institutions of higher education, and influence the relationships between public schools and institutions of higher education. Moreover, states provide most of the direct support to and oversight of public higher education institutions and also support both public and private institutions through student financial aid, tax exemptions, and sometimes direct appropriations. Thus, though federal initiatives are not without meaning, "only the states have the means and broad responsibility for assuring opportunity for education and training beyond high school" (Callan, Doyle, and Finney 2001, 12).

The different policies of the fifty states have been influential in shaping the preparation of the collective American workforce; however, this patchwork approach to higher education has created challenges for developing systems and policy approaches that advance the United States as a whole. These challenges have been exacerbated by the fact that historically states have relied on a regulatory approach to higher education policymaking and budgeting, and now must move forward with new policies that are "responsive to increased demands for more and better higher education at a time of limited institutional adaptability and of severely constrained resources" (Callan, Doyle, and Finney 2001, 18).

Creating such policies is difficult given various political dynamics and power relations within state governments and higher education institutions. Certainly, elected politicians, from governors to state legislators to local officials, need to work together to address the problems of higher education. However, these elected officials must also work with the presidents, chancellors, provosts, and governing board members of public and private higher education institutions. Although these relationships vary from state to state, it is highly likely that all the states have at least some degree of conflict in the higher education arena. This conflict might be generated from historic relations, and could, at the very least, emerge from the realities of institutional and resource constraints. Conflicts may be either mitigated or exacerbated to the extent that education networks are in place in a particular state, by the socioeconomic and cultural characteristics of the state, and / or by the degree to which those characteristics are changing.

Drivers for Higher Education Collaboration

In this case, the surrounding system context was rife with conditions that raised the profile of higher education challenges. Despite these problems, the Measuring Up reports themselves were insufficient for propelling the creation of a CGR to address the issue. It was not until all four drivers emerged that a CGR was formed.

Uncertainty was clearly present and was particularly articulated in concerns about the competitiveness of the United States in the global economy. For example, Gordon Davies (2006, 1), the director of the National Collaborative for Higher Education Policy, wrote:

> In meeting the challenges of globalization we in the United States need to mobilize our resources and adapt our public policies so that we do not fall behind other developed and developing nations in educating our population. As the global economy has developed and other nations have assumed primacy in traditional manufacturing sectors, most states in the US have had to reshape their economies. Now that several Asian nations have

developed strong capacity in high-technology industries, the effort to compete effectively in this sector has become urgent for many states as well. Yielding the advantage of a skilled and knowledgeable workforce to China and India, two emerging economic giants, or to other nations would be a strategic error with economic and social consequences.

Interdependence was also present and had several dimensions. First, the United States cannot compete in the global economy by changing the higher education systems of only one or handful of states. Rather, competitiveness must be assessed across the nation as a whole, which means that all the states needed to work on this issue. Although individual states certainly had variance in policies, a comprehensive framework that guided individual state action, particularly in relation to common needs across states, was required (Davies 2006).

Second, states generally lacked the expertise to move forward on policy change and needed to work with others. As Callan, Doyle, and Finney (2001, 19) note, "State leaders have little experience in organizing policymaking along the lines suggested here, much less in designing appropriate public policy and funding approaches for a more student-centered and market-driven environment. And there is little experience with the articulation of broad, operational public priorities for overall state performance; with designing and linking cohesive policies and accountability to priorities; or with sustaining these efforts politically." This meant that states had to develop ideas and learn best practices from each other.

Finally, there were interdependencies within the states themselves. No one person or organization could tackle the challenges of higher education alone. Within each state, government, education, and civic leaders had to work together to improve the higher education system.

Consequential incentives were also present and were strongly related to the challenges posed by inaction. For example, Davies (2006, 7) asserted, "We need to begin the hard work of maintaining the most responsible citizenry and the most skilled and knowledgeable workforce in the world. How we work together over the next few years will determine how our grandchildren live in the mid-21st century." For many, it was clear that unless political and educational leaders brought both their will and skill to developing a public agenda for higher education, appropriate and meaningful objectives would never be defined, let alone achieved.

Finally, there was initiating leadership for the National Collaborative for Higher Education Policy. Actors from the NCPPHE began the convening effort by reaching out to the Education Commission of the States and the National Center for Higher Education Management Systems. Together, these three nonprofit organizations gained support for their work from the Pew Charitable Trusts.

With this core leadership team in place, the National Collaborative reached out to states that were interested in developing new public agendas for higher education that addressed the needs of state residents and their communities. Five states—Missouri, Rhode Island, Virginia, Washington, and West Virginia—joined in the effort to develop sustainable public agendas for higher education. In addition, the National Collaborative worked informally with seven other states—Indiana, Kentucky, Louisiana, Nevada, North Dakota, South Carolina, and Tennessee. With these state partners, the National Collaborative shifted from a single CGR to a series of nested CGRs. In this nested arrangement, one could also work to identify and examine the system contexts and drivers for the state-level regimes.

In sum, this case demonstrates the importance of understanding the system context and drivers for initiating a CGR. If the groundwork had not been done on understanding the challenges in the context of US higher education, then the initiating leaders would not have been able to make a strong case about uncertainty, interdependence, and consequential incentives. Moreover, without these drivers, the National Collaborative for Higher Education would never have been formed.

Summary

In this chapter, we focused on the formation of CGRs. Specifically, we noted that the formation of a CGR (and, later, its performance) is influenced by the broader set of conditions in the surrounding system context. Some of the most salient elements of this context include public resource or service conditions, policy and legal frameworks, socioeconomic and cultural characteristics, network characteristics, political dynamics and power relations, and the history of conflict. From these and other conditions in the system context emerge four drivers of CGRs: uncertainty, interdependence, consequential incentives, and initiating leadership. We suggested that various degrees and combinations of these four drivers increase the likelihood of forming a CGR.

Next, we discussed the steps needed to actually create a CGR—such as inviting, assembling, and incentivizing potential participants—and noted that the organizational setting of initiating leaders plays an important role in CGR formation. We also introduced the three main formative types of CGRs—self-initiated, independently convened, and externally directed—which we discuss in detail in chapter 8. Finally, we illustrated the system context and drivers of CGRs with a case about the National Collaborative for Higher Education. In the next chapter we examine collaboration dynamics.

CHAPTER 3

Collaboration Dynamics

Principled Engagement, Shared Motivation, and the Capacity for Joint Action

Coming together is a beginning; keeping together is progress;
working together is success.
—Henry Ford

In chapter 2, we described how collaborative governance regimes (CGRs) emerge and function within a system context and are energized by a combination of essential drivers. CGRs may arise slowly or precipitously, intentionally or organically, and with or without third-party or bridging institutions. But then what? How does a CGR get off the ground and start moving? How do participants progress from start-up to action?

In this chapter, we describe the central components and elements of CGRs—the collaboration dynamics of principled engagement, shared motivation, and capacity for joint action. We then provide a short case illustration written by Tanya Heikkila and Andrea Gerlak that reveals the collaboration dynamics within one CGR, the Everglades Restoration Task Force. We conclude with a chapter summary.

Conceptualizing Collaboration Dynamics

The process of effective collaboration has been studied from various disciplinary lenses, through which researchers have observed numerous positive outcomes, such as improved clarity on key issues and concerns; better integration of relevant knowledge into deliberations; better-quality decisions; more effective management of differences and conflicts; enhanced trust and mutual respect between the involved parties; increased social, operational, and decision-making capacity; and greater perceived legitimacy both within and outside the collaboration (Agranoff and McGuire 2003; Bryson, Crosby, and Stone 2006; Emerson et al. 2009; Fung 2006; Leach and Sabatier 2005; Milward and Provan 2000). In general, there are two approaches to conceptualizing collaborative processes. One approach portrays collaboration as a linear sequence of cognitive steps or stages that occur over time, including problem definition, direction setting, and implementation (e.g., Daniels and Walker 2001; Gray 1989; Selin and Chavez 1995). Another approach views collaboration as consisting of progressively cyclical or iterative interactions between participants (Ansell and Gash 2008; Thomson and Perry 2006). We take the latter approach in constructing our integrative framework for collaborative governance.

Specifically, we unpack the processes at play in a CGR through an examination of collaboration dynamics across three components—principled engagement, shared motivation, and capacity for joint action (see figure 3.1). Each of these components has several underpinning elements; and each component, through its progressive and iterative cycling, also works to generate and support the other two. When successful, these dynamics reinforce what has been called a "virtuous cycle" of collaboration (e.g., Ansell and Gash 2008; Huxham 2003; Imperial 2005). By distinguishing between principled engagement, shared motivation, and capacity for joint action but still connecting them, we are able to better specify the behavioral interactions, interpersonal relations, and functional components of collaboration dynamics.

It is important to remember that though we describe collaboration dynamics in this chapter primarily as interactions between participants "at the table," there are also additional dynamics between each of the participants and those they represent. All participants' level of engagement in a CGR will be constrained by the demands and limitations of their parent organizations or constituencies. Thus, the components of collaboration dynamics apply directly to the participants but also must extend indirectly to align with and generate the "force" needed to influence their parent organizations. In this way, collaboration dynamics is not just about turning self-interested individuals into a purposeful collective; it is also about enlisting and engaging parent organizations, constituencies, or associated networks in the CGR. This issue becomes particularly salient when examining the patterns of collaboration dynamics among the different formative types of CGRs (discussed in chapter 8), as well as when assessing the process performance of CGRs (discussed in chapter 9).

Principled Engagement

Principled engagement occurs iteratively over time. It enables people with differing substantive, relational, and identity goals to collaborate across their respective institutional, jurisdictional, or sectoral boundaries to solve problems,

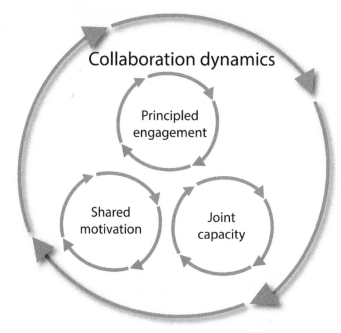

Figure 3.1   Collaboration Dynamics

resolve conflicts, or create value together (Cahn 1994; Cupach and Canary 1997; Lulofs and Cahn 2000).

Before we examine the four elements in this component, it is useful to explain why we call it "principled" engagement, because "principled" suggests certain underlying normative assumptions, particularly about the behavioral interactions between participants. Our use of this term echoes the notion of "principled negotiation," which was first heralded by Fisher and Ury (1981) in their now-classic book *Getting to Yes*. From this work, the word "principled" has developed a robust identity in the conflict resolution and public participation literatures, where it broadly means the use of processes that uphold core tenets for effective engagement. Included among these tenets are fair and civil discourse and open and inclusive communication that are informed by the perspectives and knowledge of all participants (see Ansell and Gash 2008; Carlson 2007; Henton et al. 2005; Leach 2006a; O'Leary, Gerard, and Bingham 2006; Susskind, McKearnan, and Thomas-Larmer 1999). Moreover, effective engagement typically requires balanced representation from "all relevant and significant different interests" (Innes and Booher 1999, 419). Balanced representation is an indicator of diversity—not only in terms of the participants at the table but also in terms of the ideas, beliefs, and perspectives relevant to the issue at hand. Of course, we recognize that not all CGRs will in fact be strictly "principled" in their efforts; however, the normative foundations of principled engagement are likely to advance not only this component but also the other components of collaboration dynamics—shared motivation and the capacity for joint action.

It is important to note here that the processes of principled engagement are not intended to tamp down or diffuse conflict among participants, but rather to help surface differences and create the space to acknowledge and address the tensions among diverse organizations and constituencies. These conflicts may well be interpersonal, but they are most likely to stem from structural or cultural differences among organizations, such as how each organization makes internal decisions or the extent of its representatives' delegated authority to participate or negotiate. Different organizational cultures, conversely, can lead to conflicts—for example, when there are different expectations about degrees of formality; information sharing; dealing with external actors, especially the media; and so forth. In short, collaboration can also generate conflict (O'Leary and Bingham 2007), and thus conflict management skills are requisite competencies for those leading or managing CGRs.

The principled engagement component builds on Daniels and Walker's (2001) phases of collaborative learning and consists of four basic process elements: discovery, definition, deliberation, and determinations (see figure 3.2). Together, these elements form what may be thought of as a dynamic social learning process (e.g., Bandura 1977). Principled engagement may occur between all participants in real time or between subsets of participants at different times. In both cases, engagement may occur in both face-to-face and virtual formats. Although face-to-face dialogue is advantageous at the outset, it is sometimes not essential (e.g., when conflict is low and shared values and objectives quickly surface) or feasible over time (e.g., when the CGR is operating on a large geographic scale).

Discovery

The process of discovery enables participants to reveal and explain their interests, concerns, and values, along with relevant information and its implications. The discovery process (drawn from, but not to be confused with, the legal discovery process) includes both social and scientific inquiry. In this process, participants engage in basic dialogue. They ask questions of themselves and one another, and they seek information and insight from other experts and resource persons. They explore their individual and shared perspectives through open-ended and/or very specific investigations. At the outset,

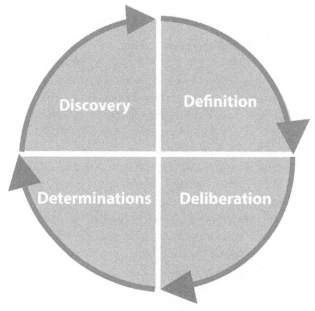

Figure 3.2   Principled Engagement

discovery may focus on identifying different and common interests; later, it may focus on joint fact finding and other analytic investigations (Ehrmann and Stinson 1999; Ozawa 1991).

Definition

As participants pursue discovery, they begin to engage in a definition process. During this process, participants build shared meaning and understanding of the concepts and terminology they are using to describe and discuss problems and opportunities, clarify and adjust tasks and expectations of one another, and set forth shared criteria for assessing information and alternatives (for discussions, see Bentrup 2001; Pahl-Wostl 2007). Although the discovery process is about opening up to and expanding sources of information, the definition process is about containing and shaping information into more tractable terms. Early on, the definitional task may mean drawing boundaries for the chosen problem or opportunity faced by the group—for example, the geographic boundary of a watershed, the limit of the regulatory or market approaches to be considered, or the aspect of health care policy to be tackled. Later, the process may focus on, for example, the specific terminology for a proposed policy provision or the language to use in a public outreach campaign.

Deliberation

As the participants make progress through the initial rounds of discovery and definition, they begin deliberation, where they engage in candid and reasoned communication and information exchange that is structured and oriented toward problem solving. Deliberation is broadly celebrated as a hallmark and essential ingredient of successful principled engagement. As Roberts (2004, 332) notes, "Deliberation is not 'the aggregation of interests.' It requires thoughtful examination of issues, listening to others' perspectives, and coming to a public judgment on what represents the common good." More specifically, deliberation requires participants to take part in open and accessible discussions, during which they "reflect carefully on a matter, [weigh] the strengths and weaknesses of alternative solutions to a problem [and] aim to arrive at a decision or judgment based on not only facts and data but also values, emotions, and other less technical considerations" (Gastil 2005, 164). Deliberation also requires all participants to have an adequate opportunity to speak, listen attentively, and carefully consider the contributions of other participants, and to treat each other with respect (Gastil 2008, 9–10).

The quality of deliberation, especially when participants have differing interests and perspectives, depends on both the skillful advocacy of individual and represented interests and the effective use of conflict resolution strategies and interventions. Moreover, hard conversations, constructive self-assertion, asking and answering challenging questions, and expressing honest disagreements are part and parcel of effective communication across boundaries—a recent National Research Council (2009) report calls this "deliberation with analysis." Thus, the deliberation process requires the creation of a safe space where participants can have a meaningful voice about issues of concern.

Determinations

Finally, principled engagement incorporates the processes of making enumerable joint determinations, including procedural decisions (e.g., setting agendas, tabling a discussion, assigning a work group) and substantive decisions (e.g., reaching agreements on action items or final recommendations). We use the general term "determinations" instead of "decisions" or "agreements" to emphasize the number and variety of group decisions that are made over time in CGRs. Although myriad determinations unfold during the progressive cycling of principled engagement, they often go unnoticed by researchers and other observers, who primarily focus on one final, often external, substantive decision that is considered to be an output or end product of collaboration or conflict resolution (Dukes 2004; Emerson et al. 2009). In an ongoing collaborative effort, however, many substantive and procedural determinations are made, which together form a critical aspect of principled engagement.

Collaboration theory and practice suggest that strong engagement will produce determinations that are fairer and more durable, robust, and efficacious (Innes and Booher 1999; Sipe and Stiftel 1995; Susskind and Cruikshank 1987). However, there has been limited research on the quality of collaborative determinations and the extent to which various kinds of determinations lead to implementation and action (Bingham and O'Leary 2008). Most practitioners and researchers, however, advance consensus building as the foundational method for making group determinations (e.g., Innes and Booher 1999; Susskind and Cruikshank 1987), although this does not mean that the decision rule of reaching a full consensus or unanimity is always required or appropriate (Choi and Robertson 2013; Susskind, McKearnan, and Thomas-Larmer 1999).

A critical threshold determination is whether and when participants can agree on a collective purpose and target goals—that is, the shared objectives they seek to accomplish together (and cannot accomplish separately). The subsequent development of a shared theory of change is another major determination made during principled engagement. We argue that a shared theory of change is critical for any collaborative endeavor, and is especially important in a CGR, given that it shapes the direction and activities of participants over the long term. Thus, although the shared theory of change is not an explicit part of the integrative framework, we give it attention in the following subsection, before moving on to the other components of collaboration dynamics.

The Shared Theory of Change

At the start of principled engagement, participants are likely to acknowledge some mutual interest, based on the drivers that have brought them together. However, they may not necessarily have shared goals, and they are unlikely to have figured out, much less agreed on, the means for achieving these goals. Identifying the "what" and the "how" of participants' collective purpose and shared goals are critical achievements in the initial rounds of collaboration dynamics, and particularly during the early steps of principled engagement. Early in principled engagement, the focus logically needs to be on exploring the range of interests and perspectives represented by the participating individuals and organizations. As the diversity of these interests and perspectives is revealed and acknowledged, so too is the potential for finding a common purpose.

Through the progressive cycling of discovery, definition, deliberation, and determinations, shared goals take shape, along with a strategy for addressing them. This strategy effectively constitutes a "shared theory of change," which better enables program evaluation through a logic model approach (see Kellogg Foundation 2005; Thomas 2003).[1] This cycling may not be an explicitly stated theory, be fully cohesive, or even be "right." But it does contain the shared ideas and underlying assumptions about what might work, and specifically about what the participants might be able to do jointly to achieve their collective purpose and target goals. Thus, at a minimum, the shared theory of change would include the group's understanding of the size of the problem or challenge it is addressing, as well as the scope and scale of its chosen actions (Koontz et al. 2004; Leach and Pelkey 2001).

Because this shared theory of change evolves and is tested over time (as we discuss in chapter 4), its consequent refining is connected to what some call "collaborative learning" (Gerlak and Heikkila 2011), or, in the context of performance management systems, "the cycle of inquiry" (Koliba, Meek, and Zia 2010). Nevertheless, despite the strength of their principled engagement process, not all CGRs are able to develop a shared theory of change. Participants may find during the early stages of engagement that regardless of the drivers motivating their initial participation, they cannot agree on a common purpose or target goals, and that consequently a shared theory of change fails to coalesce. This may lead some participants to withdraw from the collaborative endeavor. In turn, a winnowing of the group could result in a reduction of diversity or of needed representation by key interests, which in turn could lead to the CGR's demise or cause internal reflection and reconfiguration. Building shared motivation—the second dimension of collaboration dynamics—can help address these potential issues and help the CGR test any theory of change that is developed.

Shared Motivation

If the progressive cycling of principled engagement is effective, it motivates participants to continue to engage with one another across their organizational divides. Over time, participants make judgments about whether and how the collaboration will benefit them and the organization or constituency they represent. They also make judgments about whether pursuing the shared theory of change is a worthwhile endeavor given the time and resources required to participate.

Just as it is important to search for common ground and a shared purpose, it is strategically valuable to respect differences and not assume full solidarity between CGR participants. Within self-organizing networks or advocacy coalitions, it can be assumed that like-minded participants and their belief systems will be compatible, if not consonant. But this assumption cannot be made for CGRs, given their heterogeneous participants. At the outset, participants' primary, if not only, perspective and motivation stem from their own interests and those of their represented groups. If these interests are satisfied, then participants are more likely to continue working together. As the cycling of principled engagement continues, participants can also develop a shared motivation that fosters their emerging identification with, and ultimately reinforces their dedication to, the CGR (see figure 3.3). This is particularly important for encouraging informal and formal accountability for CGRs' future performance (see Radin 2006; Romzek, LeRoux, and Blackmar 2012).

In these ways, shared motivation illuminates the interpersonal and relational elements of collaboration dynamics and incorporates many dimensions of social capital (Coleman 1988; Putnam 2000; Putnam, Leonardi, and Nanetti 1993). Moreover, shared motivation is, in part, fostered by principled engagement, and in this sense it is an early indicator of the performance of collaboration dynamics. Once initiated, however, shared motivation can also reinforce or accelerate the principled engagement process (Huxham and Vangen 2005). Like principled engagement, the shared motivation component is not a static condition; instead, it is another self-reinforcing and cycling progression of four interactive elements: trust, mutual understanding, internal legitimacy, and commitment.

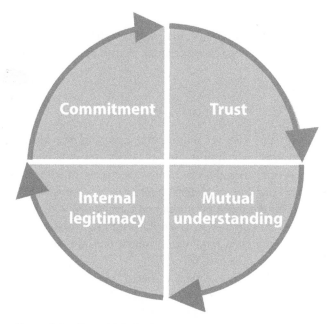

Figure 3.3   Shared Motivation

Trust

The first element of the shared motivation cycle (and the initial outgrowth of the engagement process) is the development of trust, which happens over time as parties work together, get to know each other, and prove to each other that they can be reasonable, predictable, and dependable (Fisher and Brown 1989). Trust has been a long-recognized sine qua non of collaboration (Huxham and Vangen 2005; Koppenjan and Klijn 2004; Leach and Sabatier 2005; Ostrom 1998). In networks, for example, trust has been found to be instrumental in reducing transaction costs, improving investments and stability in relations, and stimulating learning, knowledge exchange, and innovation (Koppenjan and Klijn 2004).

We conceptualize the mechanism whereby trust produces such outcomes as an initial pivotal element within the progressive cycle of shared motivation. In other words, trust generates mutual understanding, which in turn generates internal legitimacy, and, finally, commitment. Trust enables people to go beyond their own personal, institutional, and jurisdictional frames of reference and perspectives toward understanding other peoples' interests, needs, values, and constraints (Bardach 1998; Ring and Van de Ven 1994; Thomson and Perry 2006). At an interpersonal level, trust enables people to first recognize and then appreciate differences in others. It enables people to reveal themselves to others, and hence be seen and appreciated by them (Daniels and Walker 2001; Gray 1989). In short, trust forms the social bonds needed in long-term relationships, such as those present in a CGR. At an interorganizational level, trust builds through aligned objectives and consistent performance.

Mutual Understanding

Trust also forms the basis for mutual understanding, the second element in shared motivation, which grows out of respect for differences—whether differences in personalities, positions, interests, values, or some other meaningful factor. Mutual understanding should not be confused with "shared understanding," as discussed by Ansell and Gash (2008), where participants agree on a shared set of values or goals. Rather, mutual understanding refers to the ability to comprehend and respect others' positions and interests, even when one might not agree with them.

This important distinction between "shared" and "mutual" understanding is more than just semantics. In a cross-boundary CGR, diverse individual participants may develop a shared understanding about a particular goal; however, their individual interests, along with the interests and missions of their parent organizations and constituencies, may vary considerably, and may even be in conflict. Thus, though there may be shared understanding about a goal, there may not be mutual understanding about why a goal is important or about how to achieve that goal. Therefore, recognizing that participants have different rationales for engaging, as well as broader missions that are not necessarily aligned, is important in building mutual understanding.

Internal Legitimacy

Mutual understanding generates a sense of interpersonal validation and relational legitimacy—the third element of shared motivation—which is referred to as "internal legitimacy" by Provan and Milward (1995) and is viewed as a critical process factor by Bryson, Crosby, and Stone (2006). The confirmation that participants in a CGR are trustworthy and credible, with interdependent and sufficiently compatible interests, legitimizes and helps motivate ongoing collaboration dynamics. Moreover, informal interpersonal norms of trust and reciprocity further reinforce confidence in the CGR's legitimacy (cf. Thomson and Perry 2006).

In addition, participants develop confidence in the CGR's efficacy as the progression of collaboration dynamics reveals the potential for pooling and leveraging resources and for creating new capacities (discussed below), and as the shared theory of change gains traction and begins to appear feasible. This cognitive legitimacy is particularly important in a CGR because it provides the participants with specific, substantive grounds beyond relational benefits that enable them to justify their continuing engagement to those they represent.

Commitment

With the development and confirmation of legitimacy comes the creation of bonds of commitment—the fourth element of shared motivation—which enables participants to cross the jurisdictional, organizational, and/or sectoral boundaries that previously separated them and to now commit to the CGR (cf. Ansell and Gash 2008). The nature of this commitment evolves over time, as trust, mutual understanding, and internal legitimacy evolve along with, and are in turn reinforced by, principled engagement. The bonds between the participants may be initially implicit and informal, or may be contingent on the execution of specific tasks or actions. But at some point in the progression of collaboration dynamics, these ties come to be expressed in formal obligations, such as signed charters or written memoranda of understanding. At this point, the participants turn to building capacity for joint action and the emergent CGR becomes actualized.

Before discussing capacity for joint action, it is important again to note that the progression of shared motivation from trust to mutual understanding, internal legitimacy, and commitment works on two levels: directly, at the interpersonal level, between participants; and indirectly, between organizations. Again, this becomes important when assessing the process performance of CGRs (see chapter 9). Translating shared motivation at the interpersonal level into shared motivation at the interorganizational level is done vis-à-vis the communication between the CGR participants and the organizations they represent. The quality and extent of principled engagement may assist in this translation. Moreover, once generated, shared motivation at both levels can enhance and help sustain principled engagement (and vice versa), in a virtuous cycle. If this linkage between the interpersonal and interorganizational levels is not made and maintained, support for ongoing participation in the CGR may be affected.

Participants are rarely granted the same authority or degrees of freedom to negotiate by their own organization; nor will they necessarily participate to the same degree of voluntariness. These differential capacities and inclinations among participants can have an impact on the extent to which shared motivation develops at the interpersonal level and is translated from the participants to the parent organization. This underscores the importance of participants' ability not only to represent the interests of their parent organizations within the CGR but also to convey and build confidence in and commitment to the CGR by the parent organizations.

Capacity for Joint Action

As Himmelman (1994) describes it, "collaboration" means to engage in cooperative activities to enhance the capacity of both self and others to achieve a common purpose. Likewise, collaborative governance is intended to generate outcomes that cooperating parties could not accomplish separately. However, to collaborate, CGR participants must generate enhanced or new capacities for joint action that did not previously exist. Borrowing from Saint-Onge and Armstrong's (2004, 17) definition of capabilities for conductive organizations, the capacity for joint action can be seen as "a collection of cross-functional elements that come together to create the potential for taking effective action" and serve "as the link between strategy and performance." In other words, capacity for joint action is the functional dimension of collaboration dynamics that enables CGR participants to accomplish their collective purpose as specified in their theory of change.

In our integrative framework, the capacity for joint action is conceptualized as the combination of four necessary elements: procedural and institutional

Figure 3.4   Capacity for Joint Action

arrangements, leadership, knowledge, and resources (see figure 3.4). These elements reinforce one another but are not necessarily sequential, as are the elements in the other two components of collaboration dynamics. In some cases, one or more of the elements of the capacity for joint action may be offered upfront as an inducement to collaboration by the initiating leaders. Thus, some level of capacity for joint action may be present at the outset of the CGR. However, some degree of contributed or added capacity for each of these elements is needed for CGRs to function; thus, the capacity for joint action is most fully realized as an intermediate outcome of the progressive cycling of principled engagement and shared motivation.

Procedural and Institutional Arrangements

Most, if not all, collaboration frameworks recognize the importance of formal and informal rules and protocols, institutional design, and other structural dimensions. These process protocols and organizational structures are necessary to manage the repeated interactions of multiple participants over time. Many process protocols emerge from the conflict resolution literature, including arrangements such as agreements to mediate, meeting ground rules, decision rules, and operating protocols—all of which help promote stronger principled engagement. Other protocols that govern collaborative endeavors may include informal norms of reciprocity and/or more formal rules of network interactions (Thomson and Perry 2006). The common pool resource literature has contributed greatly to our understanding of the importance of rules for self-governance, including constitutional rules (laying out the basic scope and authorities for joint effort), decision-making rules, and operating procedures (Bingham 2009; Ostrom 1990). Another useful distinction is between rules that govern specific interactions between participants in networks and rules that govern the arena or institutional forum of networks (Koppenjan and Klijn 2004). As CGRs become larger, more complex, and more prolonged, they need more explicit protocols and structures for administration and management (Milward and Provan 2000, 2006). In such cases, more formal institutional instruments—such as charters, by-laws, and representational requirements—may supplement the other process arrangements and informal norms.

Again, it is helpful to define these procedural and institutional arrangements at both the intraorganizational level (i.e., how a single group or organization will govern and manage itself in the CGR) and at the interorganizational level (i.e., how the groups of organizations will govern and manage together and integrate with external decision-making authorities). In general, the internal authority structure of collaborative institutions tends to be less hierarchical and stable, and more complex and fluid, than those found in traditional bureaucracies (Bryson, Crosby, and Stone 2006; Huxham and Vangen 2005). Such structures and protocols may vary by function, for example, taking on the shape of informational, developmental, outreach, or action networks (Agranoff and McGuire 2003). They also may vary by form, for example, being administered as a self-managing system, by a designated lead agency or agencies, or with the creation of a new governmental structure (Milward and Provan 2006).

Leadership

Most researchers and practitioners would identify leadership as an important, if not the most important, element of joint capacity (e.g., Ansell and Gash 2008, 2012; Bingham and O'Leary 2008; Carlson 2007; Saint-Onge and Armstrong 2004; Susskind and Cruikshank 1987). We have already introduced initiating leadership as an essential driver of collaboration, but CGRs require that their leadership be strengthened and broadened to include many additional roles. In this way, leadership can be a significant outgrowth of collaboration dynamics (cf. Agranoff and McGuire 2003; Bryson, Crosby, and Stone 2006), and particularly of the capacity for joint action.

Box 3.1 presents a variety of leadership roles in cross-boundary governance, including initiators and champions, sponsors and conveners, facilitators/mediators, participants representing organizations or constituencies, scientific and technical experts, and public decision makers (Carlson 2007; Dukes 2001). Certain leadership roles are essential at the outset, others are more critical during moments of deliberation or conflict management, and still others are vital in championing the shared theory of change through to implementation (Agranoff 2006; Bryson, Crosby, and Stone 2006; Carlson 2007). A growing body of scholarly and professional literature examines collaborative leadership (O'Leary, Choi, and Gerard 2012; see also Emerson, Nabatchi, and Balogh 2012; Linden 2010; Morse, Buss, and Kinghorn 2007), including collaborative leadership attributes (e.g., being open minded, patient, self-confident, risk-oriented, flexible, and unselfish) and collaborative leadership skill sets (e.g., being a good communicator and listener, working well with people, and having facilitation, negotiation, and problem-solving abilities) (e.g., O'Leary and Gerard 2012).

Knowledge

"As knowledge becomes increasingly specialized and distributed and as institutional infrastructures become more complex and interdependent, the demand for collaboration increases" (Ansell and Gash 2008, 544). Scholars seem to agree, and several have studied and written explicitly about the importance of knowledge management for collaboration in networks (e.g., Agranoff 2007; Cross and Parker 2004). For Saint-Onge and Armstrong (2004), the ability to transmit high-quality knowledge effectively both within and across organizations is the essence of "conductivity" in high-performance organizations and networks. Knowledge is also the central element in adaptive resource management models, where conditions of scientific or resource uncertainty lead parties to cooperate in management experiments to test and build knowledge for better and more enduring management practices (Holling 1978).

In many ways, knowledge is the currency of collaboration. Knowledge, once guarded, must be shared with others; and knowledge jointly needed must be generated by participants working together. Contested knowledge requires full consideration, and incomplete knowledge must be balanced and enhanced with new knowledge. In essence, collaboration requires the aggregation, division, and reassembling of data and information, as well as the generation of new, shared information: "Knowledge is information combined with understanding and capability; it lives in the minds of people. . . . Knowledge guides action, whereas information and data can merely inform or confuse" (Groff and Jones 2003, 30). The term "knowledge," which has

---

Box 3.1 Key CGR Leadership Roles

Initiators or champions invest in starting a collaborative endeavor. Their direction, commitment, goodwill, and prestige attract others, both within and across different sectors, to co-lead or participate in a CGR.

Sponsors typically pay for some of the upfront costs of a CGR—for example, by providing meeting space, technology, and administrative assistance. *Conveners* assist in creating the right conditions for collaboration and in bringing diverse and representative participants to the table. The reputations of sponsors and conveners as capable, fair, and trusted leaders are especially important in motivating early commitment and establishing both the CGR's internal and external legitimacy.

Facilitators or mediators bring their professional expertise to bear as impartial managers of collaboration dynamics, working to assure transparency and to build a consensus between the group's members. They are accountable to the group, and they are particularly helpful in assuring effective and efficient processes and resolving disagreements when conflict or significant differences among the group arise.

Participants also lead, representing organizations or constituents at the table and committing to working toward joint solutions and shared benefits. Participants may lead as decision makers, planners, and/or implementers.

Scientific and technical experts translate complex information and analyses for the CGR participants and the lay public. They provide leadership in helping participants understand research findings and their implications for the issue at hand. When the science is contested, some experts can serve as interpreters of the differences and contradictions that may exist.

Public decision makers provide leadership as supporters and advocates of the CGR at the outset, and in many cases as the final decision makers and implementers of CGR recommendations or directions.

---

been called out as one of the assets of human capital by Agranoff (2008, 165), is used here to mean the social capital of shared information that has been weighed, processed, and integrated with the values and judgments of CGR participants.

Resources

One of the most recognized benefits of collaboration is its potential for sharing and leveraging scarce resources (Thomson and Perry 2006). Adequate budget support and access to other needed resources have been found to be instrumental in successful collaborative networks (Provan and Milward 1995). Included among the many needed resources are funding; in-kind support; meeting space; travel expenses; telecommunications; technical, technological, and logistical support; administrative and organizational assistance; and the requisite skills and expertise for data gathering and analysis and for implementation functions.

Most often, participants are not similarly or evenly endowed with resources; however, participants nonetheless can bring different kinds of valued resources to the table. Disparities can also exist among those benefiting from the resources garnered through collaboration. The perceived and real fairness, legitimacy, and efficacy of CGRs can depend on how well these resource differences are managed. Many researchers see the ways in which resources are marshaled and configured as critical for the success of collaboration (Milward and Provan 2000; Thomson and Perry 2006). Resource disparities can be particularly acute in cross-cultural settings, where language, customs, and culture can present barriers to engagement. Power can also be viewed as a resource; and like other resources, it is almost always distributed unevenly across participants (Bryson, Crosby, and Stone 2006; Huxham and Vangen 2005).

The four elements of the capacity for joint action—procedural and institutional arrangements, leadership, knowledge, and resources—develop through the synergistic interaction of principled engagement and shared motivation. In turn, they contribute to this synergy; as the capacity for joint action is put into effect, it further reinforces principled engagement and shared motivation, and strengthens the purpose and performance of CGRs. The appropriate levels, sequence, or combination of these elements depends on the group's purpose and shared theory of change, as well as each participant's baseline capacities. In the next section of this chapter, Tanya Heikkila and Andrea Gerlak describe collaboration dynamics through their case illustration on the Everglades Restoration Task Force.

Case Illustration: The Everglades Restoration Task Force

Tanya Heikkila and Andrea K. Gerlak

Collaborative efforts to restore the Florida Everglades emerged in the 1990s following years of conflict and concern over the degradation of this culturally and ecologically significant ecosystem (Boswell 2005; Grunwald 2006). In 1996, Congress created the Everglades Restoration Task Force—which consists of fourteen representatives from federal, state, tribal, and local agencies—to help facilitate the coordination of diverse restoration efforts and address conflicts among the different stakeholders in the South Florida region. These stakeholders included environmental groups, agricultural communities, local governments, state and federal environmental agencies, water supply and flood control managers, Native American tribes, and federal landowners and managers. In 2000, the restoration effort was further institutionalized under a federally approved plan—known as the Comprehensive Everglades Restoration Plan—that laid out a number of operational projects needed to improve water quality, water flows, and habitat protection. Since 2000, the task force has met regularly to discuss the coordination of this plan's implementation, as well as the broader restoration efforts.

This case illustration draws on research to describe how all three components of collaboration dynamics—principled engagement, shared motivation, and the capacity for joint action—are playing out in the case of restoration of the Florida Everglades. Research examining the task force's role as the central collaborative body in the restoration effort has involved in-depth analysis and coding all the task force's meetings over a ten-year period, as well as a survey of task force members and more than a dozen interviews with participants in the restoration program. Drawing from published papers and ongoing research on the task force's meetings and decision processes, this short case examines the nature of collaboration dynamics in the Everglades restoration effort, as well as some of the challenges collaborative processes may face in sustaining these dynamics.

Principled Engagement

One way the Everglades Restoration Task Force fosters principled engagement is through the discovery of the shared knowledge and understanding of the ecosystem conditions, technical challenges, and feasibility of restoration efforts. For example, within a ten-year time frame, task force meetings have included a total of 315 knowledge-building presentations (Heikkila and Gerlak 2014). This represents 20 percent of the time in meetings and averages to 6.7 presentations per meeting. Additionally, in reviewing the agenda items covered by the task force over time, about 20 percent of their discussions have focused on coordination of the broader restoration program, and another 20 percent have involved updates from advisory groups (Heikkila and Gerlak 2014). Task force members have participated in approximately ten field trips that serve to build shared experiences.

In addition, the task force has provided a formalized venue for deliberation, which is a major feature of meetings that takes up about one-third of the meeting time (Heikkila and Gerlak 2014). The task force also has a process to deliberate with non–task force members and the public. Public comments typically come at the end of meetings, where environmental nonprofits make up well over half the groups participating (Heikkila, Gerlak, and Davis 2012). However, analyses of the meetings showed that dialogues or exchanges between members of the public and the task force members are limited.

The task force also engages in the process of definition and building of shared meaning through discussion. According to their Protocol Regarding Consensus and Voting, the members of the task force are supposed to work toward a consensus (SFERTF 2002). Thus, during meetings, the task force spends most of its time in discussions, which vary quite widely by topic but typically involve multiple and diverse members. Meetings also include task force administrative issues, such as updates and procedural information from the executive director and task force chair, as well as updates from the advisory groups on their processes and duties.

Among the many determinations made by the task force include establishing shared procedures, action items (e.g., tasking one of the advisory groups with research), and approval of the task force's products, such as its strategic plan. However, the amount of time spent on these issues is minimal compared with the broader discussions and debates about the program's technical nature (Heikkila and Gerlak 2014). During the task force's early years, the most meeting time was spent dealing with administrative and governance issues—such as developing and deciding on operating rules and procedures—and less time was spent on programmatic decision making or voting.

Although these and other determinations are clear, the mechanisms for conflict resolution are unclear. In studying the meetings, concerns expressed by some of the tribal members of the task force over restoration priorities and activities do not appear to have been resolved. Furthermore, the task force does not appear to have attempted to deal with such conflicts or concerns directly—for example, by developing action items.

One example of how the task force developed a shared theory of change can be seen in its drafting and approval of a strategic plan. With a charge from Congress, the task force developed its first strategic plan during a series of several meetings and conferences. The plan included a compendium of all ongoing projects at the time, outlined how the Everglades restoration would occur, identified needed resources and responsible entities, and linked strategic goals to outcomes. The task force worked through numerous versions of the plan, incorporating comments from task force members and stakeholders in the public engagement process.

As collaboration evolved in the Everglades, the shared theory of change also evolved. For example, in the mid-2000s, in response to a lack of federal funding and engagement in the larger restoration program and concerns that public interest was waning (research interview with Ken Ammon, August 21, 2009), top officials of the South Florida Water Management District (SFWMD) led a series of internal brainstorming sessions to try to jump-start the restoration effort. Through the proposed Acceler8 program, the SFWMD proposed to design and construct restoration projects with state dollars (GAO 2007, 9). To build a shared theory of change, SFWMD leaders worked to ease concerns about the program in cooperation with federal officials and environmental groups. Some federal officials even saw the program as a way to help propel further federal investment and attention to the Everglades in the face of competing environmental crises and disasters (research interview with Dennis Duke, June 6, 2007).

Social dynamics played a role in helping not only to disseminate information and new ideas but also to garner the support, and arguably the trust, needed to translate these ideas into learning products (Gerlak and Heikkila 2011). Although the initial idea to create Acceler8 was not hatched through the broader collaborative process, multiple groups, including the task force and the various functionally specialized subgroups, provided a forum for generating new ideas, as well disseminating and translating these new ideas, before establishing and implementing Acceler8 (research interview with Ken Ammon, August 21, 2009). In this way, structural design features played a key role in shaping information dissemination in the learning process (Gerlak and Heikkila 2011).

More recently, in light of project delays and limited funding, the US Army Corps of Engineers, the lead federal agency in the restoration effort, has proposed the Central Everglades Planning Project (CEPP) as an alternative to the Comprehensive Everglades Restoration Plan. The goal of the CEPP is to deliver a finalized plan for a suite of restoration projects specifically in the central Everglades on land already in public ownership to allow more water to be directed south to the central Everglades, Everglades National Park, and Florida Bay (ACE and SFWMD 2013). It also calls for a more streamlined approach to project planning and for enhanced public and stakeholder participation in the Central Everglades restoration effort (SFERTF 2011).

Shared Motivation

In theory, the processes of principled engagement can provide the opportunity to cultivate the elements of shared motivation—trust, mutual understanding, internal legitimacy, and commitment. The meetings of the Everglades Restoration Task Force, for example, provide a venue for regular and long-term interaction for the task force's different stakeholders. The task force meets about four times a year for approximately five hours. On average, about half the fourteen regular members are in attendance, with alternates often sent as substitutes for missing members.

To date, this research only speaks indirectly to how the elements of shared motivation have evolved. At least on the surface, commitment to the process by the participants is visible. Most members have regularly participated in meetings and have maintained an active level of involvement over time. This may also speak to the legitimacy of the process. Yet, one may question whether limited funding and a lack of significant progress on the implementation of the restoration effort raise questions about the legitimacy of the broader effort.

In terms of building trust and mutual understanding, the task force's early investments in voting on process-level design features and action items may have helped build the trust needed to enable it to make more consensus-based decisions in later years. However, research has not directly measured the perceived level of trust, mutual understanding, and commitment by individual members of the task force. Survey and interview research could provide insights on whether these characteristics are currently present among task force participants, and could potentially tease out whether these perceptions have changed over time.

In addition to the task force's meetings, shared motivation may be developed and heightened among participants interacting in related venues or in more informal settings. Interview data suggest that the task force's administrative staff works on many issues behind the scenes and that task force members often communicate outside meetings. Similarly, the working group and science coordination group engage in dialogue and decision making that inform the task force. One important avenue for research would be additional surveys and interviews to find out if participants engaged in these informal and advisory processes are building more shared motivation than those who do not interact outside the formal meetings.

This research also suggests that there are many obstacles to achieving the self-reinforcing and cycling progression of trust, mutual understanding, internal legitimacy, and commitment as part of shared motivation. Conflicting agency missions pose one challenge. Indeed, the more development-minded missions of the Army Corps of Engineers and the SFWMD do not always align with the US Environmental Protection Agency's mandate to regulate water quality. Similarly, the federally recognized Native American Tribes may have land management and resource use objectives that differ from those of other actors. External events, such as lawsuits, can also stymie shared motivation. From 2000 to 2010, more than forty lawsuits regarding the restoration efforts were initiated. In addition, political turnover or an absence of funding can challenge the development of shared motivation. For example, between

2008 and 2010, while waiting for the Obama administration's appointments to the federal agencies to be confirmed, task force activity waned. Additionally, the downsizing of the state's planned buy-outs of sugar lands, which were seen as key to the restoration program, and stalled funding from the federal government have plagued the restoration effort since 2008 (Reid 2010).

Capacity for Joint Action

The capacity for joint action in the Everglades Restoration Task Force has developed over time. In terms of procedural and institutional arrangements, the task force's charter outlines the scope of membership, the powers of the task force, and its duties, such as coordinating program and strategies, sharing information on the restoration effort, and supporting science and coordination of research on restoration (SFERTF 1997). The task force is also supported by other coordinating bodies, including a science coordination group and a working group, which assists the task force in developing policies, strategies, and priorities. The task force also has established internal procedures, such as its protocol regarding consensus and voting (SFERTF 2002). Establishing these procedural elements was an emphasis in the early years of the program (Heikkila and Gerlak 2014).

Leadership is also formally established in the task force through the chair position. In the task force's early days, its leadership engaged in consensus-building and conflict resolution training sessions "in an effort to pave a path for future collaboration and help ameliorate historic conflict between some agencies and tribes" (research interview with Greg May, June 19, 2007). As a group, the task force delegates decisions and tasks to its subgroups; however, this delegation has tended to wane over time (Heikkila and Gerlak 2014).

As mentioned above, the task force fosters principled engagement through "discovery" of the shared knowledge and understanding of the ecosystem conditions, technical challenges, and feasibility of restoration efforts. Over time, knowledge-building activities have increased at task force meetings, which have contributed to the capacity for joint action (Heikkila and Gerlak 2014). These activities center on research presentations by the task force advisory groups, sharing technical studies on restoration ecology or endangered species, and reports on feasibility studies about proposed restoration projects or strategies. These knowledge-building presentations are seen as important and necessary steps in ensuring that there is technical and factual understanding across the diverse actors and stakeholders (research interviews with Dave Kimball, June 21, 2007; Greg May, June 19, 2007; and Rock Salt, June 19, 2007).

Finally, the capacity for joint action has been supported by the resources that the members contribute—especially the regular time and energy of task force members. The task force also has a staff, funded by the US Department of the Interior, that includes an executive director. The director and the staff support the organization and coordinate meetings and advisory bodies. Although these resources have allowed the task force to sustain its interactions and processes over a fairly long period of time, its biggest resource challenge has been the limited funding directed by the federal government to implement the actual restoration projects that it is supposed to coordinate. This funding primarily comes through budget priorities identified in congressional Water Resources Development Acts (WRDA), for which funds must then be allocated by Congress. The last WRDA passed by Congress was in 2007. Although the State of Florida has occasionally stepped in to invigorate the restoration effort, this funding has been limited. The challenge may be that the overall effort has been estimated to cost more than $10 billion. Whether funding will come through for the recent plans to push a more scaled-back restoration design through the CEPP is still an open question.

This case about the Florida Everglades Task Force—a federally chartered CGR involving representatives from federal, state, tribal, and local agencies—illustrated the three components of collaboration dynamics. Using empirical data, the case showed the cyclical nature of discovery, definition, deliberation, and determinations during principled engagement, as well as how the cycling of these elements helped the task force to develop a shared theory of change. Though more research is needed, the case also explored how shared motivation—including its elements of trust, mutual understanding, internal legitimacy, and commitment—was cultivated over the long term, and particularly though the purposeful design of formal task force meetings, as well as more informal interactions. Finally, the case examined the evolution of the capacity for joint action, exploring how the formalization of procedural and institutional arrangements, leadership, knowledge, and resources helped the task force meet its objectives. In addition to illustrating the central concepts in this chapter, the case also examined some of the challenges that must be faced in trying to sustain collaboration dynamics.

Summary

In this chapter we unpacked the concept of collaboration dynamics. Specifically, we suggested that collaboration dynamics involves the progressive and iterative cycling of three components: principled engagement, which involves elements pertaining to the behavioral interactions between participants; shared motivation, which involves elements pertaining to the interpersonal relations between participants; and the capacity for joint action, which involves elements pertaining to functional structures. During principled engagement, CGR participants engage in discovery, definition, deliberation, and determination. One of the most important determinations that CGR participants make concerns the shared theory of change, or the strategy that the group will use to achieve its collective purpose and target goals. An effective process of principled engagement reinforces shared motivation, which includes trust, mutual understanding, internal legitimacy, and commitment. Finally, principled engagement and shared motivation help build the capacity for joint action, which is generated through procedural and institutional arrangements, leadership, knowledge, and resources.

The components of collaboration dynamics, as well as the elements within each component, are not sequential or linear, but rather operate in vibrant and continual cycles. The elements work synergistically to enhance each component, and the components work together to enhance each other. Moreover, collaboration dynamics unfold not only between the CGR participants but also between the participants and those they represent. Finally, the case illustration by Heikkila and Gerlak demonstrated the interacting components and elements of collaboration dynamics in a case involving a federally chartered CGR that oversees the restoration of the South Florida Everglades. In the next chapter, we explore the role of actions, outcomes, and adaptation in the framework.

Note

1. Emerson, Nabatchi, and Balogh (2012) used the term "shared theory of action." Here, we have opted to use "shared theory of change," not only to be more consistent with related research in the policy sciences but also because the strategy for change extends beyond the CGR's actions to include the accomplishment of target goals through collaborative actions and outcomes. We discuss this further in chapters 4 and 9.

CHAPTER 4

Generating Change

Collaborative Actions, Outcomes, and Adaptation

> In the long history of humankind (and animal kind, too) those who
> learned to collaborate and improvise most effectively have prevailed.
> —Charles Darwin

In chapter 3, we described collaboration dynamics as encompassing the inter-active and iterative cycling of principled engagement, shared motivation, and the capacity for joint action, which respectively reflect the behavioral inter-actions, interpersonal relations, and functional components of collaborative governance regimes (CGRs). These dynamics emerge and evolve over time, and they are contingent on the system context and the set of drivers that mobilize them. These dynamics are also generative; they lead to actions that are intended to make progress toward the collective purpose of the CGR. Together, collaboration dynamics and actions shape the form and activities that constitute a CGR.

In this chapter, we focus on the collaborative actions that develop from collaboration dynamics, and we explore the resulting outcomes of these actions and the types of internal and external adaptation that can occur as a consequence (see figure 4.1). We use a case illustration of the Military Community Compatibility Committee to elucidate the roles of actions, outcomes, and adaptation in a CGR. We conclude the chapter with a brief summary.

Collaborative Actions

People and organizations collaborate across boundaries to get something done. Collaborative governance is intended to be instrumental, propelling actions that "could not have been attained by any of the organizations acting alone" (Huxham 2003, 403). Although there may be symbolic and associa-tional purposes for collaboration that some consider less directly instrumen-tal, these also result in actions that serve as means to some purposive end.

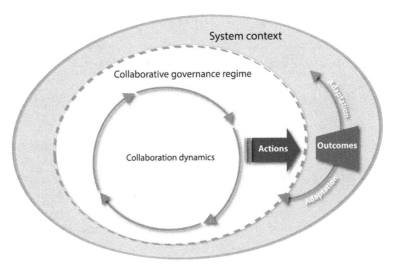

Figure 4.1   Actions, Outcomes, and Adaptation

Despite the importance of collaborative actions, they have received only limited attention from researchers and have often been left unspecified (Koontz and Thomas 2006). Collaborative actions, which are both distinct from and linked to collaboration dynamics, are intentional efforts undertaken as a consequence of the collective choices made by a CGR during collaboration dynamics. Moreover, these actions are not ends in and of themselves. They are means to an end—the CGR's collective purpose or target goal—and are based on the theory of change and an articulated strategy that participants have agreed is necessary for accomplishing that end. As discussed previously in this book, and as further examined in chapter 9, though theories of change may be assumed or implicit, collaborative actions are more difficult to agree on and accomplish, much less assess, if the shared goals and the rationale for them have not been made explicit.

Collaborative actions take many forms and vary depending on a CGR's specific context, charge, and goals. Some CGRs have very broad aims (e.g., taking actions related to strategic development or within a particular policy issue or area), whereas others have narrower goals (e.g., taking actions on a particular project or gathering and analyzing specific information) (Huxham et al. 2000). In either case, collaborative actions may include securing endorsements or educating constituents or the public; enacting new policy measures, laws, and regulations; marshalling external resources; deploying staff; siting and permitting facilities; building or cleaning up sites; carrying out new management practices; monitoring implementation; or enforcing compliance—among many other activities. Moreover, collaborative actions may be executed by the CGR participants collectively, by individual CGR participants or constituencies, by the CGR's leaders or managers, or by external agents or authorities.

Collaborative actions also vary according to their function. They may be operational actions that enable the growth or maintenance of the CGR itself. They may be developmental or revenue-generating actions that build or sustain the CGR and/or its participants. They may be networking actions that establish and build the CGR's external legitimacy and reputation. They may be substantive or purpose-driven actions that directly advance the joint mission of the CGR's participants (Agranoff 2012). In short, just as CGRs vary, so do their actions. Thus, when comparing actions across CGRs, it is useful to distinguish among particular CGR functions.

Again, collaborative actions are strategic outgrowths of the CGR's theory of change. In some cases, CGRs will choose initial actions that are easy first steps to take (so-called low-hanging fruit) based on the CGR's limited capacity at the outset. More intermediate actions (e.g., a publicity campaign) might leverage additional resources or overcome a critical barrier (e.g., debunking misinformation) and thus in turn enable a major critical or culminating action (e.g., passing legislation or a new bond issue). Collaborative actions thus occur over time in a strategic sequence that aligns with the shared theory of change.

This might suggest that we assume that CGR participants are all rational actors, and that once their shared theory of change is set, a logical series of actions will unfold. QED. Not at all. Remember, CGRs are engaged in an evolving process of problem solving. The ongoing cycling of collaboration dynamics continues to yield new information and new understanding; and as a given action takes place, it may also reshape or transform the initial theory of change. Serendipity can also play a role in CGRs; changes in the system context or drivers may lead to subtle or substantial redirections of the CGR or its participants.

When collaborative actions are effective, they are likely to reinforce the CGR's shared theory of change and to propel subsequent actions in line with this theory. However, actions that miss the mark, prove too costly, or have unintended negative consequences will require giving further attention to the CGR's theory of change, reanimating principled engagement, challenging shared motivation, and reassessing the capacity for joint action. This integral connection between collaboration dynamics and actions is why they are depicted together in the integrative framework for collaborative governance as the CGR's central, interactive dimensions.

Outcomes

The nature and quality of CGR actions, or, outputs, in turn have external effects known as outcomes. These outcomes include the intermediate changes in conditions necessary to reach target goals and the resulting effects of accomplishing these goals. These outcomes matter not only to scholars who study CGRs but also to the CGR as a whole, to its participants and to their parent organizations and constituencies, and to its potential beneficiaries (cf. Provan and Milward 1995).[1] Researchers have tended to focus on the outcomes of the collaborative process, such as trust and relationships, and on specific decisions or discrete actions or outputs (Ingraham, Joyce, and Donahue 2003; Koontz and Thomas 2012; Leach and Sabatier 2005; Lubell 2005). Our conceptualization of CGR outcomes centers on the intermediate and end effects of CGRs related to their target goals—that is, results on the ground. Although we concentrate on the intended outcomes or desired changes explicitly specified by collaborators in accordance with their shared theory of change, one should not disregard indirect, unintended, or unanticipated effects.

The potential variety of outcomes is large. Outcomes may be changes of state within the conditions of the system context, or they may be alterations in the specific, preexisting, or projected condition that prompted the formation of the CGR. Outcomes may include the improved quality or quantity of a public good, the more efficient delivery of a needed public service, or an innovative response to a new opportunity. Outcomes may be physical, environmental, social, economic, and/or political. They may be short-lived or long term, and very specific or quite broad in their reach. The less proximate the outcomes are to the collaborative action or the more dependent they are on a number of contributing factors, the more difficult it is to directly or significantly attribute them to the collaborative action(s).

The questions of which outcomes matter and to whom they matter are of ongoing interest to those who study the performance of CGRs. In chapter 9 we take up performance evaluation directly, but here it is useful to underscore the points that there are different kinds of outcomes and that different outcomes matter to different audiences (Gray 2000; Provan and Milward 1995). Thus, performance assessments should focus on outcomes in the resource or service conditions being targeted for improvement that are of value to three key constituencies: the CGR's participants, the organizations represented by the participants, and the direct and indirect beneficiaries of the targeted resources or services. The need to assess performance from multiple perspectives is true not only for outcomes but also for collaborative actions and adaptation.

Adaptation

Adaptation is a less prominent, but increasingly important, concept for understanding the evolution and performance of CGRs over time. By adaptation, we mean the potential for transformative changes, or small, but significant adjustments in response to the outcomes of collaborative action. This very simple definition draws on the literature on institutional adaptation and resilience related to climate change, which specifically defines adaptation as "a process of deliberate change in anticipation of or in reaction to external stimuli and stress" (Emerson and Gerlak 2014, 770; citing Nelson, Adger, and Brown 2007). Although collaborative governance is often argued to be more responsive to external changes than centralized, hierarchical systems, the notion of adaptation and the mechanisms that enable it are rarely specified (Bingham and O'Leary 2008; Cheng and Sturtevant 2012; Henton et al. 2005; Pahl-Wostl 2007; Wagner and Fernandez-Gimenez 2009).

Within the context of CGRs, adaptation can occur at three different units of analysis: within the CGR itself, among the CGR's participant organizations, and with respect to the targeted resource or service. Here, we are interested in the distinct and multilevel nature of adaptation, in part because of claims that in complex situations, CGRs can be more flexible and malleable than hierarchical management approaches. For example, researchers on adaptive resource management (an arena that predates the broader conceptualization of collaborative governance) have posited that more resilient, decentralized systems facing conditions of uncertainty or limited scientific knowledge may reduce the utility of permanent management investments or strategies (Holling 1978). Little is known, however, about how CGRs and participating organizations adapt to the outcomes of their efforts over time (Heikkila and Gerlak 2005; Karkkainen 2002). We discuss adaptation at these three units of analysis in further detail in chapter 9.

As noted in previous chapters, CGRs are created in response to some condition or demand in the system context to which organizations or actors cannot respond adequately on their own. Thus, CGRs themselves represent an institutional adaptation. Over time, CGRs must face and respond to the consequences of the outcomes they have created through their actions, regardless of whether these consequences are pleasing or disappointing. For example, a CGR might either expand and take advantage of momentum or contract and circle the wagons. It might either change its shared goals or adjust its theory of change. Moreover, a CGR must adapt to both ongoing changes in the external system context and to internal changes within itself and between its participants and parent organizations. In short, CGRs must manage to adapt to changes and simultaneously remain sufficiently stable to be able to perform over time. Thus, not unlike other organizations competing in the private marketplace or for public funding, CGRs must develop and retain their viability; that is, they must develop the capacity to continue to act while adapting to changing conditions.

There may also be a second level of adaptation, within and between the participants in a CGR, as well as within and between their parent organizations. Here, one focus is the extent to which the individual participants build and sustain relationships between themselves and with the CGR. Social and organizational relationships are at the heart of social capital, a concept that has been broadly and variously defined by social scientists for decades (e.g., Putnam 1995) and that is a conceptual mainstay in network theory and collaborative governance (Huxham and Vangen 2005). Perhaps more important is that the durability and elasticity of reciprocity and trust between CGR participants contribute to their ability to adapt to future conditions. In other words, their mutual reciprocity and trust help participants find a strategic balance between stasis and change that is appropriate for their internal and external environments. This equilibrium is particularly important for CGR participants because they must respond to and balance their own organizational needs along with those of the CGR.

Finally, a third level of adaptation may occur in the targeted resource and service conditions, and also in the larger system context. Here, the major focus is on sustainability—that is, whether the quality, level, and scope of a CGR's actions required for continuing to deliver the desired outcomes can be and are maintained over time. By sustainability, we mean both the robustness and resilience of a CGR's efforts, given the uncertain and changing system context and the constraints of the CGR's internal workings and resources. To assess sustainability, it may be useful to work with the beneficiaries of the targeted resource or service condition. That said, the goal of sustainability may not be of concern to those CGRs with discrete or short-term targets, and it may be a high bar for other CGRs to plan to achieve. However, the extent to which a CGR's strategy and actions respond to internal and external shifts or shocks will be demonstrated by the changes (i.e., adaptation) in these actions over time. Thus, adaptations to actions could include quality improvements, expansions or retractions, or suspension or transfer to others.

We now turn to a case illustration of collaborative actions, outcomes, and adaptation. In this case we discuss the Military Community Compatibility Committee, a CGR created to engage public, private, nonprofit, and community stakeholders around a contentious local issue concerning overflight noise from training jets flying out of the Davis-Monthan Air Force Base in Tucson, Arizona.

Case Illustration: The Military Community Compatibility Committee

The Davis-Monthan Airfield in Tucson was dedicated in 1927 by Charles Lindbergh. During the past eighty-eight years, it has grown into the large Davis-Monthan Air Force Base (DMAFB), which is home to the 355th Wing Command. Today, the base employs more than 8,500 people, and is Tucson's fourth-largest employer. Over time, the city of Tucson grew up alongside and around the base. At the time of the Lindbergh dedication, Tucson's population was between 20,000 and 30,000. Today, close to 1 million people live in Tucson's expanding metropolitan area. Among many base responsibilities, the 355th Wing Command trains air force pilots to fly A-10 and F-15 fighter jets and has been considered for future training on the new F-35 joint strike fighter jets.

In the past decade, several residential neighborhoods and businesses in midtown and downtown Tucson have become increasingly concerned about the noise of the training flights as jets take off from and land on the DMAFB's runways. In 2004, Pima County and the base published land use plans and maps showing the noise contours for areas with different expected decibel ranges related to the training flight routes. These contours then became the basis for controversial land use regulations and building codes related to future home improvements and noise insulation requirements. The residents living within or near these noise contour areas felt excluded from the land use planning process and began raising their collective voices. Adding to this, memories of a plane crash near a junior high school more than thirty years ago still conjured up community worries about public safety. The effects of the training flights' noise on the students and teachers at a nearby elementary school were also of particular concern.

The new round of recommendations from the US Department of Defense's Base Realignment and Closure (BRAC) Commission were due in 2005. (The BRAC mission is to independently assess the need for all military bases and to recommend closures, reductions, or changes in base operations and missions.) The DMAFB, along with leaders in the business community and local and state governments, including the governor's office, were quite concerned that community sentiment critical of base operations and of the potential for base expansion might affect the DMAFB's BRAC ratings and jeopardize its future. This was the setting for growing interest in a community conversation about the future of the DMAFB and its effects on the community.

Because everyone had a stake in this conflict and no one party could be trusted to assemble all the stakeholders, a neutral convener was asked to bring all the parties to the table. At that time, Kirk Emerson, the director of the US Institute for Environmental Conflict Resolution (an independent, congressionally chartered agency operated by the Morris K. Udall Foundation), started receiving calls from several different stakeholders, including the "DM 50"—an organized group that supports the DMAFB and consists of representatives of business and industry—as well as a representative of the City of Tucson manager's office, one of the key neighborhood association leaders, and a representative of the governor's office. After Emerson verified the willingness of these and other key stakeholders to consider a dialogue, and with their permission, she set up an initial meeting and invited representatives from several neighborhoods and local businesses, the DM 50, the University of Arizona, and the public school district, along with staff from the DMAFB, the City of Tucson, Pima County, and the governor's office. From this first informal meeting, cross-boundary collaboration emerged and soon fostered the creation of a more formal, voluntary CGR, which was eventually named the Military Community Compatibility Committee (MC3) (US Institute for Environmental Conflict Resolution 2014).

The subsequent collaboration dynamics progressed as the group gathered information, invited additional people to the table, created a formal organization that it named "MC3," went on numerous field trips, and conducted joint fact-finding and noise-monitoring activities. The group established ground rules and operating procedures, hired a project facilitator, structured its work through three subcommittees, and carried out formal negotiations in the committee as a whole that led to a final set of twenty-four consensus-based recommendations addressing operational, land use, and public education and outreach issues. Almost all these recommendations were implemented through subsequent actions taken by the DMAFB, the city, and the state. In addition, an ongoing liaison structure was created for a successor CGR, the Military Community Relations Committee (MCRC), which continues to operate as of this writing (MC3 2006).

MC3's Collaborative Actions

Given the highly contentious nature of the overflight issue, it took several meetings for the various parties to become willing to be participants in MC3. First, considerable remedial work had to be done for the parties to overcome past grievances and build sufficient trust to enable them to form a collaborative endeavor. Eventually, the parties agreed to work together in MC3 based on three explicit and shared principles: (1) their efforts would not jeopardize the future of the DMAFB; (2) they would work to reduce current noise levels to the extent possible; and (3) they would seek ways to minimize increases in future noise levels. The participants aspired to develop a set of recommendations to present to the public and specific official decision makers, some of whom were also MC3 participants or resource partners.

The MC3 participants' shared theory of change was straightforward and simple: if their recommendations were well founded, feasible, and supported by the full group, then they would be more likely to be accepted and enacted. The participants did not want to spend time working on a report that would not lead to change. Although the major explicit collaborative actions for this CGR became the preparation, production, and delivery of its report, the participants also took strategic actions to facilitate the acceptance of their recommendations. These actions required the continual cycling of the CGR's collaboration dynamics during more than a year and a half of meetings.

MC3 also carried out operational actions over this period—for example, it interviewed, selected, and funded a dedicated facilitator to run its meetings and coordinate its work. The institutional arrangements its members made while building their capacity for joint action enabled them to complete their preliminary work by forming subcommittees on the DMAFB's operations, land use and property regulations, and community relations. After engaging each other across several meetings and in numerous cycles of discovery, definition, deliberation, and determinations, these subcommittees created recommendations for MC3 as a whole to consider. The underlying intention for the subcommittees' work was to generate efficiencies by specializing the work on identified tasks and by doing preliminary vetting of and negotiations on recommendations to then bring to MC3 as a whole.

Internal networking action, or "inreaching," also occurred. For legal reasons, public agencies and political representatives could not participate as MC3 voting members or decision makers. However, through their presence at meetings and by sharing technical information, they participated as resource persons, sounding boards, and reality checkers. MC3 also engaged in external networking actions, initially by reaching out to additional participants to assure broad representation from the affected interests and powerful community actors who could potentially either block or leverage political support for its efforts. The shared premise behind these activities concerned the importance of reputational benefits and, specifically, transparency and external legitimacy. Though they did not use these words themselves, the MC3 participants explicitly acknowledged that these principles would be important for the future success of their recommendations.

MC3's Outcomes

In the MC3 context, the substantive outcomes can be characterized at two levels: (1) the extent to which the report's recommendations were accepted and implemented by decision makers; and (2) if a recommendation was implemented, the extent to which the current overflight noise levels were reduced as a consequence. MC3's report included recommendations focused on three areas: the DMAFB's operations, land use regulations, and future community outreach. All but one of the recommendations for operations were immediately implemented by the base—including, for example, increasing the daytime altitude from which the jets descend for landings by one-third (from 1,500 feet to 2,000 feet above ground) and by rerouting helicopters to fly over less-populated areas of the city. These changes led to measurable decreases in overflight noise. MC3's objectives also reference future noise level reductions and the base's continuing operation. Future research will be needed to determine whether these longer-term objectives have been met.

Additional outcomes occurred through enacted changes in land use regulations and the availability of additional funding mechanisms for noise buffering and soundproofing of the affected residences, businesses, and institutions. The intention behind this community outreach was to strengthen the relationship between the base and the community to assure future maintenance or reductions in overflight noise. We address this social capital outcome in the discussion of adaptation, which follows below.

As noted above and discussed further in chapter 9, one could also assess the outcomes of collaborative action for the CGR itself (in this case, how the outcomes enhanced the viability and legitimacy of MC3 and its successor, MCRC) and for its individual participants (in this case, the extent to which outcomes improved the effectiveness of the participating organizations and constituencies and how equitably the outcomes were distributed). However, for purposes of clarity, we do not cover these outcomes here.

Adaptation by MC3

The most salient adaptation by MC3 was its institutional transformation. Included in its recommendations was the formation of a standing committee to continue to monitor the overflight noise issues and to expand its mission to address other local concerns and strengthen the relationship between the DMAFB and the community. MC3 formally concluded its business after the issuance of the report and reconstituted itself as MCRC, with the blessing and participation of the city, county, and state governments, as well as the DMAFB. MCRC adopted a formal charter and bylaws, which state: "The

Military-Community Relations Committee . . . is established as an advisory committee to Davis-Monthan Air Force Base, the City of Tucson and Pima County for the purpose of providing a forum for dialogue, raising and discussing concerns, monitoring MC3 recommendations, joint problem solving, and education focusing on military and community-related issues. The MCRC may provide consensus recommendations to the DMAFB, the City of Tucson, Pima County, the State of Arizona, and other entities as appropriate" (MCRC 2014).

MCRC's members include neighborhood and business groups, nonvoting advisers, and resource specialists and staff from the City of Tucson, Pima County, the local congressional district, and the DMAFB. Its meetings are duly publicized in advance, and the public and the press are encouraged to attend. MCRC has emerged as a more formal, ongoing, and publicly recognized CGR than MC3. Although a more fine-grained analysis would be needed to explore the adaptation that has occurred at the level of each individual member, it is apparent that the DMAFB learned to take the community's concerns more seriously, acted on the advice of MC3, and now actively participates in MCRC. As Colonel Kent Laughbaum, the 355th fighter wing commander, has said, "The relationship between Davis-Monthan and the city and citizens of Tucson is 80 years strong and vital to the defense of America. I am confident that the formation of this committee will further strengthen our relationship in years to come" (DMAFB 2007).

It remains to be seen whether the maintenance of or reduction in future noise levels from overflights by the DMAFB can be sustained over time through continuing MCRC actions, given that the system context has begun to change. Three years after the formation of MCRC, a new challenge arose concerning the US military's choice for future training bases for the new F35-A joint strike fighter jets. The F35-As would be almost twice as loud as the F-15s and A-10s that are currently being flown out of Tucson, and the number of people affected by the high noise levels would increase four to twenty-plus times, depending on the number of jets being flown (Office of Public Affairs of 162nd Fighter Wing 2012). The DMAFB's supporters lobbied hard for Tucson to get one of the first F-35A training bases, and the political environment concerning this issue has heated up again.

Summary

In this chapter, we explored the collaborative actions, outcomes, and adaptations that are generated by CGRs. Specifically, we noted that collaborative actions are the steps taken to enact the CGR's shared theory of change. Such actions can take many forms and functions, depending on the CGR's specific context, charge, and goals, and they can be executed by a variety of actors. These actions generate outcomes, which may also take many forms. Moreover, these outcomes are hopefully seen within the resource or service condition targeted for change, but they may also be felt within the CGR or among its participants. In turn, these outcomes may lead to adaptation within the CGR, among its participants, and in the system context. Finally, we illustrated the concepts of collaborative actions, outcomes, and adaptation using the MC3 case. In the next three chapters, we present a series of detailed case studies that apply and illustrate the entire integrative framework for collaborative governance. These three case studies—along with the brief case illustrations in chapters 2, 3, and 4—give shape to our typology of CGRs, which is presented in chapter 8.

Note

1. The comparative value added of CGR outcomes, which are termed "impacts" in the performance literature, is also of considerable interest to researchers and has been understudied for a number of reasons, including the challenges of identification and specification; the difficulties in measurement; the absence of control groups, appropriate comparisons, or standards for assessment; and the trials of attributing causation to actions, especially over long periods of time (Turrini et al. 2010; Provan and Lemaire 2012; Koontz and Thomas 2006). In this book, we focus primarily on the direct outcomes of CGRs, as opposed to impacts.

Part III

Case Studies of Collaborative Governance Regimes

CHAPTER 5

Who Speaks for Toronto? Collaborative Governance in the Civic Action Alliance

Allison Bramwell

Around the world, city-regions are facing increasingly complex urban policy challenges that cut across levels of government, municipal boundaries, and policy silos. As a result, local institutions and actor networks are reconfiguring urban policymaking to influence the social and economic performance of city-regions (Bradford and Bramwell 2014; Clarke and Gaile 1998; Storper 2013), which in turn is stimulating experimentation with collaborative governance (Benner and Pastor 2011; DiGaetano and Strom 2003; Green and Haines 2012; Hambleton 2003; Phillips and Pittman 2009; Pierre 1999, 2005, 2011; Pierre and Peters 2012; Sellers 2002; Stone 1989, 2004, 2005).

This chapter provides a detailed case study based on thirty in-depth interviews with civic leaders in Toronto about the formation, consolidation, and evolution of the Greater Toronto Civic Action Alliance, a durable and high-performing collaborative governance regime (CGR) operating in a politically fragmented, socially diverse, and geographically large city-region (Bramwell and Wolfe 2014).[1] It draws on the integrative framework for collaborative governance (Emerson, Nabatchi, and Balogh 2012) to examine cross-boundary collaboration between public, private, and community-based leaders in Toronto, Canada's largest urban region. Although numerous regional governance challenges remain, influential multisector leadership and a nimble institutional structure interact to shape a clear, broad, actionable, and adaptable agenda. Yet the enduring questions in urban politics—Who participates, and how?—emerge as particularly salient in this case. Weak ties with municipal politicians and conflict over the question of who speaks for Toronto have important implications for understanding the prospects for cross-boundary collaboration in Canadian cities.

The Greater Toronto Civic Action Alliance: Application of the Framework to the Case

The Greater Toronto Civic Action Alliance—or Civic Action, as it is popularly known—is a rare example of a durable, influential, and high-performing CGR operating at the regional scale in Canada (Bradford and Bramwell 2014; Bramwell and Wolfe 2014).[2] This cross-boundary, multilevel initiative was formed in 2002 to address complex governance challenges and policy gaps in Canada's largest urban region. This initiative is explicitly regional in scale rather than narrowly focused on the City of Toronto, and it enjoys active support and participation from influential political and bureaucratic leaders at the federal, provincial, and municipal levels of government. But it nonetheless remains resolutely community based, initiated, driven, and sustained by local civic leaders drawn from multiple sectors.

Four features emerge as particularly salient in this case analysis. First, leadership, both as a driver and as an element within the collaboration dynamic of the capacity for joint action, was a key factor, operating in conjunction with other variables at different junctures to shape the formation, consolidation, and sustainability of Civic Action. Second, determinations and a shared theory of change are evident in Civic Action's broad, cross-boundary agenda, which targets complex policy gaps cutting across levels of government, municipal jurisdictions, and policy sectors, and which adapts and evolves according to successful project implementation and the emergence of new issues. Third, Civic Action's innovative procedural and institutional arrangements are minimalist, flexible, and adjustable, allowing this CGR to adapt to changes over time. Fourth and finally, Civic Action, which recently celebrated its thirteenth anniversary, has undertaken collaborative actions and achieved outcomes that can be measured in its longevity and performance, which have been marked by numerous and mostly successful cross-boundary initiatives—including major influence on federal and provincial tax policy for low-income families, career pathways and mentorship programs for foreign-trained professionals, an annual international performing arts festival, and other programs targeted to environmental sustainability and developing the next generation of civic leaders. These four features are further explained in the following sections, which apply the integrative framework to the Civic Action CGR.

The System Context: Challenges of Scale, Scope, and Governance

As noted in chapter 2, external political, legal, socioeconomic, and environmental, and other conditions create opportunities and constraints that shape

the formation and subsequent performance of CGRs, including public resource or service conditions, policy and legal frameworks, socioeconomic and
cultural characteristics, network characteristics, political dynamics and power
relations, and the history of conflict, among other factors in the broad system
context (see also Emerson, Nabatchi, and Balogh 2012). Although each of
these conditions is evident in the system context shaping collaborative governance in the Greater Toronto Area (GTA), it was the growing awareness
of major policy and governance gaps that provided the strongest impetus
for collaboration. Complex governance challenges cutting across municipal
boundaries, policy areas, and levels of government—such as regional economic development, increasing poverty and social polarization, and regional
transportation—became even more immediate when faced with the Severe
Acute Respiratory Syndrome (SARS) crisis and its negative global implications
for the region.

As the fourth-largest metropolitan economy in North America and "one
of the continent's fastest growing mega-regions," the economically diverse
GTA is Canada's largest and most productive city-region, with concentrations
of knowledge-intensive automotive, financial services, information and com-
munications, and life sciences industries (Bourne, Britton, and Leslie 2011).
Although its sheer size affords significant advantages, the Toronto region
lacks some key institutional supports and administrative structures that are
needed to coordinate regional social welfare and economic development
strategies. The existing geographic boundaries of the city-region—which is
currently governed by the large, upper-tier City of Toronto and is surrounded
by the four other upper-tier municipalities of Halton, Peel, York, and Durham
(which include a total of twenty-four lower-tier municipalities)—reflect an
economic geography that is anachronistic for current regional needs. The
existing municipal boundaries operate at a significantly different scale than
the "megaregional" GTA economy, seriously hampering the intermunicipal
cooperation required to address the scope of challenges facing the region,
and leaving it without a cohesive regional voice for negotiation with federal
and provincial policymakers.[3] The surrounding municipalities have tended to
compete rather than collaborate because it is "hard to get mayors to agree
that it's in the best interest of this larger area to see something happen in all
of their jurisdictions not just one of them" (confidential interview). As Sancton (2008) suggests, the region's multiple and constantly shifting boundaries
structurally limit its ability to build collaborative mechanisms for regional
government.

As outlined in the integrative framework, network characteristics, such as
the strength and density of ties within and between CGR participants, can either help or hinder collaborative efforts. Along with issues of geographic scale,

the scope of challenges facing the GTA is exacerbated by sparse networks and weak ties within and among networks, a situation that compromises regional governance capacity and presents critical obstacles to collaborative governance. To advance a variety of policy agendas, networks form between local governments and societal interests, but the active participation of nongovernmental actors requires a degree of organization that is lacking in the region.

In Toronto, both economic and social welfare interests are represented by a wide array of organizations at the municipal level, but they tend to be fragmented and weakly organized. Social service organizations belong to multiple loose networks, but there is not "one major network" or single table around which they can gather to coordinate strategic approaches to social service delivery in the city, let alone on a regional basis.[4] Citing challenges of size and complexity, one interviewee commented: "Nobody speaks for a whole lot of people in this city [because] it's just too damn big and it is really decentralized and diffuse. . . . I don't think we have institutionally developed the capacity to have a long-term conversation about the health of our city and the health of our community."

Economic development efforts also lack a number of important aspects—institutional coordination, a strategic vision sufficiently broad to unite the disconnected local business community, and cohesive political and civic leadership capable of facilitating collaboration between key economic development stakeholders—underscoring the general impression that "the economic development field [in the Toronto region] is strewn with the bodies of failed initiatives" (confidential interview).

Taken together, weak intermunicipal cooperation overlaid with fragmented political structures and weak societal networks impede efforts to coordinate, on a regional basis, strategic planning efforts for complex, crosscutting issues such as economic development, infrastructure, transit, and poverty reduction (Nelles 2012; Stren et al. 2010). One interviewee described Toronto as "a city with weak networks [that] do not hang together well. . . . It doesn't feel like a city that finds a way of having a common goal [that] everyone can contribute to and move towards."

From a governance perspective, the "almost dysfunctional" structure of municipal government coupled with a lack of "consensus on the identity of the city or the region" makes it "difficult to construct a single narrative that does justice to the highly varied and distinctive local economies, cultures, and landscapes" that make up the Toronto region. The result is an urban powerhouse struggling to implement "political initiatives and strategic planning for economic development and innovation at the regional scale" (Bourne, Britton, and Leslie 2011, 237, 241).

In summary, antecedent conditions in the system context for collaborative cross-boundary governance in the Toronto region include aspects of all the dimensions outlined in the integrative framework (see chapter 2). Political dynamics and power relations within communities and across levels of government are evident in weak efforts at intermunicipal cooperation. With weak political and civic leadership and fragmented social and economic development networks, the degree of trust and connectedness within and across existing networks is low. Most important, earlier and continuing failures to address complex challenges mean that policy gaps on key regional issues are widening. Against this backdrop, the drivers for the Greater Toronto Civic Action Alliance CGR emerged.

Drivers and Formation of Civic Action: Policy Gaps and Charismatic Leadership

As noted in chapter 2, four drivers provide the impetus for collaboration: uncertainty, the need for collaboration to reduce, diffuse, and share risk in "wicked" and complex environments; interdependence, the joint awareness that participants cannot address a challenge on their own; consequential incentives, internal or external threats or opportunities that induce leaders and other participants to engage in collaboration; and initiating leadership, a person or core group that initiates support and secures resources. All four drivers are evident in the Toronto case; however, consequential incentives and leadership played particularly powerful roles in the initial formation of the Toronto City Summit Alliance (TCSA), which later became Civic Action.

Incentives for collaboration are consequential to the extent that issues are made salient to participants and create collective awareness that inattention could result in negative outcomes. The original motivation for Civic Action is unclear, but because it provided the opportunity to establish collective awareness that did not previously exist about pressing issues, the initial City Summit in 2002 was the catalyst for the subsequent formation of the CGR. This summit was a one-day event, which was purportedly inspired by a similar event in Chicago and was organized on the initiative of then–Toronto mayor Mel Lastman. It included participation from numerous high-profile civic and business leaders, such as the chief executive officers (CEOs) of large financial services firms, unions, and community organizations, including the United Way of Greater Toronto and the Canadian Urban Institute, as well as former federal, provincial, and municipal politicians.[5]

By all accounts, however, it was the highly impactful keynote address given by David Pecaut, the CEO of the Boston Consulting Group Canada, that provided the galvanizing impetus behind the formation of the original TCSA, the predecessor to Civic Action. Pecaut would later become the TCSA's inaugural chair. Emphasizing the interdependence and uncertainty surrounding the social and economic challenges facing the region and the absence of existing community capacity to address them, Pecaut effectively "drew a picture" of potential sector failure. As one interviewee noted, swift collective reaction was evident in "the gasp that went up in the audience. Because we could see our future: a city in decline, no leadership, no fiscal authority, no fiscal tools that really meet our needs, no ideas, sort of more of the same complaining and nothing. So that was a significant moment."

 In this way, the inaugural City Summit not only outlined the negative consequences of inaction but also provided consequential incentives for action. Moreover, the summit provided the opportunity to recruit the civic leadership required for collaborative action, bringing together a diverse and representative group of leaders to identify the region's strengths and challenges and to frame an agenda to respond to them. The summit experience had a powerful galvanizing effect on a number of its participants: "People were really energized. There were breakouts and discussions. But people wanted to do something. They really wanted to tackle things. So I left that day feeling that there was a tremendous amount of goodwill in the room, a tremendous amount of interest in tackling issues and that civil society in Toronto, if you consider business, labor, nonprofits, were really ready to work together" (research interview with David Pecaut, July 9, 2009).

Following the successful conclusion of the 2002 summit, a coalition of forty civic leaders from the private, labor, voluntary, and public sectors came together to form the TCSA, which constituted a "ripe group of converts" who would form the original Steering Committee, committing to meet regularly to discuss the issues facing the Greater Toronto region and to set an actionable agenda for change. Despite an almost complete membership turnover, which was inevitable over a thirteen-year period and arguably important to the initiative's ongoing vitality, this Steering Committee continues to shape and oversee Civic Action's agenda and strategic direction.

In many ways, civic leadership represents the most critical independent variable for the CGR's—driving its formation, originally as the TCSA, and ensuring its consolidation, as Civic Action. As was explained by one interviewee, though Civic Action strived "to undermine any accusations that we were some elite or special group," encouraging broader community participation in working groups and summits and soliciting consultation and engagement with target communities, it has always essentially been a leadership group, leveraging the influence, expertise, resources, networks, and skills of high-profile leaders in the public, private, and community sectors. As Julia Deans, the founding CEO of Civic Action, put it, getting "the right people" at the table was a key strategy: "Influencing the influencers was what we were really good at. We were never a grassroots organization. It was appealing to the people at the top and saying 'we need you to play a big role.' On any initiative, we were always asking 'who are the influencers we need at this table? Who are the people who have their own networks that they can call on?'" (research interview with Julia Deans, May 8, 2013).

Yet as the integrative framework also emphasizes, different types of leadership play different roles in collaborative governance. An "initiating leader" capable of identifying and securing resources and support is essential for the formation of a collaborative governance regime (see chapter 2; see also Emerson, Nabatchi, and Balogh 2012). The inaugural City Summit also had the effect of recruiting an initiating leader, David Pecaut, who was to act as the key driver and main impetus for the establishment and consolidation of Civic Action.

Pecaut was described as "the perfect person to . . . set the stage for the summit" (confidential interview). When he was asked to deliver the keynote address, he was encouraged to "include everything, [to] tell the story of the city, how we are doing economically, socially, the environment, the whole thing" (research interview with Pecaut). He reported having put substantial time, energy, and personal commitment into the presentation: "I immersed myself and read almost everything I could get my hands on, and the more I read, the more depressed I got, . . . [and] the more concerned I was that this city—with all of this fantastic potential, wealth and creativity—was not doing so well" (research interview with Pecaut). The presentation had "an unbelievably dramatic effect," and coming out of the summit, "everybody was so impressed that they asked [Pecaut] to take the lead in setting up a citizen's movement" (confidential interview). As is discussed throughout this case analysis, until Pecaut's untimely death in 2009, a broad consensus across participants indicates that his passionate, energetic, and skillful leadership—with his lively mind, expertise in policy consulting, personal networks, and willingness to absorb the high transaction costs of initiating a regionwide collaborative effort—were one of the key reasons for this CGR's early and sustained success (confidential interviews).[6]

Collaboration Dynamics: Institutionalizing Civic Action

As the preceding analysis suggests, the genesis and formation of Civic Action were consistent with a system in which cross-boundary collaboration "represents the predominate mode for conduct, decision making, and activity" (Emerson, Nabatchi, and Balogh 2012, 10; see also chapter 1). The form and initial direction of this regional and multisector collaborative governance initiative were shaped by drivers emerging from the system context, the most critical of which were consequential incentives that made pressing issues salient and Pecaut's skilled and influential initiating leadership. However, it is one thing for a CGR to form, and entirely another for it to perform (for a discussion of CGR performance in the integrative framework, see chapter 9).

The development and effectiveness of a CGR are influenced over time by the iterative and evolutionary interplay of collaboration dynamics and collaborative actions (see chapters 3 and 4). This subsection examines the collaboration dynamics underpinning the long-term sustainability and performance of Civic Action, focusing on the processes through which principled engagement, shared motivation, and the capacity for joint action were established. It becomes evident that the components of collaboration dynamics are not linear; rather, their elements emerge at different times, reinforcing each other as they develop in an interactive manner.

Principled Engagement: Deliberative Agenda-Setting Processes

Referring to the process through which participants with differing substantive, relational, and identity goals "work across their respective institutional, sectoral, or jurisdictional boundaries to solve problems, resolve conflicts or create value," the integrative framework suggests that the effectiveness of principled engagement is partly determined by the quality of the interactive cycling of discovery, definition, deliberation, and determinations, through which participants develop a shared sense of purpose and a "shared theory of change for achieving that purpose" (see chapter 3; see also Emerson, Nabatchi, and Balogh 2012, 10, 11). According to a qualitative analysis of the interviews conducted for this case study, Civic Action experienced strong principled engagement.

Cross-boundary social learning through open and ongoing deliberation, representation of diverse interests, and the use of broad knowledge and expertise largely defines how Civic Action functions. Perhaps the primary consequential incentive stimulating its formation was the collective awareness of growing policy gaps and that "government can't solve all of the problems we have" (confidential interview). A key question arising at the early consolidation stage was where in the policy process efforts should be concentrated. Much emphasis was placed on the initial discovery and definition process, focusing on engaging diverse and influential civic and political leaders on the Steering Committee and making determinations about a common purpose and set of objectives.

The result of this discovery and definition process was the development of a shared theory of change that clearly articulated the three founding principles on which Civic Action was based. First, in the absence of a regional government, Civic Action's activities were to operate at the regional scale. Second, rather than operating in a single policy domain and addressing issues in isolation, activities were to be explicitly cross-boundary and focused on developing programs and projects that integrated social, economic, and arts and cultural issues. Third, leadership was to be explicitly multisectoral. Emphasizing the importance of establishing trust and credibility at the outset, Steering Committee members were selected based on "heterogeneous leadership" that was "demonstrably nonpartisan" and "reflected the range of civil society at the table" (research interview with Pecaut). Though there has been almost complete membership turnover since its inception, and few members of the original Steering Committee remain active, a brief scan of its current membership underscores the continued cross-sector composition of Civic Action. Members include, for example, the presidents and CEOs of large financial and professional services firms, local colleges and universities, community-based not-for-profit organizations, and postsecondary institutions, as well as municipal administrators, federal and provincial bureaucrats, and former politicians (including two sitting federal senators, two former provincial premiers, and a former mayor), arts organizations, unions, and academics.[7]

On the basis of an awareness that "problem definition is a very important starting point," the newly formed CGR's first task was to establish an evidence base or "common fact base" using "common language that everybody [could] rally around" (research interview with Pecaut). Consequently, with staff resources donated by a number of private-sector organizations, primarily the Boston Consulting Group, the TCSA worked throughout the eight months following the initial summit to produce its own analysis of the economic and social situation facing the Greater Toronto region and to formulate an action plan "that any citizen in Toronto could pick up and read and have a picture of both the vision of what is possible for the region and what was needed [as well as] something that public policymakers could get behind" (research interview with Pecaut). Representing the shared theory of change in codified form, the plan—*Enough Talk: An Action Plan for the Toronto Region*, released in April 2003—set out a broad agenda for long-term change in a number of crosscutting areas, including transportation and physical infrastructure, tourism and cultural events, research infrastructure, education and training, immigration, and social services.[8] These many years later, all current and ongoing initiatives can be traced back to this foundational report.

The *Enough Talk* report presented the evidence base and announced Civic Action's principles, purposes, and objectives, but it was—and continues to be—its deliberative process that accounts for the subsequent performance of Civic Action. In addition to a combination of skillful and representative leadership and flexible institutional design, an open and inclusive deliberation process—involving the "thoughtful examination of issues," the expression of multiple perspectives, and "public judgment on what represents the common good"—is evident in the calling of infrequent but regular summits (Roberts 2004, 332; cited by Emerson, Nabatchi, and Balogh 2012, 12). Since the original 2002 meeting, Civic Action has held three summits—in 2003, 2007, and 2011—at strategic junctures to attract leadership, build support and credibility, and refine and adapt its agenda and shared theory of change. A fourth summit is planned for 2015.

Following the release of the *Enough Talk* report in April 2003, the second summit was held in June 2003, marking Civic Action's phase of intensive early consolidation. Armed with support from federal and provincial politicians, engaged civic and business leadership, and a broad consensus on proposed initiatives, Civic Action went on to launch the Toront03 Alliance, the Toronto Region Immigrant Employment Council (TRIEC), the Toronto Region Research Alliance, and the Strong Neighbourhoods Task Force initiatives, as well as to establish an institutional structure to enable it to sustain its momentum and support its core work. With the intention of taking stock of accomplishments and identifying new areas for activity, its subsequent summits have focused more explicitly on regional opportunities and challenges. For example, in 2007 new initiatives, including Greening Greater Toronto and DiverseCity, were announced; and in 2011 the economy, transportation, employment, and immigration were identified as key issue areas to be addressed in 2012 to 2015.

Apart from Civic Action's use of summits to check its progress and adapt its agenda to reflect past accomplishments and emerging issues, the deliberative process used at the summits themselves is also significant. Not only did this process isolate, clarify, and refine actionable initiatives based on broad community input; it also provided an opportunity for interaction between people who otherwise would not have met. As one participant recalled, "There was a very powerful sense in which the city summit was a living, breathing organization and these people from very different walks of life and different roles in leadership in the city who don't know each other could sit and have really exciting conversations around these issues. . . . At one table the CEO of Manulife, one of the top five life insurance companies in the world, was sitting next to a [public] transit advocate who rides his bike to work every day discussing road tolls" (confidential interview).

In summary, multiple mechanisms have interacted to facilitate and sustain the deliberative process that continues to shape community-wide principled engagement in Civic Action. Following the initial summit, the recruitment of a broadly multisectoral Steering Committee supported the work behind the *Enough Talk* report, which outlined a shared theory of change to animate the agenda for subsequent work. This agenda is being shaped and refined on an ongoing basis through working groups and is being revisited at regular but infrequent summits. The next section examines how Civic Action developed and continues to maintain the common vision and shared motivation required for collaborative governance.

Shared Motivation: Leadership Selection and Issue-Based Organizing

Agreement on key principles, the overall strategic direction, and a shared theory of change is critical to cross-boundary collaborative governance, but a "consensus does not mean universal agreement on every issue" (confidential interview). As part of a "self-reinforcing cycle," shared motivation refers to "the interpersonal and relational elements" of collaboration dynamics that reinforce or accelerate principled engagement (Emerson, Nabatchi, and Balogh 2012, 13; see also chapter 3). Developing interpersonal trust and social capital is particularly crucial for cross-boundary collaboration between participants who are unknown to each other or are unaccustomed to working together. Interpersonal trust and social capital enable people to cross organizational, sectoral, jurisdictional, and, at times, ideological divides to commit to joint action. The integrative framework suggests that repeated, high-quality interactions through the principled engagement process foster trust, mutual understanding, internal legitimacy, and commitment, which in turn generate and sustain shared motivation. This cycle is evident in this case.

In particular, there appears to be an important relationship between leadership and the capacity to build and maintain a consensus on a collectively articulated strategic vision. As is emphasized in chapter 3, who participates and who they represent matter for cross-boundary collaboration. A major challenge in community or civil-society-based, voluntary CGRs is conflict between participants over who speaks for a particular issue, place, or set of interests, and how a particular issue is framed. Although it is important to frame issues in a collaborative and unified way to best present them to policymakers, building a consensus in ideologically divided environments underscores perhaps one of the key challenges for CGRs, and Civic Action is no exception.

Because of Civic Action's intrinsically cross-boundary nature, and its need to leverage broad support, participation, and resources from multiple sectors, establishing and sustaining shared motivation was critical to its modus operandi from the outset. Over the course of its development, three important mechanisms—an issue-based approach to organizing, an adaptable institutional structure, and a careful leadership selection process—have interacted to build trust, mutual understanding, internal legitimacy, and commitment. In this way, Civic Action has been (and still is) able to facilitate and sustain ongoing collaboration between its diverse public, private, and community-based participants, many of whom did not know each other, had no shared history of joint work, and, perhaps most important, had clashing interests or important ideological differences.

For Civic Action, value differences between business and community-based leaders and activists have been of particular consequence. Appealing to private-sector interests or "making the business case" for how activities affect the economic climate in the region is essential to the work of Civic Action; yet at times, business leaders have lacked an awareness of and sensitivity to the complexity and interdependence of regional social, cultural, and environmental issues. At the same time, it is challenging to engage activists who tend to operate on principle and who, therefore, sometimes lack the interest and motivation to engage productively with businesspeople. Because "dealing with social [or environmental] issues involves more than money, you have to use tools other than money to persuade people to do things," which is "particularly challenging in a *complex area where no one sector can do it on its own*" (research interview with Deans; emphasis added).

To build a cross-boundary consensus on crosscutting issues as well as to communicate with different levels of government, the strategic emphasis within Civic Action from the outset was focused on issue-based, rather than position-based, organizing. With this organizing approach, "You pick an issue, you convene around the table the leadership of civil society that is important to that issue, and you make sure it is inclusive and representative. You are not advocating for any specific group of people but for the public interest. . . . There is not an obvious owner of the problem" (research interview with Pecaut).

Civic Action intrinsically frames issues in a cross-boundary way, yet navigating value-based differences often requires skilled leadership. For example, among the "extraordinary range of perspectives" represented on one of the working groups focused on social welfare issues, "there were some people who were motivated entirely by principle, so you weren't going to make progress with them if you didn't deal with them on that level. The battles and the tension and the conflicts were *unbelievable*. The [co-chair] had to keep everybody moving forward while navigating these ideological clashes" (research interview with Deans).

Similarly, Civic Action attracted the participation of environmental activists, many of whom "do not work easily with business," for the Greening Greater Toronto initiative, a process that was described as "uneasy at first." Despite some "uncomfortable confrontations" they were able to identify specific issues they could work together on, and Civic Action "has since scored some big wins" on the environment (confidential interview).

In this case, the two variables of leadership and institutional structure have interacted to facilitate the development of shared motivation. The governance structure of Civic Action consists of a Board of Directors, a Steering Committee that generates ideas and selects issues for action, working groups that further refine issues and develop actionable initiatives, and a small secretariat that facilitates collective work. Broad community input and participation are solicited primarily at the summits. Due to the importance of who participates in collaborative governance and because the majority of work is accomplished at the leadership level, the leadership selection process has been of critical importance for Civic Action's formation, consolidation, and subsequent work.

Apart from being broadly representative of multiple community interests and perspectives and "not just the usual suspects at the table," participating leaders have required certain skills, such as the ability to look beyond the narrow interests of their constituencies to work across boundaries and to build trust and shared commitment to an issue. These required skills made the initial selection of the Steering Committee participants and working group leaders critical to subsequent cross-boundary consensus building. A key early challenge was to create a "sense of collective leadership"; as Julia Deans explained, "Selecting who's there to represent a set of issues is a big challenge in these processes. . . . You [need to] get people at the table who are willing to wear two hats. If you're not even willing to consider other perspectives, you probably shouldn't be at the table. They have to be open to putting things aside for the greater good" (research interview with Deans). David Pecaut observed in retrospect that "we chose wisely in getting people who were very civic-minded and ready to really participate together" for the initial leadership group, building "an incredible amount of goodwill, trust, and mutual commitment in the development of the process" (research interview with Pecaut).

Thus, the variables of skillful and committed leadership interacted with an agile institutional structure and an issue-based approach to organizing to build trust, mutual understanding, internal legitimacy, and commitment to Civic Action's cross-boundary agenda. Despite their initial misgivings about working across sectors with unfamiliar participants, many original participants were willing to stay, and many new participants were willing to join because Civic Action quickly established its legitimacy by building a track record of accomplishments on actionable agenda items. Pecaut was described as "very good at spotting opportunities" and "getting things done" in a nonpartisan way (confidential interviews), and he was also credited with setting up some "early wins" with the Toront03 and TRIEC initiatives, which established internal credibility by demonstrating Civic Action's capacity for joint action.

Capacity for Joint Action: An Innovative Institutional Structure

Emerson, Nabatchi, and Balogh (2012, 14) suggest that principled engagement and a shared motivation interact to stimulate the development of several
"cross-functional elements" that link "strategy and performance" to build,
sustain, and grow the capacity for joint action (see chapter 3). This subsection
tracks how institutional arrangements, evolving leadership, and the ability to
leverage knowledge and resources interact to explain the performance and
longevity of Civic Action. Research on the role of intermediaries in governance emphasizes the need for some level of institutionalization to sustain
collaborative momentum (see, e.g., Giloth 2004). A mixture of formal and
informal norms, decision-making protocols, and organizational structures
make up the institutional arrangements that manage and sustain repeated
cross-boundary interactions over time.

Aside from its varied and influential civic leadership, much of Civic Action's
strength is attributable to its flexible procedural and institutional structure,
which enables it to capture broad multisector input and focus efforts while
adapting to change. Over time, Civic Action has demonstrated the ability to
modify its efforts according to changing conditions in the system context,
inserting itself into the policy process in different ways that are appropriate to
evolving challenges and opportunities—ranging from time-limited projects
to address a crisis or targeted problems to coordinating multisector inputs for
direct policy advocacy to establishing programs that facilitate ongoing community development efforts.

After the second summit following the release of the *Enough Talk* report in
2003, where the CGR's future sustainability was discussed, the Steering Committee decided to develop an institutional mechanism to maintain its early
momentum and support its proposed work. What resulted was an innovative and "fairly flexible" structure that reflected its issue-based organizational
strategy and its shared theory of change. As discussed above, shortly after the
original summit, the Steering Committee of forty civic leaders was formed
to generate ideas, discuss, and select crosscutting issues for focused attention.
Issue-based working groups were subsequently formed—and new ones continue to form as issues evolve—to suggest and develop actionable projects for
issues chosen by the Steering Committee, such as innovation and competitiveness in the regional economy, transit infrastructure, financing municipal
and regional services, immigration, and poverty reduction. As is discussed
below, at successive summits Civic Action's agenda has been further refined,
new leaders have been recruited, and new initiatives have been launched.

Administratively, a small secretariat with a CEO and a few core staff
members with community development expertise builds networks, manages

project development, and plans events and meetings. Deans recalls that when she took the position as founding CEO, "There were two staff and seven dollars in the bank. . . . There was no infrastructure at all; . . . it was running completely on a shoestring." Her task was to "put some flesh around the bones without inhibiting the dynamism of the organization." The resulting institutional structure operated with a small core staff, whose members became adept at "doing everything as cheaply as possible and on a pro bono basis" and at leveraging primarily corporate support, along with some union donations of funding, time, expertise, office space, and computers (research interview with Deans). As David Pecaut described it, "I think there's a barn-raising element in all of this—everybody in the community coming together. I think that barn-raising quality of everybody pitching in is contagious when they see that something is being done with the right spirit and defining that problem the right way" (research interview with Pecaut).

In addition to Civic Action's skilled, influential initiating leadership, small core staff, and flexible structure organized on the basis of crosscutting issues, much of its capacity for joint action is also attributable to its ability to recruit leadership and resources and to leverage knowledge to develop projects for adoption by other organizations. Rather than taking on program administration itself, if there was "already a logical home for an initiative in an organization that should lead it, we would go to that organization and work with them"; and if a suitable organization did not exist, they would help create it. For example, the Toronto3 initiative for post-SARS tourism recovery and the Toronto Region Research Alliance each "needed a new table and a new structure," which "we had to create from scratch" (confidential interview). Similarly, the TRIEC was initially housed within the Maytree Foundation, but it was later established as a separate not-for-profit organization; however, the United Way, with its substantial organizational resources, agreed to house and direct the Strong Neighbourhoods Task Force.

This innovative and lean institutional structure has been a key element of Civic Action's continued impact, and has enabled its capacity for joint action in numerous ways. With minimal financial expenditures, it leverages the resources of multiple actors while maintaining agility and adaptability to changing agendas as projects are completed or housed in alternate organizations and new ones are adopted. At the same time, it acts as an organizational hub, from which the expertise, networks, and organizing capacity of the core staff facilitates idea generation and knowledge sharing between the multiple actors, working groups, and organizations launched or operating under the Civic Action initiative.

Collaborative Actions and Outcomes: Tracking Civic Action's Performance

As noted in chapter 4, if done well, collaboration dynamics will lead the CGR to take collaborative actions aligned with its shared theory of change; in turn, these actions will have outcomes in various areas. With its numerous projects, ongoing programs, and events, as well as its notable national and provincial policy influence, Civic Action has charted impressive progress on its evolving agenda. Although its strategy and leadership have undergone important recent changes, there has been little indication that its momentum is attenuating.[9] Table 5.1 provides a brief overview of Civic Action's accomplishments and outcomes over the past ten years.

Although a detailed discussion of Civic Action's long-term outcomes (and effects) is beyond the scope of the current analysis, this CGR clearly has important, successful projects and policy influence to its credit, which demonstrates its ability to go beyond the formation stage and thus to actually shape community development outcomes. For example, its early high-profile success was garnered from securing the Rolling Stones to perform in Toronto in the summer of 2003, to jump-start the city's tourism industry in the immediate aftermath of the SARS crisis; this concert attracted the largest crowd of Americans to ever gather in one place on Canadian soil. Other influential Civic Action initiatives include the Task Force on Modernizing Income Security for Working-Age Adults, which shaped federal and provincial tax policies and budget priorities for low-income adults and families; the TRIEC initiative for recent immigrants, which recently celebrated its twelfth anniversary and continues to mentor and support network building; and the international Luminato Festival, which has become an important element of Toronto's cultural infrastructure. The Emerging Leaders Network and the DiverseCity initiatives remain important ongoing priorities; and, although Civic Action's participation attenuated long ago, the Priority Neighbourhoods initiative remains an important joint social policy focus of the United Way and the City of Toronto. Civic Action's most recent initiative, What Would You Do with 32?—a slogan referring to the average number of minutes each Toronto resident would save each day in commuting time if a regional transit system were successfully implemented—seeks to influence the development and implementation of the system, whose absence severely hampers the GTA's future economic growth and compromises its quality of life.[10]

Together, these and other actions, developed in accordance with Civic Action's shared theory of change, have resulted in significant and meaningful outcomes in the GTA. In turn, these collaborative actions and outcomes have

Table 5.1   A Ten-Year Overview of the Actions and Outcomes of Civic Action

2003	Project	The Toront03 initiative was launched to revitalize the region's tourism industry in the aftermath of the Severe Acute Respiratory Syndrome crisis.
	Outcomes	The Toronto City Summit Alliance (TCSA) raised $11 million from a variety of private and public sources and invested it in branding and marketing activities for which an impact analysis indicated $70 million in economic benefits accrued to the industry.
	Project	The Toronto Region Immigrant Employment Council (TRIEC), jointly developed by the TCSA and the Maytree Foundation, was launched to help integrate skilled immigrants into the regional labor force.
	Outcomes	TRIEC has to date matched 6,000 skilled immigrants with mentors who help them build networks and career pathways leading to employment. The model has been subsequently adopted and funded by the federal government and scaled out to other Canadian cities under the Local Immigration Partnership program.
2004	Project	The United Way of Greater Toronto, the City of Toronto, and the TCSA collaborated on the Strong Neighbourhoods Task Force, which identified thirteen priority neighborhoods for revitalization and focused policy attention to broker a tripartite agreement for government investment.
	Outcomes	The United Way and the City of Toronto further developed the project into Toronto's Priority Neighbourhoods program, which almost ten years later continues to focus social investments in areas of the city that need them most.
	Project	The Modernizing Income Security for Working Age Adults Task Force was launched jointly by the TCSA and Saint Christopher House.
	Outcomes	With the participation of high-profile community, private-sector, and former political leaders, the Task Force had a major influence on tax policy for families living in poverty, contributing to the establishment of the federal Working Income Tax Benefit, the Ontario Child Benefit, and a provincial dental plan for low-income families.
2005	Project	The TCSA launched the Toronto Region Research Alliance to encourage collaboration among government, knowledge-intensive firms, and public research institutions to support regional economic development and focus the provincial research and innovation agenda.
	Outcomes	One of the few initiatives reliant on funding from the provincial government, the private sector, and various postsecondary research institutions, it was also one of the few that was not sustainable over time, and was dissolved in 2012.

Table 5.1   (continued)

2006	Project	To meet the need for next generation leadership, the Emerging Leaders Network was launched to recruit, develop, and connect young leaders to participate in future community and regional development.
	Outcomes	The network has continued to grow and now consists of more than 700 young civic leaders, who meet regularly to discuss pressing issues in the region. Their current focus is jobs and regional economic growth.
2007	Summit	The TCSA held the third summit, "Making Big Things Happen," engaging more than 600 participants. After the summit, the TCSA committed to the development of new projects in the areas of environmental sustainability and diversity in leadership.
	Project	To contribute to building the city's cultural and tourism industries, Luminato, Toronto's festival of the arts and creativity, was premiered.
	Outcomes	Luminato remains an annual festival, attracting more than 1 million people each year as one of the three top multidisciplinary arts festivals in the world.
2008	Project	Civic Action launched Greening Greater Toronto, an initiative to create a regional vision for environmental sustainability and to build environmental stewardship. Civic Action and the Maytree Foundation also jointly launched DiverseCity: The Greater Toronto Leadership Project, which includes eight initiatives to improve the representativeness of civic leadership in the region, including the DiverseCity Fellows program that each year invites individuals from various backgrounds to participate in regular meetings and events intended to build networks, leadership skills, and representation.
	Outcomes	A long-term project housed within Civic Action itself, the DiverseCity initiative remains an ongoing strategic priority.
2011	Summit	The fourth summit attracted the participation of over 800 people and launched the report "Breaking Boundaries: Time to Think and Act Like a Region," which identified the economy, transportation, jobs and income, and immigration as key issues areas for 2012 to 2015.
2012	Project	Marking a strategic shift in its activities, Civic Action spearheaded a regional transportation initiative, forming a Champions Council of over 40 leaders across the GTA to launch the "What would you do with 32?" campaign to mobilize private sector, government, and public engagement around an improved regional transit system.
	Outcomes	This initiative remains in its early stages, which makes an assessment of its impact premature.

also led to adaptation, both in the broader system context and within Civic Action itself.

Adaptation: Shifting Agendas According to Circumstances

As noted in chapter 4, collaborative actions and outcomes have the potential to foster adaptation at various levels. Moreover, a burgeoning literature on urban resilience emphasizes the relationship between economic, environmental, and social sustainability and a community's ability to collectively adapt to change (Opp and Saunders 2013). Although Civic Action remains one of many organizations active in community and economic development in the Greater Toronto region, it stands out as much for its longevity as for its comprehensive approach and cross-sector composition, having demonstrated adaptation in numerous interacting ways.

As noted above, Civic Action has a solid track record of collaborative actions, which have had meaningful outcomes for various aspects of the GTA. As particular goals have been accomplished, or passed off to other organizations for implementation, there have been corresponding changes in the system context. For example, as some issues have been ameliorated or better addressed through collaborative outcomes and actions, other issues have emerged or have taken precedence on Civic Action's agenda. These shifting priorities are clear examples of adaptation. Perhaps more interesting in this *imp.* case, however, is the adaptation that has occurred within Civic Action itself. Three features identified in the integrative framework have interacted to explain Civic Action's ability to adapt to changing circumstances and, hence, its longevity.

good leadership
First, and perhaps foremost, good leadership enabled adaptation. With its complex agenda, deliberative processes between multiple partners, and expectations of cross-boundary action, Civic Action could not rely solely on a single leader. David Pecaut's charismatic leadership was critical for Civic Action's formation and consolidation. But his untimely death in 2009 underscores the reality that the sustainability of collaborative governance depends on, among other variables, its ability to survive changes in leadership as well as to distribute responsibilities to leaders with other skills and resources. In the aftermath of Pecaut's death, Civic Action's work persisted but attenuated somewhat as it adjusted to his loss and recruited another chair.[11] In the meantime, the combined efforts of its numerous other high-profile leaders, who championed issues and chaired working groups, were critical for continuing and advancing its work. These individuals were recruited from political, bureaucratic, business, social service, postsecondary, environmental, and arts and culture sectors in the region. Each of them had different strengths and

(margin handwritten note: Cross boundary leadership)

styles—as well as substantial political, fiscal, and knowledge resources—and they participated at different junctures to shape Civic Action's formation, consolidation, and sustainability.

In a CGR, there is a particularly important relationship between leadership and the capacity to maintain a consensus on a collectively articulated strategic vision and shared theory of change. In the case of Civic Action, cross-boundary leadership "became the hallmark of all [its] activities," bringing "together the business and social communities." Although most of the people on the Steering Committee did not know each other beforehand, they were all "passionate city builders who really wanted to see the Toronto region succeed and agreed on the need for a plan" (confidential interviews). Civic Action's ability to maintain momentum after the loss of its charismatic leader as well as to continue to recruit committed and high-profile cross-boundary leadership reflects its ongoing adaptation.

A second feature that has enabled Civic Action to adapt is its innovative institutional structure, which is minimalist, flexible, and adjustable in light of change. Rather than managing programs and projects itself, Civic Action develops them for adoption and implementation by existing organizations with the requisite expertise and institutional capacity, or it develops and launches new organizational structures where none exist. Its small core staff maintains momentum, convening leaders, planning events, and managing its day-to-day operations. A core Steering Committee recommends issues for the agenda, which are further developed in issue-based working groups tasked with developing actionable objectives and then are launched in regular but infrequent community-wide summits. The process of reviewing and renewing Civic Action's collective agenda at regular summits provides additional evidence of its ability to adapt.

Finally, adaptation was enabled by Civic Action's inclusive, cross-sector, and deliberative process, which supports a broad, cross-boundary agenda focused on complex policy gaps that cut across levels of government, municipal jurisdictions, policy areas, and the public, private, and community sectors. Moreover, Civic Action's agenda is designed to evolve as its programs are successfully implemented and new issues emerge. In this way, it identifies areas of the system context where adaptation has already occurred, as well as areas where ongoing new action is required. For example, as knowledge accumulated about the challenges facing foreign-trained professionals seeking employment in the region under the TRIEC initiative, it became clear that civic leadership networks in Toronto were not broadly representative of the city's numerous ethnic, racial, and identity-based communities, which provided the impetus for the Emerging Leaders Network and DiverseCity initiatives.

Analysis: Who Speaks for Toronto?

In summary, Civic Action provides a useful illustration of the integrative framework for collaborative governance. In examining the system context, key drivers, collaboration dynamics, and the resulting actions and outcomes, this analysis of the formation and consolidation of Civic Action indicates that its inclusive leadership, institutional structure, and explicitly cross-boundary agenda have interacted to create its adaptability and long-term, if not always highly visible, impact on the greater Toronto community. At the same time, however, major governance challenges remain, which suggests that the integrative framework is less able to account for the ways in which conflict and competing interests and agendas have shaped, and in many ways have constrained, the broader context in which collaboration has occurred in this case. One of the key findings of this research suggests a governance paradox: Although the Toronto region continues to struggle with weak municipal policy capacity and a perceived lack of concerted and visionary leadership, the linkages between Civic Action and municipal politicians have remained tangential and undeveloped.

Progressive urban development occurs at the nexus of civic and political leadership (Dreier, Mollenkopf, and Swanstrom 2004). Recent empirical examinations of social and economic resilience in city-regions suggest that the most adaptable and agile places have supportive strategic governance institutions that are underpinned by high levels of civic leadership and social capital (Nelles 2012; Safford 2009; Wolfe and Bramwell 2008). Although the American urban politics literature is robust, little is known about power relations between elected municipal politicians and civic leaders in Canadian cities. The research on collaborative governance in the GTA presented in this chapter indicates that these relationships may not be as straightforward or harmonious as has often been assumed.

When asked about the main governance challenges faced by Toronto, many interviewees focused on "the absence of vision and leadership to mobilize things," the "lack of unifying ideas," and the dearth of elected politicians willing to "step up to the plate with a sense of vision and a sense of perspective and an emerging agenda around which they could build a coalition and a consensus." There was general agreement that Toronto is at a crossroads in its economic and social development, and that if it "wants to be the sort of city that everybody wants it to be, . . . it's got to change," but that there are no "mechanisms being put in place to allow that to happen" (confidential interviews). At the same time, most respondents also expressed the opinion that effective governance, even in a city-region as large and complex as Toronto, is possible with the right vision and leadership.[12]

Although Civic Action's senior administrative staff members have been actively involved from the beginning, municipal politicians have consistently opted to keep Civic Action at arm's length, outside municipal strategic planning and service delivery efforts.[13] For example, other than launching an energy reduction initiative at the 2007 City Summit, there is little evidence that David Miller, the mayor at the time, or the city councilors sought to build linkages with Civic Action. Similarly, rather than consulting or coordinating with Civic Action, Mayor Miller developed a parallel, and some would say duplicative, economic development strategy for the City of Toronto. Later, under Mayor Rob Ford, who had a patent disinterest in civic leadership initiatives, and an administration beleaguered by scandal and dysfunction, the relationship between Civic Action and the mayor was even less productive. It is significant that the current mayor, John Tory, was a founding member of the TCSA and chose to take over as chair of Civic Action after David Pecaut's death instead of running for mayor of Toronto in 2010. However, it remains to be seen how he will support the CGR now that he is in office.

The specific reasons for weak linkages between municipal politicians and Civic Action remain unclear. Although some people felt that more political bridges could have been built to support citywide and regionwide governance initiatives if there "had . . . been more active dialogue and creative relationships between the multisector civic leadership group and the mayor" to build a common purpose, others perceived Civic Action as "an anti-mayoralty-type initiative, so it was hampered by a sense of political infighting" (confidential interviews). Either way, the potential for a robust and productive partnership between the city-region's political and civic leadership remains untapped, diminishing the potential contributions of Civic Action to municipal policy capacity, and also impeding broader community awareness of its contributions and ongoing activities. Thus, though the integrative framework for collaborative governance accounts for the process through which cross-boundary collaboration occurs, it perhaps minimizes how the broader system context shapes and constrains collaborative efforts.

Conclusion

This analysis of the Greater Toronto Civic Action Alliance indicates that the integrative framework for collaborative governance provides a powerful tool for explaining this successful cross-boundary collaboration at the urban level. Taken together, the consequential drivers emerging from the broader system context shaped the formation of Civic Action, and collaboration dynamics continue to facilitate deliberative dialogue between those with multiple interests and perspectives, resulting in numerous collective actions and outcomes and a core agenda that adapts and evolves as projects are completed and new issues emerge.

With its "weak networks that do not hang together well," the Toronto region has historically lacked institutional mechanisms to facilitate cross-boundary collaboration and the development of common goals and strategic visions (confidential interview; see also Bramwell and Wolfe 2014). Despite its weak linkages with municipal politicians, the Greater Toronto Civic Action Alliance has gone a long way toward filling this governance gap in the city. It can take credit for providing visionary civic leadership, encouraging boundary-spanning and networking activity across social and economic development agendas, overseeing the implementation of innovative projects, and attracting policy attention to critical local and regional issues. Issues are generated by the core Steering Committee, and projects are developed by issue-based working groups and various other informal, ad hoc groups. The small secretariat maintains collaborative momentum as it organizes and enables the work of the various leadership groups. Agenda change occurs regularly through summits designed to check progress and adapt the agenda to reflect past accomplishments and emerging issues through community-wide consultation. Not only has this inclusive civic coalition been sustained over time; it has made tangible and durable contributions to addressing social and economic development challenges in Toronto.

Ultimately, however, engaged, collaborative, and cross-boundary leadership remains the critical independent variable accounting for Civic Action's performance and longevity. There was a strong sense that before Civic Action got off the ground, Toronto suffered from a distinct lack of civic "champions" willing to articulate and drive a visionary agenda. The late David Pecaut, who was distinguished by his strong networking skills and boundary-spanning ability, was often referred to as the civic leader who was most committed, effective, and visible in championing the interests of Toronto and the work of Civic Action. Yet as the integrative framework suggests, different types of leadership are important at different junctures in the development of a collaborative governance regime. Although some are essential at the formation stage, others deal with conflict or deliberation, and still others drive and oversee the implementation process (Emerson, Nabatchi, and Balogh 2012). With its ability to effectively leverage the participation and influence of multiple leaders—each with important skills, abilities, and resources—committed multisector leadership capable of internalizing conflict and working across boundaries is a key element accounting for Civic Action's continuing high capacity for joint action, its adaptability over time, and its discernible impact on some of the most complex issues shaping the future growth and long-term sustainability of the Greater Toronto region.

Notes

1. Key informants include David Pecaut, the inaugural chair, and Julia Deans, the inaugural chief executive officer, of the Toronto City Summit Alliance. Their comments are attributed to them throughout in this chapter. The remaining comments are drawn from confidential interviews.

2. This organization, which was originally known as the Toronto City Summit Alliance, was renamed the Greater Toronto Civic Action alliance in 2009 to better reflect its broad regional mandate, which many felt was not captured in the original name. The short name, "Civic Action," is used throughout this chapter for the sake of clarity, even though many of the initiatives were launched under the TCSA banner.

3. Scholars underscore the problems caused by the forced amalgamation of the former Municipality of Metropolitan Toronto, or Metro Toronto, into the City of Toronto by the Ontario government in 1998, which covers only a small portion of the rapidly growing regional economy, asserting that it had a questionable impact on increased efficiencies in service delivery and did little to address problems of metropolitan governance for the GTA (Boudreau, Keil, and Young 2009; Sancton 2005). Further impeding regional planning, the surrounding upper-tier governments of Halton, Peel, York, and Durham each have elected chairs and responsibilities for economic development and regional planning.

4. Although Toronto has not experienced the same levels of sociospatial segregation as some of its American and European counterparts, evidence of dramatic increases in spatial and income polarization since the 1970s has sparked increased policy activism and the development of targeted poverty-reduction initiatives (Hulchanski 2007; United Way of Greater Toronto 2004).

5. For example, the former provincial premiers Bill Davis and Bob Rae either attended the initial summit and/or participated on subsequent working groups. David Crombie, a popular former mayor of Toronto, participated on the original Steering Committee and continues to sit on the Board of Directors.

6. In recognition of his leadership and commitment to the community, the public square in front of Toronto City Hall was renamed from Nathan Phillips Square to David Pecaut Square in 2010.

7. For a complete list of the original and current Steering Committees, see www.civicaction.ca/steering-committees.

8. See Toronto City Summit Alliance (2003).

9. In somewhat of a departure from its earlier emphasis on social welfare issues, Civic Action currently focuses much of its attention on supporting the development of civic leaders and social entrepreneurs. Its efforts are also targeted at building a high-profile leadership forum to support political actions to build a regional transit system in the GTA. In terms of recent leadership changes, in addition to John Tory taking over for David Pecaut, Civic Action's chief executive officer, Mitzi Hunter, was recently elected to the provincial parliament, and her former position remains vacant.

10. As noted above, Mitzi Hunter, another former chief executive officer, was recently elected to the provincial parliament as part of a Liberal majority. A regional transit plan was a critical element of the Liberal Party's election platform, and implementation plans were announced within days of its taking office.

11. John Tory, another high-profile civic leader and politician, decided to take the position. He was a former leader of the Progressive Conservative Party of Ontario, and one of the four co-chairs responsible for the inaugural summit. He had unsuccessfully run twice

for mayor of Toronto and decided to take on the chair of Civic Action rather than running a third time.

12. Attention to Toronto's municipal institutional structure in the post-1998 amalgamated city underscores ongoing problems with transparency, accountability, and democratic representation. Taken together, a large ward system, a labyrinthine and inscrutable bureaucracy, ambiguity surrounding mayoral powers arising out of the City of Toronto Act, and the paucity of mechanisms for active citizen engagement provide serious impediments to the development of a concerted strategic vision for the future of the region (Stren et al. 2010).

13. City administrators participate on various Civic Action working groups and programs and regularly attend events and summits. For example, the city manager at the time, Shirley Hoy, was a founding member of the original TCSA Steering Committee, the current manager of economic development and tourism, and a member of the Civic Action Steering Committee.

CHAPTER 6

Collaborative Governance in Alaska

Responding to Climate Change Threats in Alaska Native Communities

Robin Bronen

Climate change is radically transforming Arctic ecosystems, threatening the habitability of the places where Alaska Native communities have lived for millennia. Several of these communities have decided that relocation is the only strategy that can protect their homes and their lives. However, with neither an institutional framework to guide the relocation process nor designated funding to pay for the relocation, residents of the Alaska Native community of Newtok are using collaborative governance to help their efforts. This chapter uses the integrative framework for collaborative governance to illustrate the work of the Newtok Planning Group (NPG), a collaborative governance regime consisting of twenty-five tribal, state, federal, and nongovernmental agencies and organizations dedicated to relocating the Yup'ik Eskimo community of Newtok, which is now living on the western coast of Alaska along the Bering Sea. Newtok's tribal government is leading this effort, in partnership with the Alaska state government.

The Newtok Planning Group: Application of the Framework to the Case

Before applying the integrative framework for collaborative governance (Emerson, Nabatchi, and Balogh 2012) to the case of the NPG, it is useful to briefly consider the ways in which Alaskan communities are being dramatically affected by climate-induced environmental change. Throughout Alaska, temperature increases are having a negative impact on the habitability of communities (GAO 2003, 2009). Alaska has warmed twice as fast as the global average during the past half century (ACIA 2004; IPCC 2007; GCRP 2009). Since the 1950s, statewide average temperatures have risen 3.5 degrees Celsius during the winter (ACIA 2004; Shulski and Wendler 2007). These increased temperatures are radically transforming the Arctic Ocean. Since 2007, the area of the Arctic Ocean covered by sea ice (i.e., the Arctic sea ice extent) has set record lows, with the six lowest seasonal minimum ice extents in the satellite record occurring since that year. The National Snow and Ice Data Center (NSIDC 2012) documented a new record for low minimum ice extent in September 2012, and a new record for low maximum ice extent in March 2015 (NSIDC 2015).

The decreased Arctic sea ice extent, coupled with warming temperatures, has caused a delay in the freezing of the Bering and Chukchi seas. Historically, the seas are frozen from early November to mid-May, but since the 1980s, the seas have tended to remain ice free approximately three weeks longer in the autumn (Hufford and Partain 2005). Coastal communities in western Alaska depend on Arctic sea ice. However, the delay in the freezing of the Arctic seas prevents the near shore pack ice from forming, which exposes many coastal communities to flooding and erosion caused by storms originating in the Bering and Chukchi seas. Although technically not hurricanes, these storms, which occur primarily between August and early December, can produce hurricane-strength winds that cause wave action and storm surges that damage the coast (Shulski and Wendler 2007).

The land itself is also affected by temperature increases. Permanently frozen subsoil—or permafrost—keeps the land intact and habitable along the northwestern Alaskan coast (GAO 2009, 7). However, this frozen subsoil is thawing because of temperature increases (Serreze 2008). According to a 2007 report by the Intergovernmental Panel on Climate Change, the temperature of the top layer of permafrost has increased by up to 3 degrees Celsius since the 1980s (Lemke et al. 2007).

The combination of repeated extreme weather events with decreasing Arctic sea ice and thawing permafrost is dramatically accelerating the rates of erosion in Alaska Native communities located along the Bering and Chukchi seas. Due to the rapidity with which these changes are occurring, communities in Alaska face imminent danger and an unprecedented need to adapt to climate change (GAO 2003, 2009; Markon, Trainor, and Chapin 2012).

The looming threat to Alaskan communities is widely acknowledged, and has been extensively analyzed. The US Army Corps of Engineers (ACE), the US Government Accountability Office (GAO), and the Alaskan Sub-Cabinet on Climate Change Immediate Action Workgroup (IAWG) have each issued numerous reports that document the increasing severity of erosion on Alaska Native villages. The reports have evaluated past efforts to protect communities in place, the costs of future protection for threatened communities through erosion control, and the costs and viability of community relocation (GAO 2003, 2009; IAWG 2008, 2009; ACE 2006, 2009).

In 2003, the GAO issued the first federal government report to document the impact of flooding and erosion on Alaska Native communities. In this report, the GAO concluded that 184 of the 213 Alaska Native villages—that is, 86 percent—are affected to some extent by flooding and erosion (GAO 2003). Four communities—Kivalina, Koyukuk, Newtok, and Shishmaref—were planning to relocate due to these environmental threats (GAO 2003). The GAO also concluded that the two federal government programs primarily responsible for erosion and flood protection, ACE and the Natural Resources Conservation Service, were unable to adequately provide these services to Alaska Native communities due to the recurring nature of the threats and funding restrictions (GAO 2003, 2–3).

The 2006 ACE report examined erosion in seven communities—Dillingham, Bethel, Kivalina, Kaktovik, Shishmaref, Newtok, and Unalakleet—and responded to questions that were incorporated into the authorizing federal legislation. These questions were: What are the costs of ongoing erosion? What would it cost to relocate a community? And how much time do these communities have left before they are lost to erosion if erosion protection is not constructed (ACE 2006)? The analysis compared the costs of prospective erosion control and relocation for three communities: Kivalina, Newtok, and Shishmaref. ACE found that the prospective relocation costs for Kivalina and Shishmaref far exceeded the cost of erosion control. However, for the community of Newtok, ACE found that the costs of erosion protection and relocation were almost equal.

After Newtok residents decided that relocation was the only climate change adaptation strategy that could protect their lives, Newtok's tribal government facilitated a three-pronged relocation process: (1) the identification of a new village relocation site, (2) Newtok residents' approval of the site, and (3) documentation to substantiate the need to relocate and the suitability of the site for the community. Newtok residents voted three times—in September 1996, May 2001, and August 2003—and overwhelmingly chose to relocate to Mertarvik on Nelson Island (ASCG 2008). However, given the lack of an institutional framework to guide the relocation process and no funding to pay for the relocation, they responded by initiating what can be described as a collaborative governance regime (CGR).

The System Context: The Challenges Facing Newtok

As noted in chapter 2, collaborative governance always occurs within a broader system context that consists of numerous political, legal, socioeconomic, environmental, and other conditions. This context affects CGRs' initial formation and their long-term performance. Although all the conditions in the system context discussed in chapter 2 are present in this case, several took on heightened importance.

Newtok and its residents are inextricably bound to the surrounding natural resource conditions which shape their socioeconomic and cultural well-being. Newtok is a traditional village inhabited by Yup'ik Eskimos, a federally recognized indigenous tribe, whose members are dependent on a limited cash economy and rely extensively on subsistence harvesting and gathering food (Bronen 2011; Fienup-Riordan 1983).With its location on the Bering Sea in far western Alaska, Newtok is small, isolated, and surrounded by water. The Ninglick River borders the community to the south and the Newtok River lies to the east, adjacent to several homes. No roads lead to or from Newtok, and there are no cars. The only year-round access to the community is by airplanes, which hold a maximum of ten passengers. In addition, the tribe has a history of forced settlement by the federal government, which ended its seasonal migrations following the movements of fish and game. The federal government chose the Newtok village site because of its ease of access for barges carrying school construction materials (Bronen and Chapin 2013). Barges historically have traveled to Newtok during the summer to bring fuel and other supplies too large or heavy to be carried by plane (ASCG 2008).

All of Newtok's four hundred residents live in a cluster of approximately sixty-three houses (Bronen 2011). Few homes have insulation to protect residents from the extreme cold. Several homes are sinking into thawing permafrost. None of the homes have complete plumbing facilities. Most residents haul water or have water storage tanks. Freshwater is pumped from a shallow tundra pond to a water treatment facility and storage tank. The treated water is available to residents at a centrally located pumping station (ACE 2008b).

A combination of gradual ecosystem changes and rapid onset extreme environmental events continues to repeatedly damage public infrastructure and endanger the lives and well-being of Newtok's inhabitants. Erosion is changing the course of the Ninglick River, moving it closer to the village of Newtok. Between 1954 and 2003, approximately three-quarters of a mile of tundra eroded in front of the village (Cox 2007). Efforts by the State of Alaska to control the erosion between 1983 and 1989 totaled approximately $1.5 million (ACE 2008b). Six extreme weather events occurred between 1989 and 2006, five of which precipitated Federal Emergency Management Agency disaster declarations (ASCG 2008). These five storms accelerated the rates of erosion and repeatedly "flooded the village water supply, caused raw sewage to be spread throughout the community, displaced residents from homes, destroyed subsistence food storage and other facilities, and shut down essential utilities." Newtok's public infrastructure was also significantly damaged or destroyed, including the village dump site, barge ramp, sewage treatment facility, and fuel storage facilities (ACE 2008b).

Political dynamics and power relations also shape the system context. As a federally recognized indigenous tribe, the Yup'ik Eskimos have the right to self-determination and self-governance. Newtok's tribal government is the community's sole governing body.

Initiating Collaborative Governance: The Drivers and Formation of the Newtok Planning Group

As was noted in chapter 2, the impetus for collaboration is shaped by four drivers: uncertainty, interdependence, consequential incentives, and initiating leadership. All four drivers are clearly present in this case.

Uncertainty is perhaps a universal theme in this case. Beyond uncertainty about environmental conditions and the speed with which future threats, conditions, and events would unfold, village relocation was (and continues to be) an unprecedented activity. No single government agency had (or has) the technical and organizational expertise to develop and manage the community relocation process, there was no funding to pay for the costs of such efforts, and there was no statutory mandate for accomplishing the task. The complexity of the endeavor resulted in inherent interdependence. No one group, organization, or agency could relocate Newtok on its own. Rather, the relocation process required that a wide variety of actors from all sectors and all levels of government work together. Thus doubt, ambiguity, and mutual reliance marked nearly every aspect of the relocation process—from determining which agency was responsible for what component of the relocation process, how decisions would be made, and from where resources would be made available to developing a basic plan for relocation, establishing a timeline for action, and determining the sequence of steps for implementation. Perhaps the only point of clarity in this case was that Newtok faced imminent threats to its security from climate change and there were no cost-feasible options to protect the community in situ. This life-threatening situation provided the critical consequential incentive for a number of parties to come together for this collaborative effort.

Although uncertainty, interdependence, and consequential incentives were important, without the strong initiating leadership of Newtok's tribal government and direct support from the Alaska state government, the NPG would never have formed. Leadership by Newtok's tribal government was a key component of the formation of this CGR. Specifically, the tribal government initiated a series of ad hoc meetings with federal and state government representatives to discuss the imminent threats of climate change to the lives of Newtok residents. These meetings led to the creation of the NPG in May 2006. The NPG's purpose was to respond to the urgent needs of the Yup'ik Eskimo community, and to develop, design, and implement a community relocation process (Bronen 2011; GAO 2009).

The NPG, which is unique in Alaska in its multidisciplinary and multijurisdictional structure, consists of approximately twenty-five state, federal, and tribal governmental and nongovernmental agencies that are voluntarily collaborating to facilitate Newtok's relocation. The Alaska Department of Commerce, Community, and Economic Development is the lead coordinating state agency for comprehensive integrated planning initiatives like the NPG (IAWG 2009; ACE 2008b). Then–Alaska governor Frank Murkowski, in a 2006 state disaster declaration, directed this department to "act as the state coordinating agency to coordinate with other state and federal agencies to propose long-term solutions to the ongoing erosion issues in . . . affected coastal communities in this state."[1] Additional members of the NPG include the Native village of Newtok, represented by the Newtok's tribal government and the Newtok Native Corporation; seven Alaska state agencies;[2] the Alaska Governor's Office; the Lower Kuskokwim School District; nine federal agencies;[3] members of Alaska's congressional delegation; and four regional nonprofit organizations.[4] In addition, the NPG has worked closely with the IAWG, a contrasting CGR that is briefly analyzed in box 6.1.

Collaboration Dynamics: Complexity and Scarcity

By the time of the first NPG meeting in May 2006, conditions in the system context had changed—in some cases dramatically. Newtok was in crisis. Erosion was claiming 70 feet of land annually, the community had major floods in September 2005 and May 2006, critical public infrastructure was lost or severely damaged, and access to the community was extremely limited due to the loss of the barge landing in 2005 (ACE 2008b). The community was also in the midst of a public health crisis. The state, federal, and nonprofit agency representatives recognized that these factors created a complex emergency and that the community needed immediate action. These issues drove home the need for a CGR to address the problems facing Newtok. They also helped shape effective collaboration dynamics.

As discussed in chapter 3, collaboration dynamics include three components, each with four internal elements: principled engagement, which includes discovery, definition, deliberation, and determinations; shared motivation, which includes trust, mutual understanding, internal legitimacy, and commitment; and the capacity for joint action, which includes procedural and

Box 6.1 A Case in Contrast: The Immediate Action Workgroup of the Alaska Climate Change Sub-Cabinet

In 2007, then–Alaska governor Sarah Palin created the Alaska Climate Change Sub-Cabinet, which was charged with developing a statewide strategy for understanding and responding to climate change. In turn, the Climate Change Sub-Cabinet established the Immediate Action Workgroup (IAWG), a multidisciplinary and intergovernmental CGR tasked with identifying the immediate needs of the communities imminently threatened by erosion, flooding, permafrost degradation, and other climate change-related effects (IAWG 2008).

The CGR and collaboration dynamics. The IAWG was co-chaired by Michael Black (deputy commissioner, Alaska Department of Commerce, Community, and Economic Development) and Patricia Opheen (chief, Engineering Division of the Alaska District, US Army Corps of Engineers). No Alaska Native organization or tribal government was an official member of the IAWG, although they were encouraged to participate (but did so infrequently).

Collaborative actions, outcomes, and adaptation. The IAWG's work occurred in three phases. In phase I (November 2007–April 2008), it focused on six Native American communities most imperiled by climate change. It released a report outlining the actions and policies needed within the next 12 to 18 months to prevent loss of life and property in these communities. In response to the report, the Alaska Legislature established the Alaska Climate Change Impact Mitigation Program (ACCIMP) to provide funding to communities imminently threatened by climate change.

In phase II (April 2008–March 2009), the IAWG researched and issued its second report, which reaffirmed the 2008 recommendations and highlighted the need to create an integrated, multiagency, and intergovernmental approach to effectively identify and address the needs of imperiled communities. It also leveraged funding to develop comprehensive emergency plans for the six communities in peril, developed flood and erosion control structures to protect community residents, and monitored the implementation of the ACCIMP.

In phase III (April 2009–March 2011), the IAWG created a system to identify imperiled communities and coordinate interagency data gathering and analysis, and commissioned additional reports about the effects of climate change on vulnerable of Alaskan communities.

The actions of the IAWG had several effects, including changes in funding and policy. However, the IAWG could not adapt in the face of political turnover. The IAWG's last meeting occurred in March 2011 because it failed to receive authorization to continue its work from newly elected governor Sean Parnell or the Sub-Cabinet on Climate Change (IAWG 2011a, 2011b). The dismantling of the IAWG creates a tremendous gap for communities faced with climate-related threats.

institutional arrangements, leadership, knowledge, and resources. Moreover collaboration dynamics do not unfold in a linear process; rather, they occur as progressive and iterative interactions between participants and their parent organizations. The cyclical nature of collaboration dynamics makes it challenging to unpack their components and elements and to present them in a straightforward manner. This is particularly true for the case of the NPG.

Principled engagement is an important feature in this CGR. As noted above, the NPG began meeting in May 2006 and continues to meet several times each year. Each meeting necessarily includes the elements of discovery, definition, and deliberation. Different agency representatives participate in each meeting depending on the particular topics on the agenda, which can vary tremendously. For example, meeting agendas have included issues such as emergency preparedness, agency updates on infrastructure development, strategic planning for relocation, and the coordination of funding and infrastructure construction at the relocation site. Some topics, such as compliance with the National Environmental Protection Act, have required repeated discussions to determine the best way to meet the requirements of this legislation. Due to the NPG's multidisciplinary nature and the breadth of issues under discussion, its participants have had to spend significant time and effort educating each other about the laws that govern their work, the available funding options, and the limitations and constraints of each organization (Bronen 2011). Again, depending on the topics being discussed, multiple kinds of determinations are made at these meetings, ranging from basic decisions about setting agendas and creating subcommittees to focus on specific issues (e.g., transportation, housing, and energy) to substantive decisions about funding, operational resources, coordination, and the design and implementation of construction and community-planning activities.

Through the process of principled engagement, the NPG developed a shared theory of change. Just as the relocation issue is extremely complex, so too is the theory of change. The NPG devised a strategy for meeting the community's immediate and long-term relocation needs. The creation of this strategy was an intense multiyear process that directly reflected the complexity of the relocation process.

The process of principled engagement was critical to developing the shared motivation that generated and maintained the NPG's momentum. Over the course of numerous meetings, trust began to develop between its members. Rich discussions led to greater mutual understanding about the capacities and constraints of the individual organizations at the table. Transparent decision making, as well as the close working relationship between the tribal and state government representatives, gave internal legitimacy to the group's efforts. Together, these features, along with the dramatic need for the relocation of the Newtok community, enhanced the parties' commitment to the CGR.

Over time, the NPG has also developed the capacity for joint action. Coordinating the activities (and resources) of multiple parties from all sectors and all levels of government necessitated the creation of procedural and institutional arrangements; however, there was never any attempt to strictly formalize the process. Indeed, because of the breadth, interconnectedness, and complexity of the issues being tackled by this CGR, no single entity had complete decision-making authority. Thus, the procedural and institutional arrangements had to remain flexible.

Given the diffuse nature of decision-making authority, leadership played a critical role not only in the NPG's creation but also in its success. From the NPG's inception to its continuing efforts, Newtok's tribal government has led the relocation effort and approved all decisions related to relocation, including choosing the relocation site, developing the strategic management plan, and constructing the pioneer infrastructure. A state government representative from the Alaska Department of Community and Regional Affairs implements these decisions by coordinating the efforts of the other state, federal, and nongovernmental agencies. No state or federal statutes or regulations govern or guide the NPG's work. Instead, the members of the NPG are guided only by their collective desire to provide technical assistance to the Newtok tribal government. Statements and actions of state and federal agency representatives have repeatedly affirmed the importance of working with Newtok's tribal government (Bronen 2011; ACE 2008b).

This multilevel leadership structure enabled the effective sharing and generation of knowledge and the leveraging of scarce resources—including time, technical and logistical support, administrative and organizational assistance, requisite skills for analysis and implementation, and other needed expertise. This willingness and ability to leverage resources was particularly important because of the remote locations of Newtok and Mertarvik and the enormous expense of transporting technical equipment and materials to the relocation site.

The issue of financial resources is particularly interesting in this case. Funding limitations have made it extremely difficult to facilitate coordination, particularly of other resources and when taking collaborative actions. In fact, not one agency involved in the NPG has funding designated for Newtok's relocation. In 2008, the IAWG noted: "The Newtok experience [shows] that there are so many unknowns that it's . . . very difficult to track information and to project and plan for what's needed with the relocation effort. Funding sources are iffy, and [it's] difficult to get a handle on who is going to fund and what the requirements of the project [are] and what agencies' requirements are. Everyone has a different tracking system, and so the site is being developed piecemeal."[5]

Moreover, every aspect of the relocation requires state and federal agencies to identify and secure funding in phases and to coordinate their funding efforts, including sharing equipment costs and coordinating the usage of funds. To put together the relocation puzzle, the NPG has been extremely creative in its use of existing revenue sources from funds generally available for community projects throughout Alaska.

Collaborative Actions, Outcomes, and Adaptation: Creating the Village Infrastructure at the Relocation Site

The NPG was able to take several collaborative actions—that is, intentional efforts that were in line with its shared theory of change for achieving the CGR's collective purpose. As noted above, the NPG developed—and continues to have—a complex shared theory of change. Obviously, several factors have contributed to this complexity; however, early during the collaboration, the members of the group discovered (perhaps not surprisingly) the need for flexibility in their strategy so they could adjust to changes in the system context. Of particular concern to the group—and one of the primary reasons for flexibility—was the issue of funding. As noted above, no single agency or organization had funding specifically dedicated for the relocation. Rather, parties to the NPG have used existing revenue sources to fund specific elements of the relocation plan. This added to the intricacy of the CGR's collaborative actions.

One of the main features of the CGR's theory of change was the need to begin the relocation process with the construction of primary infrastructure at Mertarvik—the community relocation site. Accordingly, the NPG engaged in a multiyear effort to determine what should be built, with specific attention being given to the design and construction of infrastructure that not only created the foundation for the community over time but also provided emergency evacuation facilities. To meet these objectives, the NPG decided that the first infrastructure built at Mertarvik needed to be an evacuation center, a barge landing, a staging area, and an access road between the barge landing and the evacuation center.[6]

Seven different federal, state, and tribal entities were involved in the construction of these facilities, but no agency was authorized as the project's lead supervisor.[7] In October 2006, the Department of Commerce, Community, and Economic Development and the Newtok tribal government both applied for and received funding from the Economic Development Administration of the US Department of Commerce to build a barge landing and staging facility at Mertarvik.[8] The Alaska Department of Transportation and Public Facilities provided additional funding to satisfy the state matching requirement.

ACE then planned and designed the road connecting the barge landing to the evacuation center pad, with construction performed by the State of Alaska (ACE 2008a). The US Department of Defense's Innovative Readiness Training Program (IRT) assisted with the construction (Bronen 2011). The IRT is a military program to improve military readiness while simultaneously providing services to communities throughout the United States. ACE worked with the IRT to provide the necessary documentation to complete all permitting requirements, including National Environmental Policy Act documentation, a Coastal Zone Consistency Determination, and Water Quality Certification. During the summer of 2009, the Alaska Department of Transportation and Public Facilities built the barge landing (IAWG 2009). The US military built the road during the summer of 2010.

In addition to these efforts, the Newtok Traditional Council decided to build some initial housing at the site. Newtok residents received vocational training specifically for this construction effort. As of 2014, six houses had been built at the relocation site.

These and other collaborative actions have had multiple outcomes. For example, the ability of diverse parties to work together under complex and difficult circumstances has strengthened their commitment to the NPG and to collaborative governance more generally. It has also shored up support from the participants in the CGR as well as from their parent organizations. Most important, the NPG's actions have provided numerous benefits to the current residents of Newtok as well as to the current and future residents of Mertarvik. In turn, these outcomes have led to adaptation both within the CGR itself and also in the broader system context.

One of the clearest examples of adaptation can be seen in how the NPG has responded to barriers and obstacles. Although the NPG has made significant progress toward Newtok's relocation, the policy and practical challenges have been enormous. Existing federal and state statutes and regulations, such as postdisaster recovery legislation, have impeded their efforts (IAWG 2009). For example, the design and development of a comprehensive relocation plan was an essential first step in Newtok's relocation effort. However, because no funding was specifically available for this activity when the NPG began its work, the group had to compartmentalize its efforts instead of executing one streamlined relocation plan. The several agencies involved used existing revenue sources within the mandate of their respective agencies to fund specific projects from the initial relocation community layout plan. As a result, the first plan focused exclusively on a master plan for water, sewer, and solid waste in Mertarvik, because Village Safe Water, the state agency, dedicated to the design and construction of sanitation systems in rural Alaska, received a grant in 2006 to fund this work (GAO 2009).[9] Several months later, the Division of Community and Regional Affairs (DCRA) of the Alaska Department of Commerce, Community, and Economic Development received funding to supplement the Village Safe Water work by developing a comprehensive community layout plan to determine the specific location of homes and public infrastructure (Bronen 2011). Subsequently, the DCRA received funding so that a comprehensive strategic management relocation plan, the Mertarvik Strategic Plan, could be completed in 2012. Numerous additional examples exist showing how the NPG—as a CGR—adapted in response to emerging obstacles and opportunities.

Adaptation as a result of the outcomes of collaborative action can also be seen in the broader system context. Newtok is not the only community in Alaska to have decided that relocation is the only strategy to protect it from climate-induced threats. Although extremely challenging, the Newtok case has revealed the necessity and promise of using collaborative governance to address village relocation due to climate change. After seeing success in this case, the DCRA received funding to build collaborative interagency working groups to assist other communities in need of relocation. Such funding will be critical to future collaborative endeavors and may mitigate many of the challenges faced by the NPG. At this time, it is unknown whether the tremendous social and human capital generated by the NPG will transfer to these other collaborative governance endeavors.

Analysis and Conclusion

The NPG has worked diligently for eight years—and will continue to work—to relocate Newtok residents to their chosen site in Mertarvik. Moreover, the NPG has been successful both in the work it was able to accomplish vis-à-vis relocation, and also in its model of an effective response to the unprecedented environmental changes threatening Alaskans' lives and livelihoods. Thus this case not only provides an example of a successful CGR but also demonstrates the applicability of the integrative framework to even the most complex cases.

From numerous challenges in the system context emerged all four of the drivers (uncertainty, interdependence, consequential incentives, and initiating leadership) that led to the formation of the NPG. From a series of ad hoc meetings emerged a robust, voluntary CGR consisting of more than two dozen federal, state, and tribal governmental and nongovernmental agencies and organizations. Through the cycling of collaboration dynamics over several years, the NPG practiced principled engagement that included discovery, definition, deliberation, and the making of innumerable determinations; built shared motivation that cultivated trust, mutual understanding, internal legitimacy, and commitment; and created the capacity for joint action that leveraged leadership, knowledge, and resources, while keeping procedural and institutional arrangements informal and flexible. The many parties to the NPG were able to develop a sense of purpose and a shared theory of change that guided its collaborative actions to relocate Newtok to Mertarvik. The outcomes of these actions, as well as the resulting adaptations, have been felt not only in the Newtok and Mertarvik communities but also in and between the CGR's members, in the broader system context, and in other Alaskan communities facing threats from climate change.

Despite the fact that the integrative framework applies well to the NPG as a CGR, it is perhaps limited in its ability to capture all the dynamism and complexity of collaborative governance—particularly when collaborative governance is being used in response to wicked problems. It is a challenge to break down the facts of a case into neat and distinct components. This is particularly evident in the case of collaboration dynamics, where the components (principled engagement, shared motivation, and the capacity for joint action) and their internal elements do not emerge and appear in a linear fashion. For example, in the case of the NPG, the ability to leverage particular resources (an element of the capacity for joint action) sometimes led to deliberation and the making of specific determinations (elements in principled engagement), which in turn led to the building of shared motivation. It is difficult to capture this leapfrogging among components and elements within the confines of a chapter. Nevertheless, the integrative framework does provide the scaffolding for robust case descriptions—and in doing so, meets both practical and research needs.

In this case, the application of the framework highlights three significant issues: the importance of leadership; resource challenges, particularly in terms of funding; and the potential for adaptation—in this case, adapting to large-scale changes in the system context resulting from the outcomes of successful collaboration. First, multilevel and multisectoral leadership was essential for the NPG's creation and success. The Newtok tribal government took the lead in bringing the parties together. Over the course of the collaboration, different entities also took on leadership roles—for example, in terms of securing funding and implementing actions—but respected the authority and rights of Newtok's tribal government. Collectively, these leadership efforts helped to generate transparency, trust, and commitment to the effort, which in turn generated legitimacy not only for the NPG but also for its relocation decisions. This leadership was thus perhaps the most important element of creating a successful CGR.

Second, funding continues to be a central issue. No organization had funds specifically approved and allocated for the relocation process. Thus, collaboration was needed to leverage resources (financial and otherwise) among the parties; however, the inflexibility of agency funding streams and budget processes hampered efforts. In part, this is because the "State of Alaska, just like the federal government, plans for and manages programs primarily through individual departments. The priorities are set usually during budget formulation for the next budget cycle. However, many capital projects need years of planning for engineering study and design and for the identification of federal funding. These funding decisions occur for each individual agency and often are without consideration of other state or federal projects that may be in potential conflict for the same community or region" (IAWG 2009). Nevertheless, through extensive coordination and collaboration, the NPG was able to overcome this and other resource barriers; and in doing so, it was able to generate recognition of this issue and action to address it.

This connects to the third issue: the potential for adaptation to changes resulting from the outcomes of successful collaborative actions. As noted above, after seeing the NPG's success, the DCRA secured funding to build a collaborative interagency working group. In its investigation of the needs of Alaskan communities in peril, the IAWG (2009) noted that "state and federal agencies are severely limited by this lack of integration for data, research, and program or project development. This environment of uncertainty increases the risk of many communities of facing extreme risks from the unknown effects of natural disasters. The traditional 'stove-piped' approach of creating and managing government programs ensures a narrow, myopic view of community needs and places the individual programs in competition for approval and funding. This segregated approach increases the uncertainty of funding but decreases the potential for meaningful and comprehensive assistance."

As a result of this finding, the IAWG (2009) recommended an integrated, interagency systemic framework to respond to communities imperiled by climate threats to "save money on public infrastructure, avoid costly delays, save funds through economies of scale and combining mobilization, mitigate the effects and costs of disaster relief and recovery" (IAWG 2009). The work of the IAWG has led to significant policy-level recommendations that respond more broadly to the climate threats faced by Alaskan communities. Hopefully, these recommendations, which have reshaped the system context, will make collaborative governance for Alaskan community relocation easier and timelier.

In sum, collaborative governance has clearly played a significant role in the state and federal government responses to the climate-induced environmental changes threatening Alaskan communities. Moreover, the NPG has emerged as a model for CGRs in this important area of work. Although the NPG was created in an ad hoc manner, it continues to collaborate to assist with the relocation of Newtok to Mertarvik. Because the NPG does not have a formal institutional structure, it is unclear whether the tremendous social and resource capital generated through its efforts can be replicated for other imperiled communities. However, this CGR's success has been widely recognized. Hopefully, this case study will lead to changes that will enable government agencies and other organizations to more flexibly leverage resources and expertise and develop strategies and actions that will respond effectively to the unprecedented changes occurring in Alaska. Only time will tell if this hope becomes a reality.

Acknowledgment

I am indebted to the work of the Newtok Planning Group and the willingness of state, federal, and tribal government representatives to allow me to observe dozens of meetings to understand the enormous challenges involved in relocating Newtok. Their work is inspirational and provides a model for other communities that are faced with unprecedented climate change threats and need to relocate in order to protect lives and livelihoods.

Notes

1. Alaska Administrative Order 231, November 29, 2006, www.gov.state.ak.us/admin-orders/231.html.

2. The state agencies include the Alaska Department of Commerce, Community, and Economic Development, Division of Community and Regional Affairs, which is coordinating the Newtok Planning Group; the Alaska Department of Environmental Conservation Village Safe Water Program; the Alaska Department of Transportation and Public Facilities; the Alaska Department of Military and Veterans Affairs, Division of Homeland Security and Emergency Management; the Alaska Department of Natural Resources, Division of Coastal and Ocean Resources; the Alaska Department of Education and Early Development; the Alaska Department of Health and Social Services; the Alaska Industrial Development and Export Authority; and the Alaska Energy Authority.

3. Federal agencies include the US Army Corps of Engineers, Alaska District; the US Department of Commerce; the US Economic Development Administration; the US Department of Agriculture, Rural Development; the Natural Resources Conservation Service; the US Department of Housing and Urban Development; the US Department of the Interior, Bureau of Indian Affairs; the US Department of Transportation, Federal Aviation Administration; the US Environmental Protection Agency; and the Denali Commission.

4. The regional nonprofits include the Association of Village Council Presidents Regional Housing Authority, the Coastal Villages Region Fund, the Rural Alaska Community Action Program, and the Yukon-Kuskokwim Health Corporation.

5. Immediate Action Workgroup, Meeting Summary, January 18, 2008, 7, www.climate change.alaska.gov/docs/iaw_18jan08_sum.pdf.

6. Newtok Planning Group, Meeting Summary for Friday, June 9, 2006, 4, www.com merce.state.ak.us/dca/planning/pub/June9_Newtok_meeting_summary.pdf.

7. Newtok Planning Group, Mertarvik Barge Landing and Staging Area, www.com merce.state.ak.us/dca/planning/BargeLanding.htm.

8. Ibid.

9. See GAO (2009, 30), where it is noted that the "completion of a preliminary layout of water and sewer infrastructure by the Alaska Department of Environmental Conservation's Village Safe Water Program" was a sign of "significant progress." See also Newtok Planning Group, Meeting Summary for Friday, June 9, 2006, www.commerce.state.ak .us/dca/planning/pub/June9_Newtok_meeting_summary.pdf; and Newtok Planning Group, Meeting Summary for Friday, December 11, 2006, www.commerce.state.ak.us /dca/planning/pub/December_2006_meeting_notes.pdf.

CHAPTER 7

Power and the Distribution of Knowledge in a Local Groundwater Association in the Guadalupe Valley, Mexico

Chantelise Pells

Collaborative governance of groundwater resources in Mexico began in 1992 with the passage of the new National Water Law (Ley de Aguas Nacionales, LAN). The law required administrative decentralization to improve water use efficiency, and devised a range of new institutions to carry out the goals and objectives of the National Water Agenda through collaboration between local-level groundwater users, water officials, and technical experts.[1] The central water authority was renamed the Comisión Nacional del Agua (CONAGUA) and was divided into thirteen hydraulic administrative regions (Organismos de Cuenca), with a central office in Mexico City. State and municipal governments were given greater autonomy, and in areas dependent on groundwater resources, water-user participatory institutions were created at the basin scale (Consejos de Cuenca) and subbasin scale (Comités Técnicas de Aguas Subterraneas, COTAS).

Collaboration and coordination at each administrative level—federal, regional, state, municipal, and basin—were to bring about efficiency and equity improvements in the management of Mexico's water resources. In the initial implementation phases, Mexico was heralded internationally as a successful model of transference of water management authority (Global Water Partnership 2000; Kemper 2007; Shah, Scott, and Buechler 2004). Over twenty years later, however, effective collaboration across government scales, sectors, and social groups continues to be a work in progress that is plagued with social injustices, bureaucratic gridlock, and environmental exploitation (Scott and Banister 2008; Wilder and Whiteford 2006).

A variety of explanations are cited as the cause of ineffective governance, such as the central authority's reluctance to relinquish control (Acheson 2006; Wester, Sandoval Minero, and Hoogesteger 2011), institutional fragmentation due to inadequate cross-scale coordination, vague administrative and regulatory roles, and the limited autonomy of decentralized bodies (OECD 2013; Wilder and Romero Lankao 2006; Wilder and Whiteford 2006). However, these explanations ignore or sidestep the core issue of power in political processes and the argument that those who benefit from these institutions are those who have the power to assert their will (Moe 2005; Purdy 2012).

Key features of decentralization include the delineation of administrative power (Ribot, Agrawal, and Larson 2006; Schneider 2003) and the direction of accountability either to the political authorities or lower-level constituencies. Although these are often the topic of analyses about decentralized institutions (Agrawal and Gibson 1999; Agrawal and Ribot 1999; Wester, Sandoval Minero, and Hoogesteger 2011), few investigations delve into the degree of local representation (Schlosberg 2003; Swyngedouw 2005) and the distribution of knowledge about the new institutional rules and functions that emerge from decentralization (Foucault 1978, cited by Ribot and Peluso 2003). Instead, in the adoption and mobilization of new institutional arrangements, it is commonly assumed that there is equitable dissemination of information about the new governance structure, which in turn influences individuals' decisions to participate and cooperate (Agrawal 2003; Hardin 1968; Ostrom 1990). However, in some cases, the new institution creates (or recreates) power relations by identifying the most visible and dominant stakeholders, and thus further entrenches the underrepresentation of economically disadvantaged groups (Beck and Ghosh 2000; Purdy 2012; Swyngedouw 2005; Wilder and Romero Lankao 2006; Wilder and Whiteford 2006).

This chapter uses the integrative framework for collaborative governance (Emerson, Nabatchi, and Balogh 2012) to explore some of these power dynamics in the context of groundwater resources management at the local scale in Mexico. Specifically, it examines COTAS Guadalupe, a local collaborative governance regime (CGR) in the Guadalupe Valley—Mexico's most productive viticulture region—created in response to the decentralization that occurred under the new water law, LAN. COTAS Guadalupe was intended to facilitate the information flow and to ultimately increase groundwater users' cooperation with the new institutional rules following decentralization. However, this research shows that power dynamics and control over institutional knowledge have resulted in the asymmetric flow of information concerning the role and function of the local groundwater CGR, which in turn has led to the capturing of benefits by the economically powerful.

COTAS Guadalupe: Application of the Framework

El sistema de gobernabilidad es burocrático y kafkiano:
diseñado para no funcionar al servicio de la sociedad.
[Mexico's] governance system is bureaucratic and Kafkaesque:
designed to not benefit society.
—The author's translation of a statement made by
a Guadalupe Valley informant

Before assessing the COTAS Guadalupe CGR, it is useful to address the bigger picture of groundwater governance in Mexico. Under the direction and with the financial support of the World Bank and Inter-American Development Bank, Mexico restructured its government to assist in the shift toward a market-oriented economy (OECD 2013; Randall 1996; Wilder and Whiteford 2006). As in other Latin American countries and developing nations, this shift required Mexico to move toward decentralization and concomitantly required the nation to initiate major reforms and develop intergovernmental collaboration (Agrawal and Ostrom 2001; Lubell et al. 2002; Ribot, Agrawal, and Larson 2006). For the purposes of this case, some of the most prominent reforms were the transferring of water supply provisions to municipal—and sometimes state—water commissions, the establishment of tradable water usufruct rights, and the deployment of participatory institutions at the basin and subbasin scales.[2]

Mexico's model of water resources administration applies the principles of integrated water resource management (IWRM)—an internationally recognized approach that employs cross-boundary collaboration at the national, regional, basin, and subbasin levels, and is promoted as a mechanism to achieve environmental sustainability, economic efficiency, and social equity (Lubell and Edelenbos 2013). Under the integrated water resource management model, local-level participation is viewed as a critical component of achieving water management goals (Global Water Partnership 2000).

In accordance with the 1992 Water Law (LAN) and the move toward decentralization, Mexico's water resources were reorganized into set of nested institutions comprising thirteen hydrological administrative units, twenty-six watershed councils, and eighty-two subbasin committees. Under this structure, CONAGUA, the national water authority, maintains its role as the administrator of water rights allocation, duty collection, and enforcement. CONAGUA's thirteen regional hydrological administrative units (Organismos de Cuenca) are responsible for the water management plans in their region, which are integrated into the national, state, and municipal plans. The twenty-six watershed councils (Consejos de Cuenca) are represented by local water users and coordinate with the regional units. The eighty-two COTAS (Comités Técnicos de Aguas Subterráneas) are groundwater committees organized at the subbasin scale.

The COTAS are most frequently found in communities where groundwater is the primary water resource—and in most cases, under stressed conditions. Being represented by local water users, the COTAS are to operate in coordination with the regional watershed council, and to advise and collaborate on local issues with regional, state, and local planners. Specifically, these citizen-based COTAS are to serve as a public interface, where office spaces, regular meetings, and technicians are available to local groundwater users, primarily to inform them about current regulations and assist in documenting water rights and usage. In some cases, the COTAS monitor groundwater conditions by measuring changes in levels over time and providing this information to CONAGUA and water management planning officials.

Despite the logic of this decentralized structure, there are a number of problems with its implementation. For example, the role and function of the watershed councils in water management are limited by a lack of legal authority, inadequate administrative capacity, conflicting objectives, and coordination gaps with administrative bodies (OECD 2013). Although the prerogatives of the watershed councils were strengthened in 2004 by legislative reform to LAN, the lack of political legitimacy continues to plague their relevance and effectiveness in water management.[3]

As auxiliary bodies to the watershed councils, the COTAS also suffer from organizational challenges. In contrast to the watershed councils, the role of the COTAS is *not* defined in LAN. Consequently, the COTAS are treated more like watershed council programs than autonomous institutions. For example, enforcement measures such as fines, well closures, and regulatory changes are overseen and implemented by CONAGUA, in most instances without consultation with COTAS officials. The absence of a clearly defined purpose for groundwater management pervades the COTAS' capacity to garner support and cooperation from local groundwater users. Ultimately, the COTAS' influence on water policy and management in Mexico is marginal due their indirect management position. Thus, decentralization in this case has not rerouted the direction of water rights and revenue responsibilities to subsidiary levels of government, but rather remains deeply rooted in CONAGUA, which is located in the nation's capital, Mexico City (Scott and Banister 2008).

As evident in the case, this reality has important implications for the collaborative governance of Mexico's groundwater resources. Specifically, the COTAS represent an institutional link to the new rules of the game, where the access to water resources is controlled by the assignation and allocation of water rights. Those with power seek to secure (and sometimes to increase) their assets by controlling access to water through knowledge of the new rules and their positions of power. Moreover, the privatization of water extends their power, presenting an opportunity for capital accumulation via water rights trading (Guarneros-Meza and Geddes 2010). Under these auspices, actors on the periphery of the knowledge–power nexus have little opportunity or incentive to participate. With this background, the chapter now turns to an analysis of the system context for COTAS Guadalupe.

The System Context: Turning Water into Wine

As noted in chapter 2, collaborative governance efforts are made within a broader system context, which consists of numerous interrelated conditions that shape and constrain the work of CGRs. This is certainly true in the case of COTAS Guadalupe. Several factors within the system context interacted to create complex conditions that shaped collaborative governance within COTAS Guadalupe, both at the outset and over time. It is important to note that in this case, the system context has been overtly shaped by the history of Mexico. At the time Mexico shifted to decentralized governance, it had experienced decades of centralized control, a fact that is still evident in the saying "All roads lead to Mexico City." Past and present political–economic polarities undergird institutional outcomes, and thus they influence the extent of integration in collaborative endeavors (Bryant 1998; Saravanan, McDonald, and Mollinga 2009; Shah 2008). Indeed, the history of colonialism and oppression permeates present-day political processes, and thus poses a challenge to collaborative (and other democratic) initiatives.

The socioeconomic and cultural characteristics of the Guadalupe Valley (GV) are particularly interesting. The GV is an agricultural inland valley located in Baja California, Mexico, 120 kilometers from the US border and 35 kilometers from the coastal city of Ensenada. The valley includes the rural communities of San Antonio de las Minas (Villa Juarez), Colonia Articulo 115, Francisco Zarco, Ejido El Porvenir, and Ejido Emiliano Zapata; the indigenous community (*comunidad indigena*) of San Antonio de Necua; and other outlying areas.[4] The average population of the valley is 5,110, and is expected to increase to 7,544 by 2030 (CONAPO 2005). The area has a unique and rich cultural heritage of agrarian livelihoods, indigenous populations, and Russian immigrants.

The GV is also the most productive viticulture region in Mexico, producing 90 percent of domestic wine, and is part of the regional Wine Route (Ruta del Vino), a popular national and international tourist destination. Viticulture in the valley has a long history dating back to the Spanish mission era of the mid-1800s. In the last thirty years, the GV landscape has transformed from small-scale agriculture to large-scale viticulture production. The rapid development into an internationally renowned wine region has intensified and increased irrigation and fertilization, which has consequently created substantial demands on local water resources (CONAGUA 2007; Kvammen 1976). In 1999, CONAGUA and the state government of Baja California jointly formed and funded the watershed council for Baja California (Consejo de Cuenca de Baja California).

The decreasing availability of groundwater as a public resource is a primary condition affecting all the COTAS in Mexico, including COTAS Guadalupe. Due to the semiarid climate, groundwater is the primary water source for domestic, agriculture, viticulture, winery, service, and other uses in the GV. The city of Ensenada also extracts groundwater from the valley to support its burgeoning urban population.[5] However, the limits of available water resources present an obstacle to further viticulture and tourism expansion. As a result of the growing water demands, water balance studies indicate a groundwater decline and an overconcession of water use rights, which is two times greater than water availability (CONAGUA 2007). According to estimated water extraction rates, water use is currently classified as having reached prohibited use status, further restricting groundwater development (CONAGUA 2009). The declining water table is most evident in the decreased water volume flow and duration of the Guadalupe River (Rio Guadalupe), the loss of watering holes (*ojos de aguas*; Kvammen 1976; Schmieder 1928; interviews with GV informants, 2009-2011), a deterioration of riparian plant species, degraded water quality (Daesslé et al. 2006), dry or drying wells, and increasing costs to pump water and reposition wells.[6]

These issues are exacerbated by the policy and legal frameworks governing groundwater use. Before decentralization, attempts by the central water authority to restrict groundwater extraction in some cases resulted in twofold increases in clandestine well digging. This increase was due, in part, to the race to establish new wells before a federal ban was decreed (Foster, Garduno, and Kemper 2004). In 1962 a federal ban on new well drilling was issued; however, due to the ban's weak enforcement, it did not deter further development. In 1989, CONAGUA was established as the new national water authority.[7] By 1990, there had been a rapid, almost twofold, increase in new wells, perhaps in anticipation of water volume restrictions and enforcement by CONAGUA. In light of the central government regulations inducing overuse, and the incapacity to effectively monitor and sanction the vast number of groundwater wells, water management took a new direction. Specifically, and as described above, the 1992 LAN created groundwater user-based institutions at the basin and subbasin scale to foster user cooperation and eventually self-regulation. Figure 7.1 shows well development in the GV following major water management transitions.

Today, regardless of the use category, water users must hold a volumetric title (concession) to legally pump groundwater from a private well. Priority is given first for domestic and urban water users, followed by livestock, agriculture, environmental, electric energy generation, and industry uses. Agriculture and multiple uses constitute the largest allocation, with 82 percent of the total concession volume.[8]

Political dynamics and power relations are also integral features of the system context. All levels of government actively support viticulture production and wine tourism as central to rural and regional economic development. This has created a divide between small-scale water users and economic interests responding to the allure of wine tourism and economic development. Consequently, small-scale producers and *ejido* farmers—relics of the Mexico's socialist past—have been squeezed out by a policy that tacitly gives preference to the economic gains of a select few winery owners (Wester, Scott, and Burton 2005). As a result, the major viticulture producers and owners of large wineries have become powerful political and economic figures in the GV, and in the region at large. These individuals have been able to leverage their strong ties to the government, which has directly affected the leadership and direction of COTAS Guadalupe.

Finally, these and other issues served to foster and aggravate numerous social conflicts. Survey research in 2011 revealed numerous water-related conflicts centered on issues such as opposition to the continuation of the City of Ensenada's concession, decreasing water availability, water contamination, excessive sand removal from the arroyos in the watershed, channelization of the Guadalupe River, and land and water monopolization by the largest viticulture producers located in the upper valley. These and other conflicts over water have inspired the organization of social movements throughout the GV. They have also shaped the drivers leading to the creation of COTAS Guadalupe, as well as the CGR's initial form and function.

Initiating Collaborative Governance: The Drivers and Formation of COTAS Guadalupe

Chapter 2 identified four drivers that help initiate the formation of a CGR. All four drivers were present in this case, helping to shape the formation of collaborative COTAS Guadalupe. There was uncertainty about the future of water resources, and interdependence was implicit between groundwater users. Moreover, the newly institutionalized role of local-level water management

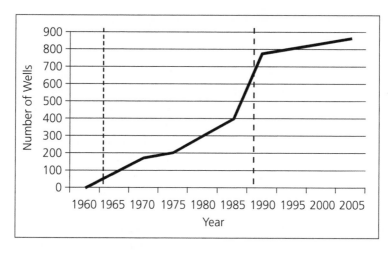

Figure 7.1.   Groundwater Wells and Development Restrictions in the Guadalupe Valley of Mexico, 1960–2005

Note: Groundwater development restrictions are indicated by the vertical lines. The first vertical line indicates the ban on new wells in 1962. The second vertical line indicates the shift to the new water authority, CONAGUA, in 1989.
Source: Programa Integral del Agua del Municipio de Ensenada, 2010.

provided a consequential incentive for forming COTAS Guadalupe, which in turn created an opportunity for leadership to initiate the formation of the local CGR.

Uncertainty is an implicit feature of groundwater governance. In the GV, this uncertainty was evident in concerns about future groundwater supply and the sustainability of the area's agrarian culture. Such concerns were exacerbated by the fact that groundwater is a classic common-pool resource. Groundwater resources are inherently interdependent (i.e., one's use of groundwater affects another's use) and are difficult to manage due to issues of scale and complexity. It is also difficult to restrict access to common-pool resources, including groundwater, which makes them vulnerable to overuse. In groundwater-dependent regions, cooperation between users is necessary to address the challenges of intensive resource use (Ostrom 1990; Schlager 2007).

Although the need to have access to and conserve groundwater was certainly an incentive for collaboration, the more meaningful consequential incentive was created by LAN (the 1992 new water law). Specifically, and as discussed above, LAN provided a range of newly devised, nested institutions to carry out the goals and objectives of the National Water Agenda. It also provided the opportunity for local groundwater users to organize into COTAS, with which they could establish a local office and gain access to government support and resources.

The initiating leadership for COTAS Guadalupe emerged in 2004. Specifically, a GV viticulturist who was concerned about the local groundwater deterioration and volume restrictions decided to take advantage of the opportunity to organize, and created COTAS Guadalupe.[9] This initiating leader is one of the largest landowners in GV and is a lifelong resident,[10] whose family history dates back to the Russian Molokan emigration of the early 1900s.[11] Without institutional guidelines or training, this local leader designated the most prominent individuals in the GV community to participate as officiants. As a result, the initial governing body of COTAS Guadalupe was dominated by some of the most powerful water players in the region. The president (COTAS initiator) and treasurer are large-scale viticulturists, and the secretary was the director of the Baja California state water service provider for the municipality of Ensenada (Comisión Estatal Servicios Publicos de Ensenada).[12]

COTAS Guadalupe's first governing body developed and voted on its organizational statutes that laid out its roles, duties, and objectives, which were subsequently ratified into an official civil association. Federal and state funds supported the COTAS' operations, including an administrative office, official vehicle, personnel, and equipment, as well as ongoing groundwater monitoring and water efficiency studies.

In addition to the president, secretary, and treasurer, the COTAS Guadalupe governing body is presided over by a technical analyst, operations agent, and up to three representatives of the different water user categories: agriculture, industry, livestock, and urban public.[13] The general assembly comprises the groundwater users in the GV, who can vote the members of the governing body in or out. The main objectives of COTAS Guadalupe, as outlined in its organizational statutes, are to (1) promote democratic participation in the sustainable management of the GV aquifer; (2) ensure democratic representation; (3) promote and create a sustainable water culture through education; (4) investigate and monitor groundwater conditions; (5) mediate and represent water user needs to CONAGUA; (6) prevent conflicts and collaborate on resolutions; and (7) create a fund for studies on water efficiency.

However, the composition of COTAS Guadalupe and its governance structure limited its abilities to meet the goals outlined in the statute in at least two important ways. First, although the COTAS are initiated by and within local communities, they are devised by, and hence accountable to, CONAGUA, the central water authority. This accountability to CONAGUA compromises the perceived legitimacy of the COTAS, especially in communities that are already suspicious of CONAGUA and its agenda. In the GV, the allegiance to CONAGUA is clearly demonstrated by the street-view office sign that displays the two institution titles—COTAS Guadalupe and CONAGUA—together. This does not convey to the public that COTAS Guadalupe is a community-based or grassroots institution, and consequently it confounds and deters some residents of the local community from participating. Second, and relatedly, because the governing body of COTAS Guadalupe was dominated by the most powerful economic actors in the region, the benefits of the cooperative work in COTAS Guadalupe were skewed toward the large viticulture producers and not toward the majority of GV groundwater users. Together, these limitations had numerous implications for the functioning of the CGR.

Collaboration Dynamics: Soy *COTAS (I am COTAS)*

Once a CGR is formed, it engages in an iterative and cyclical process of collaboration dynamics, which includes principled engagement, shared motivation, and the capacity for joint action (see chapter 3).[14] Collaboration dynamics certainly happened in the case of COTAS Guadalupe, albeit not as the proponents of collaborative governance would have it. To understand the collaboration dynamics of COTAS Guadalupe, it is important to remember two related points. First, although Mexico's national water law supports institutional collaboration between the decentralized governance bodies, it relegates all the COTAS to serving as informational and advisory bodies with limited to nonexistent power to influence policy decisions and regulations. It also provides insufficient guidance on how to design and manage the internal and external processes of COTAS. Second, this lack of authority and guidance, coupled with the fact that COTAS Guadalupe (at least in its initial formation) was directed by power holders, meant that the CGR was able to use collaboration to reinforce and strengthen the power of elites. Together, these issues had a significant bearing on the collaboration dynamics within COTAS Guadalupe.

In this case, principled engagement was not really principled. As noted in chapter 3, the word "principled" suggests that a CGR should "uphold core tenets for effective engagement." Key to these tenets is the idea of balanced representation among all relevant interests. However, in the case of COTAS Guadalupe, all interests and voices were not included. The reasons for this are at least threefold. First, the initiating leader invited and selected many of the participants on the basis of their power status; those without status were generally not included. Second, under LAN, the COTAS have limited authority, which gave many the impression that these would be toothless organizations and reduced people's willingness to participate. Third, the underlying objective of the COTAS is to reduce groundwater use, which for many was another significant deterrence to participation. Together, these issues had the effect of excluding many perspectives from discussions, which lessened the ability of COTAS Guadalupe to engage in robust processes of discovery, definition, and deliberation, as well as to make determinations based on the knowledge of all those affected. This lack of principled engagement also affected shared motivation and the capacity for joint action.

Shared motivation is central to the functioning of a CGR. Without shared motivation, the evolution of social learning—which is gained through the development of trust, mutual understanding, internal legitimacy, and commitment—cannot proceed (Lubell 2005; see also Emerson, Nabatchi, and Balogh 2012). Shared motivation is particularly important for all the COTAS, given the diverse interests and contentious nature of groundwater rights. COTAS Guadalupe, however, was unable to develop a healthy and vigorous sense of shared motivation, at least in the way for which advocates of collaborative governance would hope. Rather than building shared motivation to tackle a collective action problem, COTAS Guadalupe succeeded only in building a shared motivation between some of the powerful members of the COTAS Guadalupe governing body. And, at least on the surface, this shared motivation appeared to be oriented toward reinforcing the power of elites.

Finally, the inability of COTAS Guadalupe to foster the principled engagement and shared motivation weakened its overall capacity for joint action. In part because of statutory and administrative restrictions, and in part because of limited participation, COTAS Guadalupe was able neither to develop effective procedural and institutional arrangements and leadership nor to foster sufficient sharing of knowledge and resources. In light of these deficiencies in collaboration dynamics, COTAS Guadalupe never really devised a shared theory of change to address groundwater issues in the area. Instead, and as discussed in the next section, the CGR took actions to reinforce existing power arrangements.

Collaborative Actions and Outcomes: Ipsa Scientia Potestas Est (Knowledge Itself Is Power)

The integrative framework suggests that a CGR will take collaborative actions based on its shared theory of change, and that these actions will in turn have a variety of outcomes (for a discussion, see chapter 4).[15] In the case of COTAS Guadalupe, its limited authority and capture by elites meant that an effective theory of change was not developed during collaboration dynamics. Not surprisingly, then, the collaborative actions and outcomes of the CGR are also limited.

The minimal authority of the CGR has meant that the primary collaborative actions of COTAS Guadalupe centered on educating the public about newly imposed regulations and CONAGUA crackdowns on illegal groundwater use. For example, current management requires water volume metering of every registered well. COTAS Guadalupe provides government-subsidized meters and assists groundwater users with their positioning and implementation. Another important function mandated in the COTAS Guadalupe statutes is to monitor groundwater levels and report the information to CONAGUA and local water users. The CGR also conducts irrigation water efficiency experiments and reports its findings to local irrigators, and it advises groundwater users in the local office on CONAGUA document preparation and new requirements. In addition to information sharing and groundwater investigations, COTAS Guadalupe participates in water management planning venues; however, it lacks the decision-making capacity (and funding) to devise and carry out strategies for the Guadalupe watershed. Still, like its counterparts throughout Mexico, COTAS Guadalupe did offer previously nonexistent opportunities to improve awareness and knowledge about groundwater conditions, which may, in the long term, contribute to groundwater sustainability.

The outcomes of these and other actions on water resources are questionable. Various regulations encourage the "use or lose it" principle, which deters users from conserving water. Water rights are revoked when water use falls below the concessioned volume, encouraging farmers to overirrigate. Large farmers also receive an electrical subsidy for groundwater pumping when wells are registered; however, for small-scale producers and domestic water users, electrical use is minimal, and the provision of a subsidy is less of an incentive to register. In light of these issues, COTAS Guadalupe has not improved the benefits for lower-income water users, and especially for those who are experiencing water shortages due to level and quality declines and those who lack the resources to reposition wells for better access.

There is also doubt about the outcomes of actions for the education of water users. Research shows that in most cases, water users are unaware of COTAS Guadalupe and its services, including document preparation assistance, well registration, and subsidized meters. An analysis of an in-person survey of GV groundwater users demonstrated that knowledge of COTAS Guadalupe was dominated by economic interests.

Table 7.1 displays the results of a binary regression model of the characteristics of groundwater users who are most likely to be aware of COTAS Guadalupe. The results show that awareness of COTAS Guadalupe is greatest between users with strong economic interests, including those who own large parcels of land and/or wineries, who are large consumers of water, who believe groundwater is low, and who are located in the upper valley.[16] As measured, however, awareness of COTAS Guadalupe does not indicate what the groundwater users know or how accurate their knowledge is. For example, some respondents were aware of COTAS because they had seen the office sign or the COTAS logo on the official vehicle. In most cases, however, knowledge of COTAS was in name only. In other words, many of the respondents who were aware of COTAS were unfamiliar with or ignorant about the CGR's specific role and duties in groundwater governance.[17]

In addition to awareness, survey respondents were asked a series of questions to test their actual knowledge about the function and role of COTAS Guadalupe. A knowledge score was calculated based on the number of accurate responses. The results, shown in table 7.2, demonstrate that knowledge about COTAS Guadalupe is again greatest among those with strong economic interests, including those who use large amounts of water, own wineries and farms, are wealthy, and believe that groundwater levels are decreasing.[18]

The results from the two analyses show an asymmetric distribution of knowledge; affluent groundwater users, such as owners of large properties and/or wineries, are better informed about COTAS Guadalupe, and consequently they are better informed about the new groundwater rules than are lower-income users. Thus, wealthy landowners have an advantage over lower-income and *ejidatario* groundwater users, in that they can stay better informed on requirements and profit from potential water rights trading. Indeed, one GV winery owner remarked, it is "their business to know." In contrast, those left out of the loop—primarily, lower-income users—are vulnerable to exorbitant fines or the termination of their water rights and access. This has played out in the GV. The actions of the CGR—particularly those related to fines and well closures—have created and exacerbated social conflicts. For some valley farmers, the costs of the fines imposed on them by the government for doing what they have been doing for years—irrigating their crops with water from their private well—represent the ultimate betrayal of the government.

Adaptation: ¡La Union Hace la Fuerza! United We Stand!

In 2011, a household survey of the GV increased awareness about COTAS Guadalupe.[19] One year later, perhaps in response to the broadening of general knowledge about the CGR, the COTAS Guadalupe president stepped down after an eight-year residency, and a new governing body was elected.[20] This has led to significant changes or adaptation in the CGR. Large viticulture producers no longer dominate the governing body, which has become more representative of the region's diverse interests. Each category of water user type is represented in the new governing body—agriculture, industrial, multiple, urban public, livestock, domestic, and service. Moreover, groundwater users of diverse backgrounds, such as residents of the local *ejido* and those

Table 7.1 **Regression Results for Awareness of COTAS**

Measure	Result	Standard Error
Water use amount	0.085**	0.044
Winery	1.363**	0.595
Hectares owned	0.030**	0.016
Upper valley	0.666*	0.434
Believe groundwater is low	1.639***	0.435
Constant	−2.321	0.207
$N = 167^a$		

Note: The magnitudes of the coefficients do not indicate importance; *, **, *** indicate significance at the 90, 95, and 99 percent levels, respectively.

[a]Some of the observations were imputed to increase statistical power. Imputed data were verified using Monte Carlo error and other diagnostics.

Table 7.2 **Regression Results for Knowledge about COTAS Guadalupe**

Measure	Result	Standard Error
Water use amount	0.050***	0.016
Winery	1.006***	0.420
Farmer	0.631**	0.301
Income	7.08e.06*	3.85e.06
Believe groundwater is low	0.815***	0.259
Constant	−.027	0.422
$N = 167^a$		

Note: The magnitudes of the coefficients do not indicate importance; *, **, *** indicate significance at the 90, 95, and 99 percent levels, respectively.

[a] Some of the observations were imputed to increase statistical power. Imputed data were verified using Monte Carlo error and other diagnostics.

of lower economic status, are now members of the new COTAS Guadalupe. Some of the members of the new governing body are community leaders who are using COTAS Guadalupe as a venue to unite and speak out about water management issues.

The first meeting held under the new governing body was attended by more than 100 valley residents (five times more than a typical meeting)—a hallmark for COTAS Guadalupe and emblematic of the representativeness and potential effectiveness of the governing body. According to the new president, COTAS Guadalupe increased participation by notifying groundwater users of the meeting door to door—the only reliable method in a rural and resource-limited region—about important regulations that affect their lives and livelihoods.

The adaptive capacity of COTAS Guadalupe to mobilize and take ownership of the democratic venue bodes well for future collaboration on groundwater governance issues in the GV. Some outcomes of a stronger collaborative effort with greater community participation could be improvements in information sharing about current regulations, groundwater conditions, and water planning events. A stronger voice may eventually lead to greater institutional autonomy and improved internal and external legitimacy. Improved autonomy could also result in more effective collaboration dynamics and in the development of groundwater plans that reflect the community's demands. Greater representation could also ensure more equal distribution of institutional benefits, such as information on water rights, government subsidies, document assistance, and ultimately the reduction of fines and well closures. With effective leadership and collective action, self-governance through government support may be the optimum outcome for COTAS Guadalupe, especially in terms of groundwater resources that necessitate cooperative actions to achieve sustainability. Only time will tell whether the newly reformed CGR can take actions that have positive outcomes for water users and groundwater resources.

Analysis: The Power–Knowledge Nexus in Collaborative Governance

> Ultimately, power is not just what planning and management attempt to exclude. Rather, power and politics imbue the process of management thoroughly and unavoidably.
> — Arun Agrawal, "Sustainable Governance of Common-Pool Resources"

According to Harvey (2005, 11; 19 cited by Guarneros-Meza and Geddes 2010), Mexico's decentralized governance has paved the way for the "'process of neo-liberalization to re-establish the conditions for capital accumulation and to restore the power of economic elites,' and specifically to disembed capital from the constraints of the 'embedded liberalism' of social democracy and the Keynesian welfare state." The case of COTAS Guadalupe seems to support this assertion. For example, the application of the cap-and-trade principle to groundwater rights provides economic incentives that promote capital accumulation in the form of water rights. Currently, there is minimal water trading in the GV; however, this is likely to change as the enforcement of water use regulations increases in tandem with economic development.[21] Moreover, as the GV's wine industry and tourism continue to develop, the value of water will invariably increase, and so too will the opportunity to control and monopolize the water market by those who can afford to pay. Indeed, as groundwater levels decline and the cost to extract water increases, the poor and *ejidatario* producers have little choice but to sell their water rights and abandon their land into the hands of the wealthy. In this regard, COTAS Guadalupe represents the locus of control in the valley for the emerging market and economic interests.

The asymmetric flow of benefits that favors the economically powerful counters the democratic imperative of collaborative institutions and is an obstacle to achieving distributional equity, water resource sustainability, and ultimately governance efficiency (Agrawal 2003; Wilder and Romero Lankao 2006). Such control not only limits institutional benefits for a select few but also restricts the social learning capacity and development of social capital that are crucial for achieving the potential benefits of collaborative governance (Mostert, Craps, and Pahl-Wostl 2008; Pahl-Wostl et al. 2007). Social learning through vertical and horizontal information flows can improve users' opinions of governance, and may also improve resource conditions by enhancing cooperation through gains in social capital (OECD 2013; Randall 1996; Wilder and Whiteford 2006).

Although COTAS Guadalupe embodies a strand in a "bundle of powers" by providing a new avenue for actors to acquire benefits, survey research revealed that knowledge about the function and role of this local CGR was limited to the most powerful viticulture producers (Ribot and Peluso 2003). On the surface, organizing the largest water consumers around the issue of the sustainable management of water resources appears to be a logical strategy. However, the inclusion of all water users and uses is not only an imperative for a democratic institution but also necessary for ensuring mutually beneficial returns (Berkes and Turner 2006; Moe 2005). In the case of COTAS Guadalupe, the influence of power and knowledge enabled cooptation by elite interests and resulted in an unequal allocation of water rights and institutional representation. This is not surprising, because control over the flow of knowledge and institutional access by the economically powerful is tantamount to control over the governed resource (Ribot and Peluso 2003; Wilder 2005).

These and other issues suggest that in planning and implementing a CGR, overlooking the potential for knowledge inequities and power disparities jeopardizes success, especially when democratic representation is lacking. In the case of COTAS Guadalupe, limited authority, coupled with the direction of accountability to the central government rather than to local groundwater users, obfuscated the potential mutual gains of collaboration by disincentivizing democratic representation and the equitable distribution of benefits. In turn, this calls the relevance of the local CGR into question—COTAS Guadalupe may have only earned the image of collaborative governance to satisfy a political agenda.

Conclusion and Recommendations

This chapter used the integrative framework for collaborative governance to illustrate the COTAS Guadalupe CGR. In doing so, it identified factors critical to understanding the processes and outcomes of collaboration. In particular, it revealed the power dynamics in the inner cogs of the COTAS Guadalupe CGR, and it focused on the external knowledge inequities that produce or reinforce power relations by limiting the capacity of some participants to benefit from collaborative efforts. Although the integrative framework for collaborative governance offers many analytic benefits, it does not adequately deal with the influence of knowledge and power in the design and implementation of CGRs. A central conclusion of this chapter is that because *all* CGRs are vulnerable to the influence of power, power must be carefully considered and explicitly examined at the outset and overtime.

Arun Agrawal (2003, 258–259) expands on this idea of power bounded by the collaborative governance processes for environmental resources that are inherently difficult to manage—such as water, forests, and fisheries—and he asserts the need for additional research on this issue: "A greater focus on how power works within communities and in the governance of common-pool resources can help strengthen greatly the force of writings on common property. On the one hand, such a shift in focus would facilitate a better understanding of how power and status are related to access and use of resources; on the other hand, it would complement the exclusive focus of common-property theorists on institutions and rules. . . . Without attention to the politics that generates underdevelopment and environmental degradation as universal problems, it may be impossible to address poverty, underdevelopment, and environmental degradation effectively."

In addition to demonstrating the need to give more attention to knowledge and power asymmetries, the COTAS Guadalupe case study advances the integrative framework in four important ways. First, the analysis shows that it is important to distinguish between collaboration that is initiated top-down by upper-level government institutions and bottom-up through grassroots organizations (see chapter 8). A government-imposed collaboration may be less successful than a community-initiated collaboration, because the community motivation may arise from an agreed-upon mutual need. In contrast, the government's agenda for fostering collaboration may not adequately consider community needs or provide guidance for sufficient representation within the collaborative effort.

Second, identifying where the accountability lies—upward to administrative authorities, or downward to the local constituencies—is a critical factor in gaining internal and external legitimacy. Without authority, CGRs are likely to suffer from limited funding, inadequate administrative capacity, conflicting objectives, and coordination gaps with administrative bodies. Together, these issues create substantive obstacles for the work of CGRs—ranging from fostering equitable outreach and representation to engaging in effective collaboration dynamics to taking meaningful actions to achieve targeted goals and collective purposes.

Third, it is necessary to understand the motivation for initiating a CGR. A central government's agenda for its collaborative policy can include ideas that are very distinct from a community's agenda for its collaborative vision. A central government may perceive participatory institutions as ways to extend power at a reduced cost (e.g., organizational expenditures; Agrawal and Ostrom 2001), whereas community members may view collaboration as a means to advance their interests and resolve conflicts. Because the central government does not have the same goals as the community, it may not make available the discretionary powers and resources necessary to meet the community's agenda.

Fourth and finally, as has been made clear by this chapter's main theme, understanding the context—and particularly in less developed nations, the political-economic legacy—is critical for ensuring the identification and representation of *all* interests, both at the initial stages of collaboration and over time. Thus, when devising and implementing CGRs it is imperative to take into account and mitigate barriers to the degree of democratic cohesion represented by the level of political autonomy (Ribot, Agrawal, and Larson 2006), horizontal and vertical information flows (Andersson 2006), and equal representation and the distribution of benefits (Geddes 2006; Guarneros-Meza and Geddes 2010). At every stage of collaboration, careful attention must be given to the process of equitable representation to mitigate the impact of social inequities that impede social learning and obstruct the achievement of the benefits of collaboration.

To offset the vulnerability of local-level collaborative governance, two policy recommendations are apparent. The first is to strengthen the autonomy and legitimacy of local CGRs by giving them a political role defined in legislation. The second is to provide guidelines and support through central government or third-party programs. For example, hiring well-trained collaborative governance coaches or facilitators who can work with communities and local institutions to craft an inclusive, equitable collaborative process may well be a crucial first step toward achieving effective collaboration to govern groundwater sustainability.

Notes

1. Mexico's National Water Agenda has a five-year planning horizon, and each subnational administrative entity is responsible for creating a planning document in accordance with the national plan established in the agenda.

2. According to Mexico's Water Law, water is the property of the nation; thus, private water use is a right to use, or usufruct right (Agrawal and Ostrom 2001; Guarneros-Meza and Geddes 2010).

3. As of September 2013, a revision to the National Water Bylaws was still in draft form.

4. The *ejido* is a communal land tenure system that was put into Agrarian Law (Ley de Agraria) in 1917 following the reform of Article 27 of the Mexican Constitution. In 1992, Article 27 was amended and a new Agrarian Law was enacted to privatize *ejidal* lands and make them available as a commodity as part of Mexico's adoption of neoliberal free trade policies. The *ejidal* lands can now be sold, rented, and held as collateral—a radical departure from the previous socialist model. *Ejidos* may opt to disband and divide the land or continue to manage land and resources communally. If *ejidatarios* choose to continue as an *ejido*, decisions about land and resource use are subject to the *ejido*'s assembly approval process. The Kumiai of San Antonio Necua chose the legal identity of an *ejido* rather than *comunidad indigena*.

5. Currently, the Ensenada concession is 11 percent of the total concessions for the groundwater basin; however, the extraction rate can exceed (and has) the concession, depending on demand rates. The city of Ensenada's population is expected to increase from 307,000 to 422,000 by 2030. This rate of growth presents a challenge for water managers and the region's already stressed groundwater resources.

6. This is based on survey and field research conducted by the author in the Guadalupe Valley from 2009 to 2011.

7. Secretaría de Recursos Hidráulicos was the federal water agency that preceded CONAGUA.

8. Multiple-use water users are typically small-scale agriculture, livestock, and domestic users. The figure of 82 percent is based on COTAS Guadalupe figures.

9. COTAS Guadalupe was first initiated in 1999, along with eight other COTAS offices within the watershed council of Baja California; however, it was not formalized with procedural statutes until 2004.

10. Currently, he lives in his urban residence in Ensenada, which is located 35 kilometers from the Guadalupe Valley.

11. The Molokan are members of a Russian Christian sect who fled Russia to escape the Russian Orthodox Church. They settled in the Guadalupe Valley through the Mexican government's land grants and private purchase arrangements. The Molokan are known for their communal organization and farming.

12. The former secretary is the Guadalupe Valley's "water baron" and the largest viticulture producer in the valley.

13. These are the represented water user categories named in the 2004 statutes. In 2012, a new governing body was organized that is representative of all water uses and now includes domestic and multiple users.

14. This section is based on a statement made by a former COTAS Guadalupe governing body member during an interview in 2011.

15. The saying *ipsa scientia potestas est* is a quotation from Sir Francis Bacon, 1597.

16. Some of the largest wineries and viticulture are located in the upper valley. The COTAS Guadalupe office is also located in the upper valley.

17. Just 38 percent of the total survey respondents were aware of COTAS. Most of these had no knowledge of the purpose of COTAS.

18. The variable "believe groundwater is low" could also be tested as a dependent variable. Knowledge about groundwater conditions may also be an outcome of participating with COTAS Guadalupe.

19. The saying "¡La union hace la fuerza!" is a quotation from a Guadalupe Valley resident. This household survey was administered during a period of CONAGUA "sweeps" of illegal groundwater use and improper documentation. As a result, some residents were understandably outraged and suspicious that the survey was another CONAGUA intrusion. In the end, some of these individuals participated in the survey and shared their experiences.

20. The COTAS president's resignation was voluntary. Although term limits exist, these are not enforced.

21. Although it is currently illegal to buy or sell a water right, there are examples of illegal water markets in other parts of Mexico (personal communication with Nadine Reis, 2014).

Part IV

Collaborative Governance Regimes

CHAPTER 8

Moving from Genus to Species
A Typology of Collaborative Governance Regimes

> It is once again the vexing problem of identity within
> variety; without a solution to this disturbing problem,
> there can be no system, no classification.
> —Roman Jakobson

The previous two parts of this book defined and illustrated collaborative governance regimes (CGRs) as vibrant configurations of collaboration dynamics that respond to system contexts and drivers, and result in actions, outcomes, and adaptation. Specifically, part II of the book individually examined the key dimensions, components, and elements of the integrative framework for collaborative governance, illustrating each with a brief case. Part III shared a series of case studies, written by contributors, which applied the entire integrative framework to a variety of CGRs. At first, the variety of CGRs covered in these case illustrations and case studies may appear to be infinitely varied and far too contingent for systematic or comparative study. This raises a question: Is there a way to characterize distinctive types of CGRs that can then allow for further specification and comparison? This chapter, which turns from describing the general CGR genus to characterizing key CGR species, focuses on answering this question.

We first review other typologies developed for studying cross-boundary collaboration and collaborative governance. Building on these, we then present our typology, which is based on the way CGRs are formed and assumes a path-dependent approach to their development and performance. Specifically, we identify and describe three formative types of CGRs: self-initiated, independently convened, and externally directed. Each of these by CGR "species" is distinguished by a set of prevailing conditions and characteristics, as well as by different patterns of collaboration dynamics. We conclude with a chapter summary.

Approaches to Typologies

Borrowing from biological taxonomy, it is useful to begin our discussion at the most general, family level of classification. Some juxtapose the pattern of policymaking in collaborative governance with adversarialism and managerialism (Ansell and Gash 2008). Others contrast collaborative governance as an institutional arrangement with authority-based government hierarchies and with market-based arrangements (Tang and Mazmanian 2010). This family-level approach to classification has its obvious merits, but we argue that distinguishing collaborative governance from competitive or coercive systems is likely to discourage more integrative approaches to both practice and research. As we have defined it, collaborative governance commonly involves crossing sectoral boundaries, not separating them. Furthermore, collaborative governance does not exist in a vacuum with no connection to markets or regulation. Rather, collaboration dynamics are shaped by both the marketplace and governmental frameworks.

In addition, though engagement in cross-boundary collaboration is often characterized as voluntary, this is not always the case. Motivations for participation range broadly within any given CGR and across all CGRs, and, as we discuss below, externally directed collaboration is only one type of CGR. Thus, though the voluntary nature of markets may distinguish them from governmental actions, this is not a useful distinction for collaborative governance. Likewise, competition can serve cooperative ends and play a useful role in collaborative governance. Similarly, regulatory constraints can limit the cooptation of collaborative intentions. Thus, for the time being, we put aside such family distinctions and start with collaborative governance as the genus from which to further develop helpful classifications of species. Many approaches to classifying the different species of CGRs can be taken. Scholars working in collaborative resource management, community engagement, conflict resolution, and public networks have offered a wide variety of typologies reflecting their particular theoretical lenses or applied perspectives. In turn, these efforts have informed our development of a CGR typology.

Some scholars categorize collaborative processes on the basis of their specific contexts. For example, in her early typology of collaborative processes, Gray (1989) distinguishes between two contexts—those that arise from conflict, and those that start with a shared opportunity or vision. She suggests that these two contexts affect participant motivation. She then crosses these contextual dimensions with two distinct outcomes—information exchange and joint agreement—to classify four different forms of collaboration: dialogues, negotiated settlements, information forums, and collective strategies.

Although this typology is useful when describing differences in collaboration dynamics, it does not fully describe differences among CGRs, because these activities (or forms of collaboration) are not mutually exclusive.

Other scholars use functional typologies to categorize collaborative arrangements. For example, Agranoff and McGuire (2003) organize their network governance cases according to four primary functions: planning, education, outreach, and implementation. Similarly, Henton and colleagues (2005) divide collaborative governance approaches into three different forums based on specific functions: deliberation, community problem solving, and multistakeholder dispute resolution. The challenge with such functional typologies is that collaborative systems tend to change over time—starting out, for example, as a planning group but then evolving into an outreach center. Again, these categories are not mutually exclusive and do not capture the full variety among CGRs.

Some scholars focus on scale, distinguishing between collaboration at the community level, where place-based concerns are paramount, and collaboration at larger scales, where interest group negotiation is used (Cheng and Daniels 2005; Cheng, Kruger, and Daniels 2003). Scholars taking this approach suggest that the nature and quality of collaborative processes become fundamentally different as the scale increases. Although scale certainly matters in CGRs, it may not explain other, more fundamental differences between collaborative systems.

Still other scholars use the locus and nature of decision making as the basis for their typologies. For example, Margerum's (2011) typology of collaborative planning and management stems from Ostrom's (1990) Institutional Analysis and Development (IAD) framework. He distinguishes between the action, organization, and policy levels of collaborative decision making, which correspond to the IAD's hierarchy of constitutional, collective choice, and operational rules. This is a helpful instrumental approach for differentiating collaborative endeavors based on what they do and what kind of decisions they make. However, many CGRs may engage in decision making at multiple levels, which means that this approach is less useful for identifying various species of CGRs.

Finally, some scholars emphasize the governance or management of collaborative processes. For example, Moore and Koontz (2003) classify collaborative watershed groups based on the roles played by citizens and government. They identify three types of collaborations: citizen-based, agency-based, and mixed-partnership. Similarly, the nature of the governing arrangement has been used to distinguish between different types of public service networks. For example, Provan, Kenis, and Human (2008) compare participant-governed networks with those governed by a lead organization and those managed by a network administrative organization. We build on these approaches, but we use a formative perspective rather than a management perspective.

Although all these typologies provide insights into the workings and performance of CGRs and reflect a range of practice and research traditions and theoretical frameworks, none fully capture and distinguish between the range of CGR species. Some typologies explain only one variation, and cannot or do not account for other differences among CGRs (e.g., Cheng and Daniels 2005; Cheng, Kruger, and Daniels 2003). Some focus on specific policy domains, like collaborative watershed partnerships (e.g., Moore and Koontz 2003), or on specific applications, like public service delivery (e.g., Provan, Kenis, and Human 2008). Others contain categories that are not mutually exclusive when placed in the context of CGRs (e.g., Agranoff and McGuire 2003; Margerum 2011). Still others categorize processes that are frequently apparent in the collaboration dynamics of CGRs (e.g., Gray 1989; Henton et al. 2005) but do not include other important dimensions of ongoing collaborative systems. Thus, though all these typologies are useful and provide glimpses into important collaborative governance processes and practices, none of them constitutes a typology that adequately allows for differentiation among the variety of CGR species.

Our CGR Typology

Louis Agassiz (1857, 170) defines a "species" as characterized by "the relations of individuals to one another and to the world in which they live, as well as by the proportions of their parts, their ornamentation, etc." This early typological characterization fits our understanding of CGR species quite well. Specifically, our typology for CGRs is based on formative type, or how individuals come together to form and direct a CGR.

Our premise is that the way in which CGRs are formed influences their composition and their collaboration dynamics as they evolve over time. Specifically, we suggest that CGRs form in one of three different ways—they can be self-initiated, independently convened, or externally directed. In self-initiated CGRs, participants come together after being inspired and galvanized by a set of core stakeholders. In independently convened CGRs, an autonomous third party assembles participants and designs processes for interaction. In externally directed CGRs, outside entities with sufficient authority or resources incentivize or mandate participants to work together in a preset manner. Moreover, the three formative types of CGRs respond to distinct conditions and possess distinct characteristics at the outset. Likewise, and consistent with general path-dependence theory, each formative type influences the nature and development of CGRs at their start and also as they evolve over time.

In the following sections, we lay out our CGR typology. We begin by exploring the prevailing conditions for each formative type, and then turn to their distinguishing characteristics. We use the case illustrations and case studies from the book to further illustrate the CGR types. Table 8.1 presents the typology of CGRs, and box 8.1 provides thumbnail sketches of these cases to refresh readers' memories.

Table 8.1 Typology of Collaborative Governance Regimes

Formative Type	Self-Initiated	Independently Convened	Externally Directed
Prevailing Conditions			
Policy challenge	Acute	Complex	Extensive
Determining authorities	Diffuse	Mixed	Concentrated
Characteristics			
Initiating leadership	Direct stake	Independent	Official stake
Initial structure	Ad hoc and emergent	Designed	Preset
Participant volition	Voluntary	Induced	Incentivized or mandated
Group autonomy	High autonomy	Assisted autonomy	Constrained autonomy
Common Examples	Community-based collaboratives, ad hoc working groups, planning committees, informal partnerships	Independent fact-finding commissions, community visioning processes, bipartisan policy coalitions, Policy Consensus Initiative's Public Solutions model	Federal advisory committees, grants requiring collaboration, regional planning or operating authorities, legislatively mandated collaborations
Book Case Studies and Illustrations	Toronto Civic Action; Newtok Planning Group	National Collaborative for Higher Education; Military Community Compatibility Committee	COTAS Guadalupe; Everglades Restoration Task Force

Box 8.1 Case Sketches

The National Collaborative for Higher Education was convened by the National Center for Public Policy and Higher Education to help states improve their higher education performance. Representatives from the Education Commission of the States and the National Education Center for Higher Education Management Systems, worked formally with five states and informally with seven states on state-based higher education policy and statewide priorities for improvement (see chapter 2).

The Everglades Restoration Task Force was created by Congress in 1996 to guide restoration efforts and address conflicts among multiple governmental and nongovernmental stakeholders. Fourteen representatives from federal, state, tribal, and local agencies worked together under the co-leadership of the US Department of the Interior, the US Army Corps of Engineers, and the South Florida Water Management District to facilitate the coordination of several operational projects to improve water quality, water flows, and habitat protection in South Florida (see chapter 3).

The Military Community Compatibility Committee was convened by the US Institute for Environmental Conflict Resolution in Tucson, Arizona, to address community concerns over noise levels produced by training jets at the Davis-Monthan Air Force Base (DMAFB). Representatives from residential neighborhoods, the real estate and business community, supporters of DMAFB, advisers from DMAFB, and state, city, and county governments collaborated to develop a set of recommendations to minimize current and future noise levels while assuring the continued viability of DMAFB (see chapter 4).

The Greater Toronto Civic Action Alliance was initiated by regional leaders to address complex governance challenges and policy gaps in Canada's largest urban region. Political and administrative officials from federal, provincial, and municipal governments, along with business and community leaders, were engaged to promote community-based civic action in a politically fragmented and socially diverse metropolitan region. Civic Action evolved over time to address several critical crosscutting challenges (see chapter 5).

The Newtok Planning Group is an ad hoc group of twenty-five tribal, state, federal, and nongovernmental agencies and organizations dedicated to relocating the Yup'ik Eskimo community of Newtok, Alaska, to higher ground. Newtok's tribal government is leading this effort in partnership with Alaska's Department of Commerce, Community, and Economic Development. Acute environmental conditions affecting the public health and safety of the community required action despite the absence of any one responsible public agency (see chapter 6).

Box 8.1 (continued)

COTAS Guadalupe is a local collaborative groundwater institution in Mexico's most productive viticulture region. As a result of the decentralization required by Mexico's 1992 Water Law, COTAS Guadalupe was created to improve water user coordination through broader participation in the subbasin. With increased autonomy, but little guidance, collaborative governance has proven to be challenging and continues to evolve (see chapter 7).

Prevailing Conditions

Drawing from the elements of the system context described in chapter 2, we identify two related prevailing conditions that give rise to a CGR's formative types: (1) the nature of the policy challenge and (2) the configuration of the determining authorities. The nature of the policy challenge concerns the problems or service conditions for which CGRs are created to respond. These policy challenges can be quite varied, particularly in terms of the range and intensity of their outcomes, which may be acute, complex, or extensive. Acute policy challenges affect a narrow or localized set of diverse stakeholders in extreme or severe ways, such as the imminent demise of the Alaska Native coastal village due to environmental stressors in the Newtok Planning Group case. Complex policy challenges are felt more broadly and with more contention between stakeholders about their interests and preferences for needs or solutions, such as in the Military Community Compatibility Committee (MC3) controversy over the noise levels produced by air force training jets. Extensive policy challenges are recurring situations across multiple settings or contexts that warrant similar approaches for policy and governance, such as the structured decentralization of the 1992 Mexican water law in the Comités Técnicas de Aguas Subterraneas (COTAS) Guadalupe case.

Determining authorities refers to the relevant jurisdictions and decision-making powers, whether in the public, private, or nonprofit sectors. The determining authorities may be diffuse, mixed, or concentrated. Diffuse authorities describe a configuration where there are multiple, disconnected, or fragmented authorities with limited or uncertain decision-making roles or responsibilities—as, for example, in the Greater Toronto Civic Action Alliance. Mixed authorities refer to a pattern that includes both diffuse and concentrated authorities, as in the National Collaborative for Higher Education. Concentrated authorities describe a situation where one or a small set of coordinated authorities are clearly the responsible decision makers, as the intergovernmental stakeholders were in the Everglades Restoration Task Force.

The distinct combinations of these specific policy challenges and determining authorities set up the prevailing conditions for the three CGR types. Self-initiated CGRs form in response to an acute policy challenge where the authorities are diffuse. Independently convened CGRs form around more complex policy challenges with mixed authorities. Externally directed CGRs form in response to extensive and recurring policy challenges with a concentrated core authority or set of authorities.

Distinguishing Characteristics

By virtue of the differences in their prevailing conditions, these three formative types of CGRs also vary according to several characteristics, including the initiating leadership, initial structure, participant volition, and group autonomy. Given the nature of the policy challenge and the determining authority, the locus of the initiating leadership, one of the four essential drivers for CGRs, varies among the three formative types. Leaders of self-initiated CGRs, like those in the Greater Toronto Civic Action Alliance and the Newtok Planning Group, have direct stakes in the substantive outcomes of their collaborative efforts and reach out directly to other leaders and potential participants across the divides of interest, values, geography, or policy perspective, or other gulfs. Initiating leaders of independently convened CGRs do not have a direct, vested interest in the specific policy outcomes, but, by virtue of their individual reputation or the standing of their organization, they can serve as impartial yet motivated conveners, creating the necessary bridging function to bring together multiple, diverse stakeholders, as did those in the National Collaborative for Higher Education. Externally directed CGRs are initiated by entities with an official stake in the outcomes, such as those in the Everglades Restoration Task Force. Sometimes, this official stake is indirect and removed from the immediate locus of action; other times, this stake is direct and connected with jurisdictional, oversight, or other responsibilities.

Each formative type of CGR is also associated with a different initial structure. Self-initiated CGRs, like the Greater Toronto Civic Action Alliance and the Newtok Planning Group, arise in a more ad hoc and emergent fashion as core leaders coalesce around a shared problem. Independently convened CGRs are more intentionally designed from the outset to assure that the collaborative process and structure attract and accommodate stakeholders with diverse and often contenting interests or conflicts, as is true in both MC3 and the Higher Education Policy Collaborative. Externally directed CGRs, like COTAS Guadalupe and the Everglades Restoration Task Force, are formally authorized or sanctioned from the start, which means that the collaborative process and structure are preset to some degree and are often more formal.

Consistent with, if not as a consequence of, these prevailing conditions and characteristics, the extent to which stakeholders voluntarily engage at the outset—the participant volition—varies across each CGR type. Although the degree and basis for participation will differ among participants in self-initiated CGRs, individuals are more likely to voluntarily engage on the basis of their own self-interests and shared interests. Independently convened CGRs often require additional inducements for individuals to participate—for example, assurances of fair and open consideration of specific issues or the inclusion (or exclusion) of specific individuals or groups. Externally directed CGRs attract participants through positive incentives (e.g., grant money, reputational benefits, and relief from certain requirements) or through regulatory mandates (e.g., state and federal laws requiring collaborative engagement and multiparty negotiations or sanctions). These distinctions in participant volition are also consistent in our six cases.

The final distinguishing characteristic of these three CGR types is group autonomy. The importance of participant autonomy and the tension between maintaining it while building group cohesion are carefully discussed by Thomson and Perry (2006). Here, we refer more specifically to the nature and extent of the group's ability to make its own rules and guide its own determinations and actions. Group autonomy is highest in self-initiated CGRs, where the principal participants are creating their own rules and capacities to act together, as they did in the Greater Toronto Civic Action Alliance. Independently convened CGRs have somewhat fewer degrees of freedom, because they require assistance through facilitated processes and structures, and in some cases initially borrow legitimacy from their convener, as happened in the MC3 case. Group autonomy is most constrained by formal structures and requirements in externally directed CGRs, as seen in the COTAS Guadalupe case.

In sum, self-initiated CGRs are formed by initiating leaders with a direct stake in addressing acute policy challenges where responsible authorities are diffuse and fragmented. These CGRs develop in an ad hoc, emergent manner, and engage stakeholders who participate voluntarily and have a high level of group autonomy. Typical examples of self-initiated CGRs include community-based collaboratives, ad hoc working groups, planning committees, and informal partnerships. The Greater Toronto Civic Action Alliance and the Newtok Planning Group exemplify self-initiated CGRs.

Independently convened CGRs are formed by initiating leaders who can bridge differences to address complex policy challenges where multiple, often overlapping authorities are involved. These CGRs are intentionally designed to provide a process and a structure that are attractive to the disparate stakeholders who are being encouraged or induced to participate. The group's autonomy is assisted by the impartial facilitation and guidance of the third-party convener. Typical examples of independently convened CGRs include independent fact-finding commissions, community visioning processes, and bipartisan policy coalitions. The Public Solutions model advanced by the Policy Consensus Initiative uses a design template akin to independently convened CGRs (www.policyconsensus.org/publicsolutions/index.html). The National Collaborative for Higher Education and MC3 exemplify independently convened CGRs.

Externally directed CGRs are formed by initiating leaders with a more removed or indirect stake in addressing extensive, recurring policy challenges. These leaders are situated in agencies or organizations that possess explicit, concentrated authority in the subject policy area. These CGRs develop through a formally structured approach that creates incentives or mandates for participants whose collective autonomy is constrained or directed to some extent by the authorized collaborative structure. Typical examples of externally directed CGRs include federal advisory committees, grant programs requiring collaboration, regional planning or operating authorities, and legislatively mandated collaborations. COTAS Guadalupe and the Everglades Restoration Task Force exemplify externally directed CGRs.

Before moving on to an exploration of collaboration dynamics according to the formative type of CGR, it is useful to note that within each formative type, there can be wide variations. In table 8.2 we examine the case illustrations and studies presented in this book across common variables, including CGR policy area, scale, size, and lead organizations. As per the discussion about others' typologies, there is no apparent pattern across these descriptors. This suggests that each formative CGR type can occur in any policy area, function at any jurisdictional scale, engage any number of participants, and be led by a variety of organizational forms and types.

Collaboration Dynamics by Formative Type

Given the variations in their prevailing conditions and characteristics, there are also variations in the initial patterns of collaboration dynamics for each formative type of CGR (for more on collaboration dynamics, see chapter 3). As we have noted throughout this book, CGRs are not static—they are continuously evolving. Moreover, our typology assumes a path-dependent model. Each CGR formative type sets up different patterns of collaboration dynamics at the outset that unfold over time, influence the CGR's subsequent development, and pose different kinds of challenges for CGR leaders and participants. The variations in the initial collaboration dynamics for each formative type (including principled engagement, shared motivation, and the capacity for

Table 8.2 CGR Case Summary by Formative Type

Case and Features	Self-Initiated		Independently Convened		Externally Directed	
Case	*Greater Toronto Civic Action (chapter 5)*	*Newtok Planning Group (chapter 6)*	*National Collaborative for Higher Education (chapter 2)*	*Military Community Compatibility Committee (chapter 4)*	*COTAS Guadalupe (chapter 7)*	*Everglades Restoration Task Force (chapter 3)*
Policy area	Community development	Community health / emergency planning	Education policy	Community health / noise abatement	Groundwater management	Natural Resource Protection
Scale	Regional	Local	National	Local	Local	Regional
CGR size	40	25	22	23	100–150	14
Lead organization	Steering committee with a chair position	Newtok tribal government; state DCCED facilitated	NCPPHE, Education Commission of the States, and National Center for Higher Education Management Systems	US Institute for Environmental Conflict Resolution	CONAGUA and leading local water users	Department of the Interior, ACE, and SFWMD

Note: For the meanings of the abbreviations used here, see the chapter where the case is given.

joint action) are shown in table 8.3. We discuss each formative type individually in the following subsections.

Self-Initiated CGRs

Self-initiated CGRs are formed through the voluntary association of stakeholders who engage directly with one another based on self-interests and shared interests. In this type of CGR, principled engagement is initially generated by and grounded in social and relational exchanges. Given that participants already have some degree of shared interests, principled engagement is likely to evolve on its own over time, and be only a moderate challenge as participants discern the potential for collaboration through discovery, definition, deliberation, and determinations. Moreover, through principled engagement, which may be aided by already-established relationships, the participants stimulate the surfacing of common objectives, which helps them to generate a shared theory of change, although elements of these agreements are likely to be present at the outset, given shared interests.

Given the common interests of the participants, shared motivation is likely not only to be present but also to be the most developed component of collaboration dynamics—at least initially. Moreover, this shared motivation (including its elements of trust, mutual understanding, internal legitimacy, and commitment) will be reinforced once participants have decided upon the CGR's collaborative potential, collective purpose, and shared theory of change.

The capacity for joint action is likely to be less developed at the start, and the most difficult to cultivate. The key element of this capacity in self-initiated CGRs is the group's core leadership, who must instigate the ongoing voluntary engagement of participants in the face of an acute problem or worsening condition for which there appears to be no formal or dedicated institutional leadership or authority. Without this core leadership, it will be difficult to further build the capacity for joint action, particularly in terms of procedural and institutional arrangements, knowledge, and resources.

In sum, at their outset, self-initiated CGRs are likely to have participants who share common interests. This generally aids principled engagement, which reinforces the already-extant levels of shared motivation. However, given their characteristics, self-initiated CGRs are less likely to initially emerge with a strong capacity for joint action. Thus, this CGR type depends on how well principled engagement and shared motivation develop the capacity for joint action. Of particular importance to the capacity for joint action is the cultivation of leadership, which may take a considerable time to develop and mature.

Table 8.3   Initial Patterns of Collaboration Dynamics by CGR Type

Collaboration Dynamics	CGR Type		
	Self-Initiated	*Independently Convened*	*Externally Directed*
Principled engagement (PE)	Internally generated and grounded in social/relational processes	Facilitated by third party neutral	Constrained or enabled by preset terms
	(PE is somewhat developed at the outset)	(PE is more developed at the outset)	(PE is less developed at the outset)
Shared motivation (SM)	Centered on common interests	Created over time through demonstration of good-faith participation	Contingent on incentives or mandates
	(SM is more developed at the outset)	(SM is less developed at the outset)	(SM is somewhat developed at the outset)
Capacity for joint action (CJA)	Leadership is key	Knowledge is key	Procedural/institutional arrangements and resources are key
	(CJA is less developed at the outset)	(CJA is somewhat developed at the outset)	(CJA is more developed at the outset)

As noted above, two of the cases discussed in this book exemplify self-initiated CGRs: the Greater Toronto Civic Action Alliance and the Newtok Planning Group. In the Civic Action case, many public leaders shared a "collective awareness of growing policy gaps" and recognized the need to better integrate the city of Toronto with its surrounding region. Thus, when the CGR was formed, there were well-developed levels of shared motivation, on which Civic Action capitalized to stimulate regional engagement and commitment. Although principled engagement was not particularly challenging at the start, the CGR had to be extended over time to include a broader, more heterogeneous group. The introduction of new participants stimulated conflict, which was overcome by rearticulating the CGR's collective purpose and the three founding principles of their shared theory of change: to operate regionally; to focus on multiple, cross-sector programs; and to assure multi-sectoral leadership. The CGR's leadership was, and continues to be, the key capacity for joint action cultivated by Civic Action (for more about this case, see chapter 5).

In the Newtok Planning Group case, participants realized that the community was in crisis, and immediate steps were needed to begin relocating the village. The core participants were directly affected by the critical environmental stressors and thus had well-developed levels of shared motivation from the start. Principled engagement was not contentious, given that all the participants appreciated the current and imminent threat conditions. Nevertheless, through an intense, multiyear process, the Newtok Planning Group was able to devise a shared theory of change for meeting the community's immediate and long-term needs. Building the capacity for joint action was very difficult in this case, particularly given the large and diffuse numbers of determining authorities involved. However, over time and with the leadership of key community leaders, the planning group was able to build the capacities needed to assure community relocation (for more about this case, see chapter 6).

Independently Convened CGRs

Independently convened CGRs face complex policy challenges, generally with a history of contending interests that need to be overcome or remediated. This history of conflict often necessitates calling upon an independent convening leader or institution. In such settings, the convener often conducts an informal or formal assessment of the situation and the affected and interested stakeholders to learn how to create the conditions for effective principled engagement. Thus, principled engagement is likely to be strong, given that it arises from intentionally designed and structured interactions that lead participants through the processes of discovery, definition, deliberation, and determinations. Over time, strong facilitated processes may help participants internalize the norms associated with principled engagement, thereby reducing their reliance on independent conveners. Regardless, as group norms, ground rules, and protocols are developed with facilitative assistance, participants in the CGR will also develop shared objectives and a theory of change.

In this CGR type, shared motivation may be slower to arise and is likely to be the least developed component of collaboration dynamics—at least initially. Brokers need to create conditions or assurances that induce the participation of key stakeholders; and in some cases, this depends on effective conflict management. Effective conflict resolution strategies not only help with principled engagement but also gradually lead to the progression of shared motivation and the building of trust, mutual understanding, internal legitimacy, and commitment. In short, over time the demonstration of good faith participation in principled engagement can enhance shared motivation.

Finally, the initial potential for a capacity for joint action is likely to be modestly developed for this CGR type, in part because the conveners will have identified and included all the necessary players. That said, knowledge is the key initial element in the capacity for joint action—knowledge leads participants to understand that the complex policy challenges they all face require collaborative action to overcome, particularly given the multiple authorities—formal and diffuse—that must be brought together or coordinated.

In sum, at their outset, independently convened CGRs bring together diffuse participants who often have conflicting interests. The convener aids in principled engagement, which is not only particularly strong at the beginning in this type of CGR but is also important, given the initially low levels of shared motivation. Because of their characteristics, independently convened CGRs are likely to have a modest initial capacity for joint action, which can be further cultivated with facilitative assistance. Doing so depends on the ability of the convener to activate the knowledge of participants, which can take time.

Two of the cases discussed in this book exemplify independently convened CGRs: the National Collaborative for Higher Education and MC3. However, given the lack of research on the National Collaborative for Higher Education, we cannot fully examine that case in light of our typology. Therefore, we only discuss MC3, where principled engagement was strong from the start, despite the contentious relationships between the participants. The strength of principled engagement can be attributed to the presence of an independent third party that provided facilitative assistance to the CGR. Through facilitated processes, participants were able to engage in discussions, establish ground rules, and reach an agreement on the CGR's collective purpose and shared theory of change, which focused on operational changes, land use and zoning options, and public education. Professional and independent convening helped bridge initial gaps in interpersonal trust, and repeated interactions slowly built the shared motivation of the participants during a two-year process. Shared knowledge about community concerns and the sensitivity of the Davis-Monthan Air Force Base's Base Realignment and Closure Commission standing were the basis for the key capacity for joint action, and enabled the CGR to focus on providing recommendations to public decision makers (for more about this case, see chapter 4).

Externally Directed CGRs

Externally directed CGRs, through appointed or legislated means, often establish the structure for collaborative groups, such as who can participate, how participants can interact, and what participants are authorized to do.

As a result of these and other preset terms for collaboration, principled engagement may be either constrained or enabled during initial interactions. In either case, this component of collaboration dynamics is likely to be only moderately developed at the outset; participants must show good faith participation over time to further cultivate principled engagement.

Similarly, in many instances, the problem set has already been defined and the group's collective purpose and theory of change have already been selected, though this need not always be the case. Regardless, participant buy-in or acceptance of the objectives and strategy will likely take time. Thus, the incentive or mandate for collaboration requires this type of CGR to create or strengthen the shared motivation of participants to engage. Trust is leveraged, rather than created, by the degree of transparency, breadth of representation, level of fair dealing, and other procedural and structural arrangements afforded by the predetermined structure for engagement. The same is true for mutual understanding, internal legitimacy, and commitment. Thus, shared motivation may be moderately developed at the start of the CGR, but its development over time is contingent on numerous factors.

Finally, the capacity for joint action is also frequently determined by the structure of the incentive or mandate in externally directed CGRs, and therefore is likely to be well developed (for better or for worse) at the outset. Two initial elements of this capacity are particularly important and must be drawn on at the start of such CGRs: the procedural and institutional arrangements provided by the preset structure, and the resources that incentivize and support collaboration.

In sum, at their outset, externally directed CGRs bring together selected participants under present structures for engagement. Although the collective purpose, shared theory of change, and capacities for joint action are often predetermined by these structures, CGR participants need to work to find ways to foster principled engagement and build the levels of shared motivation needed to accomplish their goals. Moreover, given the preset structures, the capacity for joint action in this type of CGR is likely to be well developed; however, participants still need to work to activate these capacities, paying particular attention to procedural and institutional arrangements and resources.

Two cases in this book exemplify externally directed CGRs: COTAS Guadalupe and the Everglades Restoration Task Force. In the COTAS Guadalupe case, the national water law created the incentives and authorization to establish the CGR; however, the absence of guidance for setting up a collaborative body opened the group to cooptation by more powerful local interests and weakened effective representation. Thus, principled engagement was manipulated to serve the interests of powerful participants, but not the broader community. Similarly, shared motivation was diminished by the constraints on the structure and responsibilities of the group and its limited authority, which in turn affected the CGR's capacity for joint action. Specifically, the lack of effective procedural and institutional arrangements and resources meant that COTAS Guadalupe was unable to cultivate a theory of change and carry out collaborative actions. Therefore, this case provides an example of a situation where the preset structures did not work to promote effective collaborative governance (for more about this case, see chapter 7).

In contrast, the preset structures of the Everglades Restoration Task Force had very different consequences. The task force was created in 1996 at the direction of Congress, which required the participation of representatives from fourteen different governmental agencies and authorities, as well as outreach to an array of other nongovernmental stakeholders. Moreover, the CGR's collaboration dynamics were formally structured and professionally staffed as a result of the congressional mandate. Discovery processes were led primarily by agency experts, and the solving of disagreements about definitional issues was facilitated by staff-level subgroups. Robust deliberation occurred within the task force meetings, whereas determinations were more formally made through voting procedures. Although the CGR's collective purpose was outlined by Congress, its shared theory of change was developed through a strategic planning process between task force members and was informed by a public engagement effort. Conflicts between agencies and related litigation raised challenges for the development of the virtuous cycle of shared motivation. Consistent with this CGR type, the procedural and institutional capacity, along with funding and staff resources, were essential capacities that enabled joint action by the task force over time (for more about this case, see chapter 3).

Challenges and Implications for Design and Management

As illustrated in the discussion above, the three formative types of CGRs are all path dependent; that is, each type takes on an initial pattern of collaboration dynamics that strongly influences its future development. These initial patterns create different kinds of challenges for CGRs, which in turn affect the likelihood of positive (or negative) changes in collaboration dynamics over time. Thus, those who design, lead, manage, or participate in CGRs can benefit from understanding the general tendencies of each CGR type, so they can better anticipate and prepare for the corresponding challenges. In chapter 9, we explore CGR process and productivity performance in detail. In the conclusion, we explore issues pertaining to CGR design and management. Here, we review briefly some of the most salient challenges vis-à-vis collaboration dynamics that each formative type is likely to face.

Self-Initiated CGRs

Self-initiated CGRs face significant timing pressures. On one hand, they must confront time-sensitive, acute issues and conditions, where no determining authorities are readily apparent or able to take action. On the other hand, they must overcome the time-intensive challenge of organizing for voluntary collaboration. Although many participants' initial motivation for joining the CGR is likely to derive from their overlapping interests, it can be challenging to sustain their motivation and participation. Efforts to maintain voluntary participation may be eased to the extent that the CGR is able to engage with the diffuse and fragmented determining authorities, because doing so suggests to participants the potential of the collaborative endeavor to effect change.

Leadership is particularly key to this formative type for many reasons, but especially because it is central to generating and sustaining voluntary participation and building the capacity for joint action. However, as exemplified in the Greater Toronto Civic Action Alliance case, leadership burnout (and turnover for other reasons) is a common occurrence for these CGRs as they develop over time. The need to replace the founding leadership should be anticipated, and succession planning could be very helpful. Moreover, given the diffuse nature of the determining authorities, these CGRs face the challenge of connecting and engaging with the available authorities, as well as creating and supporting new decision-making actors. Although this work certainly requires skillful leadership, it may also require forging new networks and perhaps even shaping a new role for the CGR within broader networks.

Self-initiated CGRs also tend to be limited in their initial capacity for joint action, not only in terms of leadership but also in terms of procedural and institutional arrangements, knowledge, and resources. After it builds its leadership, its leveraging of joint and external resources to support collaborative action becomes essential. This is dependent in large part on building the external legitimacy and standing of the CGR within the larger community and potential donors or funders, as was successfully done by the Newtok Planning Group. In addition, this CGR type faces challenges in transitioning from its ad hoc, informal initial formation to more stable, routine, and formal operations over time. Sharing management responsibilities, rotating chairs, selecting professional managers, and engaging in other activities that allow the CGR to evolve in a positive manner all pose new collective management challenges that should be anticipated and planned for.

Finally, the strength of self-initiated CGRs lies in their shared motivation, which is typically strong at the outset, in large part because participants come to the table with an overlapping set of interests. These shared interests often translate easily into at least the core elements of the CGR's collective purpose and shared theory of change. Leveraging the common interests of participants and reinforcing their collective purpose and shared theory of change can help self-initiated CGRs overcome these and other design and management challenges.

Independently Convened CGRs

Independently convened CGRs are likely to encompass the most diverse set of participants, at least in the beginning, and these participants are likely to have a preexisting conflict history about the problem or condition at hand. These conflicts are likely to persist and be manifested as significant differences in interests and perhaps values, as was demonstrated in the MC3 process. Conveners must continue to manage these differences through principled engagement. Moreover, the conveners—with the assistance of CGR managers, leaders, and participants—will benefit to the extent that they can anticipate ongoing challenges and foresee disagreements. Conflict management skills will be particularly useful for this CGR type. Recognizing and appreciating differences, rather than assuming them away or focusing exclusively on achieving a consensus, is important for these CGRs, particularly to generate a collective purpose and shared theory of change and to build shared motivation.

Participation is induced by the conveners of these types of CGRs, and changing external events or shifts in participating organizations can easily affect the participants' motivations; therefore, keeping the participants at the table can be another significant challenge for these CGRs. The conveners need to continually monitor the participants' volition and to ask all the participants how well the CGR is meeting their needs. Moreover, given the substantive differences between participants, coalitions or factions within the CGR are likely, if not inevitable. Coalitions per se are not a negative development. Coalitions formed between like-minded participants can empower those who, on their own, might not have much influence. Coalitions within large groups can also help distinguish key interests and strengthen constructive advocacy. Conveners should anticipate, and guide where appropriate, the development of such coalitions. The initial selection of participants and their composition should be made with coalition formation in mind.

As with self-initiated CGRs, independently convened CGRs must build and coordinate decision makers. Given the mixed authorities required to address the CGR's goals, the convener may also need to activate the existing networks or broker the formation of new networks to address the complexity of the policy challenge. For example, although many informal and formal networks exist in higher education, the convener of the National Collaborative for Higher Education had to galvanize and stimulate the participation of specific groups and organizations.

Implementation is also a concern for this CGR type, given problem complexity. Again, the convener needs to think about implementation (and raise questions about implementation to participants) at the very early stages of CGR formation, not only to assure the right composition of participants but also to provide ample opportunity for discovery and deliberation about how to carry out the CGR's plans. Although these CGRs are likely to have a modestly developed capacity for joint action, the sharing, building, and expansion of knowledge will be critical, particularly in strategic thinking about the challenges of implementation.

Finally, the strength of this CGR type lies in the quality of principled engagement, which is cultivated by the presence of the convening person or organization. Selecting a convener with the experience and skills necessary to manage the participant interactions over time can help independently convened CGRs overcome these and other design and management challenges.

Externally Directed CGRs

Externally directed CGRs require considerable strategic thinking at the design stage, particularly in creating the appropriate set of incentives or mandates to foster productive collaboration dynamics. If the intent is to reap the benefits of cross-boundary collaboration, then the preset structures and frameworks need to stimulate authentic collaboration dynamics; they need to create conditions that not only allow for, but also encourage, robust participant selection, principled engagement, shared motivation, and the creation of new collective capacities for joint action. There is a fine line between criteria and guidelines that are too rigid and constraining, and criteria and guidelines that are too flexible and easily manipulated. Often overlooked is the fact that the preset parameters for collaboration can recreate, reinforce, or reanimate existing power asymmetries, leading to imbalances and unproductive collaboration.

Preset agendas and narrowly focused objectives can also discourage participants from buying into collaboration. In turn, without such buy-in, it can be difficult to cultivate individual and collective advocacy and shared motivation for the CGR's collective purpose and theory of change, as was the case with

COTAS Guadalupe. However, careful balancing between needed guidance and group autonomy can be designed into the directives, with safeguards for assuring experienced process management and even participant training. For this reason, it is not only important to pay attention to the preset conditions for the CGR, but also for managers and leaders to work to create procedural and institutional arrangements that will allow the group to function over time.

Externally directed CGRs can be resource rich, as was the case with the well-funded Everglades Restoration Take Force. However, they can also become overly resource dependent. This is especially the case when CGRs are initiated with start-up funds but are expected to quickly transition to self-sustaining entities before participant volition and internal leadership are sufficiently strong. It is therefore important for CGR participants to give sustained and meaningful attention to the cultivation of joint and new resources.

Finally, the strength of this CGR type lies in its capacity for joint action, which is present (at least to some degree) by virtue of its preset structure. Leveraging and building on these initial capacities over time can help externally directed CGRs overcome these and other design and management challenges.

Summary

In this chapter we first reviewed several related typologies for collaborative processes. We then presented our own typology of CGRs, which is based on formative type, that is, how individuals come together to form and direct a CGR. We identified three formative types—self-initiated, independently convened, and externally directed. We also described the nature of two prevailing conditions—the policy challenge and the determining authorities—that give rise to each of the three formative types, and we explained each type in terms of a broad set of characteristics, including initiating leadership, nascent structure, participant volition, and group autonomy.

Consistent with path-dependence theory, we asserted that how CGRs are formed influences their composition and their collaboration dynamics as they evolve over time. We described the nature of the initial collaboration dynamics within each type of CGR, and we concluded the chapter with a discussion of the challenges and implications for CGRs' design and management. In the next chapter, we tackle issues of performance assessment for CGRs.

CHAPTER 9

Assessing the Performance of Collaborative Governance Regimes

The only man I know who behaves sensibly is my tailor; he takes
my measurements anew each time he sees me. The rest go on with
their old measurements and expect me to fit them.
—George Bernard Shaw

Thus far in this book, we have described, illustrated, and categorized collaborative governance and collaborative governance regimes (CGRs). The growth in collaborative cross-boundary approaches to complex or seemingly intractable problems would appear to attest to their effectiveness. There is certainly a strong normative appeal to such approaches, which many characterize as being more democratic, inclusive, and transparent than traditional hierarchical approaches. Indeed, collaboration may often seem the right thing to do in addressing many problem-ridden issues; however, "there is perhaps no topic . . . where the level of interest is so high and evidence so low as for cross-boundary collaborations" (Kelman, Hong, and Turbitt 2013). Although it is certainly true that experiments in collaborative governance have evolved over the last several decades, and, in some cases, have transformed the way the public's business is getting done, empirical research on the performance of cross-boundary collaboration continues to lag. Scholars and practitioners are working hard to understand how such systems emerge, what makes them work, and whether they are indeed producing their intended effects (Andrews and Entwistle 2010).

In this chapter, we review some of the challenges associated with assessing CGR performance and introduce the central aspects of an integrated approach to performance assessment.[1] We then turn to issues of measurement, providing potential indicators, data sources, and methods for assessing the antecedents and formation of CGRs, as well as for appraising their process and productivity performance. We conclude with some observations about connecting the process performance of CGRs to the productivity performance of CGRs.

The Challenges of Assessing CGR Performance

In recent decades, performance has become the prevailing concept for assessing the work of government and governance (Gormley and Balla 2004; Radin 2006). In the United States, performance measurement and management first gained prominence with the publication of Osborne and Gaebler's (1992) best-selling book *Reinventing Government*, and have since become standard, yet evolving, practices. In 1993, President Bill Clinton created the National Performance Review and Congress passed the Government Performance and Results Act (GPRA), which later provided the foundation for the Program Assessment Rating Tool (PART), an Office of Management and Budget process that attempts to link executive branch budget recommendations to specific federal programs (Radin 2006). Although President Barack Obama discontinued use of PART, he too has focused on performance management with the creation of performance.gov and the signing into law of the GPRA Modernization Act in 2010. Indeed, performance measurement and management have become key features of governance not only at the national level in the United States, but also at the state and local levels, as well as in nations around the world (Yang 2011; for a comparative discussion of performance systems, see Bianchi and Riverbank 2012).

Over time, the government's "performance rhetoric" has led to a number of approaches for assessing the outcomes of intergovernmental cooperation (Radin 2000), which have in turn been extended to assessing the outcomes of collaborative governance and CGRs. Few would stand against the argument that assessing the performance of interorganizational, multistakeholder collaboration efforts is a critical public management task (cf. Frederickson and Frederickson 2006; Goldsmith and Eggers 2004; Koliba, Meek, and Zia 2010; Turrini et al. 2010). Nevertheless, measuring the performance results of cross-boundary collaboration efforts remains difficult and complex (Agranoff and McGuire 2001b; Cheng and Daniels 2003; Kettl 2005; Provan and Milward 2001; Radin 2006). For example, despite the "legitimate concerns" that motivate performance measurement and management, these approaches often "create problems" that "inhibit the achievement of performance" (Radin 2006, 3). Included among the many problems seen in performance regimens are "relying on formal analytical approaches without attention to the political context in which they occur, jumping to measure outcomes without attention to decision processes, highlighting efficiency goals without including a focus on equity questions, a reliance on a one-size-fits-all approach, difficulty finding a decision process that will use the information developed, and separating management activities from substantive program concerns" (Radin 2006, 7–8).

The task of assessing the performance of collaborative governance and CGRs is complicated by several additional challenges. The normative appeal of collaborating across boundaries to solve complex public problems or deliver public goods and services may have slowed the needed scrutiny of these rapidly proliferating forms of governance (Kettl 2006; Koontz and Thomas 2012). Moreover, the orthodoxy of collaboration and collaborative governance often prevents critical assessments and evaluations of performance. Instead, we get stories and anecdotes about the benefits and positive outcomes of collaboration. Indeed, "the literature on collaboration is often celebratory and only rarely cautious" (O'Leary et al. 2009, 6).

We also have lacked consistent definitions for important terms such as "governance," "collaboration," and "networks," which are often used interchangeably or in conjunction with one another (Ansell and Gash 2008; Emerson, Nabatchi, and Balogh 2012). In part, this is due to the fact that collaboration is examined within many different research traditions and lineages, and these traditions are not well connected (see chapter 1). Understandably, scholars studying networks, conflict resolution, institutions, and management, among other topics, approach and assess collaboration differently. Moreover, scholars tend to operationalize different discrete aspects of collaboration (e.g., leadership, management, and relationships), but they do not often examine systemic issues or collaborative governance regimes as a whole. Together, these issues make it difficult to operationalize and measure collaboration and collaborative performance.

This leads to the additional challenge of defining the performance of interorganizational collaboration. Although there is general agreement that traditional approaches to performance assessment do not transfer easily or appropriately to collaborative governance systems (Kim, Johnston, and Kang 2011; Mandell and Keast 2008), there is little agreement about what constitutes effective performance in collaborative arrangements (e.g., Koliba, Meek, and Zia 2010; Provan and Milward 2001). Some assess collaborative performance in terms of relational outcomes, such as increased social capital, enhanced conflict management (prevention, reduction, and resolution), and better knowledge management (including generation, translation, and diffusion), whereas others believe the appropriately measured outcomes are improved coordination of efforts, better leveraging and pooling of resources, greater risk sharing in policy experimentation, and increased policy compliance (e.g., Agranoff 2008; Agranoff and McGuire 2003; Leach and Sabatier 2005; Provan and Milward 1995). The interaction and feedback between these different aspects of performance further complicate this definitional challenge.

These differences are in part related to another important challenge in measuring CGR performance: the temporal nature of these systems. The performance of CGRs not only occurs over time but also changes over time, making it difficult to observe and evaluate. CGRs are fluid, generative, and evolving, and there are multiple levels of short-, intermediate-, and long-term performance. As the performance dimension being measured moves further away in time from the CGR action, it becomes more difficult to attribute specific accomplishments solely to the CGR. In addition, the limited availability of longitudinal data often constrains researchers' ability to study longer-term performance effects. Finally, many studies are based on post hoc perceptions of what happened and what was accomplished by a CGR. This leads to concerns about the halo effect, whereby recent successes influence reported impressions and perceptions (Sabatier et al. 2005), along with the recall effect, whereby the accuracy of participants' reports on past events diminishes or becomes biased over time.

To further complicate CGR assessment, various perspectives on the relevant dimensions of successful performance need to be addressed, a point that is well documented in a recent review of interorganizational networks (Popp et al. 2014). There are multiple participants in CGRs, each of whom may have a different view on CGR performance. Emerson and her coauthors (2009) found, for example, that there can be considerable within-group differences between diverse stakeholders in environmental collaboration and conflict resolution processes as to whether a group even reached agreement. The more diverse the group, and certainly the more conflictual, the more likely there will be divergent perspectives on performance.

The organizations or constituencies that participants represent are also likely to have different perspective and priorities about what aspects of CGR performance matter, and these perspectives may be different from those of individual participants. Looking at performance from the perspective of the CGR as a whole may reveal other dimensions of performance that are important. The broader community and public at large—perhaps as recipients or beneficiaries of CGR actions—are also likely to have different views that might even be mediated by the media or other opinion leaders. External funders will certainly look for their own relevant performance benchmarks. Finally, and perhaps most important, performance matters in terms of direct measures of targeted changes in the nature or condition of the public problem that constitutes the focus of the CGR. In sum, assessing CGR performance is complex and is made particularly challenging because of conceptual and definitional inconsistencies, the temporal nature of CGR activities, and the multiple pertinent perspectives from which performance is viewed and valued.

An Integrative Approach to Collaborative Performance

To better handle these and other challenges, we recommend an approach to CGR performance assessment that incorporates (1) the use of a logic model structure to clarify the constituent components of CGRs and the relationships between these components, (2) recognition of the distinctions and connections between CGR process performance and productivity performance, (3) the use of multiple units of analysis, and (4) temporal awareness and longitudinal attention.

First, when we introduced our integrative framework for collaborative governance in chapter 1, we noted that it uses performance logic, which is easily translatable into a logic model approach. Logic models are essentially evaluation tools that trace the causal connections between inputs, processes, outputs, and outcomes. They provide a conceptual guide or road map for program evaluation and are used extensively in policy analysis, in fields ranging from education to public health, and from environmental conflict resolution to public participation (Emerson et al. 2009; Kellogg Foundation 2005; Mayeske and Lambur 2001; Nabatchi 2012; Orr, Emerson, and Keyes 2008).

Recent calls for using logic models to inform performance measurement for collaborative governance underscore their potential value (Koontz and Thomas 2012; Thomas and Koontz 2011; see also Emerson and Nabatchi 2015). In this chapter, we draw on the logic model approach to CGR performance assessment and present indicators for the components of our framework that represent antecedent conditions, process performance, and productivity performance.

Second, given a logic model approach to collaborative performance, it is necessary to parse out input, process, output, and outcome variables. This is not an easy task. On one hand, the performance movement tends to focus almost exclusively on outcomes; it largely skips over the importance of the inputs, processes, and outputs (Radin 2006). On the other hand, these variables are often conflated—with good reason. As others have noted, "processes and [productivity] outcomes cannot be neatly separated in consensus building [and CGRs] because the process matters in and of itself, and because the process and outcome are likely to be tied together" (Innes and Booher 1999, 415). In our formulation of collaboration dynamics, we recognize the essential value of process, and we realize that it generates its own set of performance results; however, by including both collaboration dynamics and collaborative actions as the constituent features of a CGR, we also recognize that process spawns the production of actions (which we sometimes refer to as outputs in this chapter, to be consistent with logic model terminology), as well as outcomes and adaptation, which in turn matter on their own.

Thus, we recommend differentiating between process and productivity performance. We define process performance as the level of functioning of collaboration dynamics that emerges from the combined interactions of principled engagement, shared motivation, and the capacity for joint action. We define productivity performance as the actions (or outputs) of the CGR and the resulting outcomes and adaptation they generate. The framework illustrates the dynamic causal connections between collaboration dynamics and collaborative outputs, between outputs and outcomes, and between outcomes and adaptation, as well as subsequent feedback to collaboration dynamics.

Although integrative, this approach still requires separating and specifying both the process and productivity sides of the collaborative performance equation. Formative evaluation, which examines performance during the operating cycle of a program, is likely to be a valuable approach for assessing process performance; summative evaluation, which examines performance at the end of an operating cycle, is likely to be a valuable approach for assessing productivity performance. Although it is clearer and more tractable to separately assess process and productivity performance, it is also important to examine the interaction between the two, particularly because process performance directly affects productivity performance. Thus, we distinguish between the two performance areas, but we also connect them to develop a fuller understanding of the overall performance of CGRs. Later in this chapter, we illustrate how some researchers are studying these causal connections and interactions.

Third, just as there are different types of collaborative performance, there are also different units of analysis that can be examined to better explain the complexity of CGR performance. As suggested above, there are many possible units of analysis at which CGR performance can be assessed, and we encourage researchers to assess CGRs using more than one. For example, process performance can be studied at the CGR level (a group, or system, unit of analysis) and at the participant level (an individual unit of analysis). Productivity performance can be studied at a minimum of three levels: the CGR level (a group, or system, unit of analysis), the participating organization level (an individual unit of analysis), and the target goal condition level (a substantive change unit of analysis). These three units of analysis are central features in our approach because they most directly contribute to and reflect CGRs' performance. However, other relevant units of analysis may also be of interest; obvious examples include the primary manager of the GCR, the network within which the CGR operates, the media covering the CGR, the community at large, and external funders.

Finally, because CGRs evolve and work over time, performance assessments can be conducted at various stages of their development. In their examination of collaborative networks, Mandell and Keast (2008) suggest four stages of collaborative development:

1. Formation, where the focus is on getting participants together, agreeing on a common goal, deciding what to do, and building the relationships, trust, norms, and commitment needed to enable collaboration;
2. Stablization, where participants work to gain external legitimacy for their efforts and develop and nurture the skills needed to sustain collaboration;
3. Routinization, where cooperation becomes the norm, and participants develop rules and guidelines for continued cooperation; and
4. Extension, where the collaborative effort becomes seen as a viable operation.

In some ways, these stages are captured in our integrative framework for collaborative governance. We, too, talk about formation in terms of the drivers for collaboration that emerge out of the system context. Formation, stabilization, and routinization are also captured in our notion of collaboration dynamics. Extension is, in some ways, akin to our idea of collaborative actions or outputs. To this list, we might add at least one additional stage of development: adaptation, where the CGR or its participants respond to the outcomes that arise from collaborative actions.

This temporal awareness requires attention to longitudinal issues and analyses. Time series analyses, panel studies, retrospective approaches, and other methods that appraise temporal issues would be particularly useful for assessing collaborative performance; however, we recognize that it is not always feasible to study CGRs over time, either continuously or at different intervals. At the very least, however, CGR managers and researchers should be aware of the CGR's developmental stage when analyzing and interpreting performance findings.

We now turn to issues of CGR performance measurement. We begin with the antecedents and formation of CGRs, and then proceed to process and productivity performance. For each of these three areas, we provide potential indicators, data sources, and methods for assessment.

Measuring the Antecedents and Formation of Collaborative Governance Regimes

As we have specified in our integrated framework, cross-boundary collaboration does not just happen; rather, conditions in the broader system context prompt a perceived need for collaborative governance, and four specific drivers trigger and energize the formation of a CGR. The complex system context that shapes CGRs at the outset and over time includes, among other possible elements, public resource or service conditions, policy and legal frameworks, socioeconomic and cultural characteristics, network characteristics, political dynamics and power relations, and the history of conflict. Of these, public service and resource conditions are particularly important, because they often form the substantive policy setting within which CGRs forge a common purpose and set target goals. These conditions also provide the basis for the discovery and definitional elements that occur within principled engagement.

We argue that the four drivers—including uncertainty, interdependence, consequential incentives, and initiating leadership—are needed in various degrees and combinations to propel the formation of CGRs, regardless of whether the CGR is self-initiated, independently convened, or externally directed. Moreover, launching any type of CGR takes effort—participants must be invited and assembled (either voluntarily or by mandate); attention must be paid to issues of diversity and representation; and thought must be given to who will bring the right motivations, attitudes, and resources to the table.

Although many might ignore these antecedents and formative conditions in assessments of collaborative performance, we believe they are critical, for three main reasons. First, assessments of the system context, presence of drivers, and CGR formation provide the basis for overall case documentation, as well as for the determination of the formative type, which in turn can enhance theory, research, and practice. In comparative research, for example, certain system context elements may be useful as control variables. Second, for those wishing to engage in collaborative governance, such an examination is useful for determining a CGR's potential practicality, viability, and sustainability. Third and finally, such assessments can establish the baseline conditions from which to assess the effectiveness of CGR productivity—the change in targeted conditions based on CGR outputs (actions), outcomes, and adaptation. In short, an analysis of the system context, drivers, and regime formation at the start, over the course, and at the close of a collaborative endeavor can help one analyze the overall productivity of the CGR.

Given the variety among CGRs, no one set of indicators will be applicable to all regimes. However, in table 9.1 we identify several illustrative indicators that capture elements of the system context, drivers, and CGR formation, and might be found across most, if not all, CGRs, along with several potential data sources for capturing these and other indicators, including archival documentation, interviews, surveys, network analysis, and geographic information system tools. We discuss some of these indicators below.

In assessing the system context, one might look at data on public resource

Table 9.1   Indicators and Data Sources for the System Context, Drivers, and Regime Formation

Dimension	Elements	Sample Indicators	Potential Data Sources
System context	Public resource or service conditions	State of depletion, pollution, or extraction of environmental and natural resources Inadequacy, deterioration, or risk to public health/safety of physical infrastructure Quality, extent, and distribution of public services	Archival data and documentation; interviews with key parties/researchers; survey data; network analysis and mapping; geographic information system tools
	Policy and legal frameworks	Nature and bearing of pertinent laws, rules, regulations, and policies Extent to which frameworks are established, newly formed, or in process of change Degree to which decision making and action are enabled or constrained by frameworks	
	Socioeconomic and cultural characteristics	Income and education levels Community health index Ethnic and racial diversity	
	Network characteristics	Network density (e.g., dense or sparse) for community of interest Strength of ties (e.g., weak or strong) within networks	
	Political dynamics and power relations	Degree of access to and support from public decision makers Degree of partisanship and political polarization Stability/turnover in public leadership Sources and distribution of power across stakeholders	
	Conflict history	Perceived levels of trust, litigation history, prior CGR experience	

Table 9.1   (continued)

Dimension	Elements	Sample Indicators	Potential Data Sources
Drivers	Uncertainty	Existing or expressed need to reduce, diffuse, and share risk Existing or expressed information asymmetries	Archival data and documentation; interviews with key parties/researchers; survey data; direct observation
	Interdependence	Existing or expressed need to "work together" to make progress Evidence of "sector failure" in solving problem or meeting needs	
	Consequential incentives	Effects of not collaborating on key actors and organizations Level of external situational or institutional crises, threats, or opportunities Issue salience and ripeness for collaboration	
	Initiating leadership	Presence/absence of one or more leaders and number of leaders/ leadership roles filled Available leaders with key attributes (e.g., broadly respected, fair-minded, neutral as to solution, ability to support initial transaction costs)	
CGR formation	Conditions and characteristics of formative type[a]	Evidence about the nature of the policy challenge (acute, complex, or extensive); the nature of the determining authorities (diffuse, mixed, or concentrated); the structure of the CGR (emergent, designed, or preset); participant volition (voluntary, induced, or incentivized or mandated); the level of group autonomy (or the nature and extent of the group's ability to make rules and determinations and take actions).	Archival data and documentation; interviews with key parties/researchers; survey data; direct observation

Table 9.1   (continued)

Dimension	Elements	Sample Indicators	Potential Data Sources
CGR formation	Additional descriptive variables	Number of participants and sectors/organizations represented Baseline information about participant attributes, attitudes, and motivations (credibility, level of resources, level of talent, team spirit, beliefs about the necessity of a CGR); participant resources and needs (available or needed resources, time, power)	Archival data and documentation; interviews with key parties/researchers; survey data; direct observation

[a]Definitions and indicators for the prevailing conditions and characteristics of self-initiated, independently convened, and externally directed CGR types are provided in chapter 9.

conditions (e.g., the state of depletion, pollution, or extraction of environmental and natural resources; the inadequacy, deterioration, or risk to public health/safety of physical infrastructure; or the quality, extent, and distribution of public services), socioeconomic and cultural characteristics (e.g., income and education levels, community health, and ethnic and racial diversity), and network characteristics (e.g., the density of networks and their strength of ties), among other issues.

In terms of the four drivers, one might measure uncertainty by gauging the perceived need to reduce, diffuse, and share risk; interdependence by the perceived need to "work together"; consequential incentives by the perceived salience and ripeness of issues; and initiating leadership by perceptions about the presence (or absence) of people who could perform requisite tasks.

Finally, one might examine CGR formation by identifying the prevailing conditions and distinguishing characteristics related to the formative type of the CGR. For example, it is possible to find a priori evidence for the nature of the presenting policy challenge (i.e., whether it is acute, complex, or extensive) and determining authorities (i.e., whether they were diffuse, mixed, or concentrated). Post hoc, after the formation of the CGR, one can assess additional characteristics, such as the structure of the CGR (emergent, designed, or preset), participant volition (voluntary, induced, or incentivized or mandated), and the level of group autonomy (or the nature and extent of the group's ability to make rules and determinations and take actions). In addition, one might assess other common descriptive information about the participants themselves—for example, by examining the number of participants and sectors/organizations represented; the specific attributes, attitudes, and motivations of the participants; and the level of their available and needed resources.

Measuring the Process Performance of Collaborative Governance Regimes

Turning now to process performance, we unpack and suggest indicators for the elements of collaboration dynamics, including principled engagement, shared motivation, and the capacity for joint action. We also discuss several approaches to process performance assessment, and we provide innovative examples of how others have tackled this issue. Finally, we suggest several areas where researchers could advance our knowledge about collaboration dynamics and process performance—for example, through use of multiple cases, longitudinal studies, and multiple units of analysis.

Principled engagement captures the behavioral interactions between CGR participants and consists of four elements: discovery (i.e., the identification and analysis of relevant information); definition (i.e., efforts to build shared meaning around the issues at hand); deliberation (i.e., candid and reasoned discourse about the issues, information, target goals, alternative approaches, and theories of change); and determinations (i.e., the multiple operational and substantive decisions reached by the CGR participants). In table 9.2 we identify and define each element of principled engagement, provide a list of potential indicators, and offer suggestions about potential data sources. For example, discovery could be measured by the extent to which participants reveal interests, concerns, and values; recognize shared goals; or identify, share, and analyze relevant information. Definition could be measured by the extent to which parties articulate a common purpose, target goals, and a shared theory of change. Deliberation could be measured by the extent to which parties have fair, civil, inclusive, and candid discussions. Determinations could be measured with the number and type of procedural, operational, and substantive decisions. Data for these and other indicators could be gathered from archival sources, surveys, interviews, and direct observation.

Shared motivation captures the interpersonal relationships between the CGR participants and their attitudes toward one another and the CGR, and consists of four elements: trust (i.e., confidence in the reliability, truthfulness, and abilities of others); mutual understanding (i.e., appreciation and tolerance of differences); internal legitimacy (i.e., beliefs about the worthiness and credibility of the CGR and its participants); and commitment (i.e., the dedication and responsibility to the CGR, its collective purpose, and shared theory of change). In table 9.3 we identify and define each element of shared

Table 9.2 Indicators and Data Sources for Principled Engagement

Component	Element	Definition	Sample Indicators	Potential Data Sources
Principled engagement (captures the behavioral interactions among participants)	Discovery	Identification and analysis of relevant information	Extent to which participants reveal interests, concerns, and values; recognize shared goals; recognize how their own interests are served by participation in group; identify, share, and analyze relevant information	Archival data (e.g., meeting minutes, reports, case documentation); surveys or interviews of participants; direct observation at meetings
	Definition	Effort to build shared meaning around issues relevant to the CGR	Extent to which participants articulate common purpose and target goals; arrive at shared problem definition and theory of change; define concepts and terminology; clarify tasks and expectations; develop evaluation criteria	
	Deliberation	Use of candid and reasoned discussion to address issues	Extent to which participants engage in fair and civil discourse; are open and inclusive during communication; have candid and reasoned discussion; offer individual opinions; thoughtfully listen and examine perspectives; manage conflicts and disagreements; change their perspectives after discussion	
	Determinations	Decisions reached by the CGR	Explicit agreement on common purpose, target goals, and shared theory of change Number and type of procedural and operational decisions (e.g., setting agendas, tabling discussions, assigning work groups) Number and type of substantive determinations (e.g., technical or policy-related decisions, decisions on future actions) Acceptability and fairness/equity of agreements reached Durability, robustness, and efficacy of agreements reached	

motivation, provide a list of potential indicators, and suggest potential data sources. For example, trust could be measured by the extent to which parties perceive other participants to be reasonable, predictable, and dependable. Mutual understanding could be measured by the extent to which parties respect one another or feel comfortable revealing information. Internal legitimacy could be measured by assessing the degree to which participants believe that the CGR and its parties are useful, worthy, and credible. Commitment could be measured by the degree to which participants are committed to the CGR and its collective purpose, target goals, and shared theory of change. Data for these and other indicators could be gathered from archival sources, as well as from surveys, interviews, and focus groups.

The capacity for joint action captures functional assets available to the CGR, and consists of four elements: procedural and institutional arrangements (i.e., the protocols for managing the CGR over time); leadership (i.e., the variety of roles taken on by CGR participants to carry out various functions); knowledge (i.e., the generation and sharing of information, data, and expertise); and resources (i.e., the acquisition of people, technology, finances, and other resources needed to achieve the CGR's collective purpose). In table 9.4 we identify and define each element in capacity for joint action, provide a list of potential indicators, and suggest potential data sources. For example, procedural and institutional arrangements could be measured by the nature and quality of the CGR's ground rules, operating protocols, decision rules, charters, bylaws, rules, and regulations. Leadership could be measured by examining the number and types of leaders and leadership roles filled. Knowledge could be measured by the extent to which information was generated, presented, shared, and understood by participants. Resources could be measured by the extent to which parties leveraged or contributed funding, administrative support, expertise, tools, and so forth. Data for these and other indicators could be gathered from archival sources, surveys and interviews, and direct observation.

Assessing the level of process performance starts with selecting appropriate indicators for these multiple elements and components. Depending on the available access to data and time for data collection, one signal indicator may be selected for each element. For example, in their work on interorganizational engagement in the Everglades Restoration Task Force in South Florida (discussed in chapter 3), Berardo, Heikkila, and Gerlak (2014) focused on the effects of specific issues and actor characteristics on the level of engagement. To do so, they conducted microanalyses of meeting minutes over a five-year period. They operationalized engagement—what we would call deliberation—as the time spent voicing individual opinions during the discussion of a specific agenda item divided by the number of meeting attendees. Then they

Table 9.3 Indicators and Data Sources for Shared Motivation

Component	Element	Definition	Sample Indicators	Potential Data Sources
Shared motivation (captures the interpersonal relationships)	Trust	Confidence in the reliability, truthfulness, and abilities of others	Level of perceived trust among participants Extent to which they believe each other to be reasonable, predictable, and dependable	Archival data (e.g., charters and references to participant organization commitments to the CGR); surveys or interviews of participants; focus groups and other formal and informal conversations with the CGR participants
	Mutual understanding	Appreciation and tolerance of differences	Extent to which participants can identify and respect differences among participants; are comfortable revealing information to others; appreciate and feel appreciated by others	
	Internal legitimacy	Beliefs about the worthiness and credibility of the CGR and its participants	Extent to which participants deem the CGR and its parties to be useful, worthy, and credible	
	Commitment	Dedication and responsibility to the CGR, its collective purpose, target goals, and theory of change	Extent to which participants are committed to the CGR, its collective purpose, target goals, and shared theory of change; are motivated to achieve outcomes together; feel responsible and accountable for outcomes	

Table 9.4 Indicators and Data Sources for the Capacity for Joint Action

Component	Element	Definition	Sample Indicators	Potential Data Sources
Capacity for joint action (captures the functional assets available to the CGR)	Procedural or institutional arrangements	Protocols for managing the CGR over time	Nature and quality of ground rules, operating protocols, decision rules, charters, bylaws, rules, regulations Extent to which arrangements enable effective administration and management of the CGR Extent to which individual organizations in the CGR have protocols and institutional arrangements	Archival data (e.g., meeting minutes, reports, case documentation); surveys or interviews of participants; direct observation
	Leadership	Variety of roles taken on by the CGR participants to carry out various functions	Number and types of leaders and leadership roles filled and unfilled (e.g., champion, sponsor, convener, facilitator/mediator; expert)	
	Knowledge	Generation, sharing, and analysis of information, data, and expertise	Extent to which relevant knowledge was generated and developed (and how it was developed); explicit and tacit knowledge management was manifested; high-quality and trusted information was presented, made accessible, and understood by the participants; technology was used to aid in knowledge generation and management	
	Resources	Acquisition of human, technological, financial, and other resources needed to achieve the CGR's collective purpose	Extent to which funding, administrative support, expertise, tools, and other resources were acquired; all parties contributed to and leveraged various resources; parties made efforts to accommodate the diversity of resources and capacities of others	

used these data in a series of regression analyses, finding that contributions made by less powerful attendees can increase levels of engagement.

Alternatively, data on multiple indicators could be aggregated into indices for different components. For example, in her exploration of collaboration in the Federal Energy Regulatory Commission's hydropower licensing process, Ulibarri (2015a) used various indicators from survey data to create reliable indices for principled engagement, shared motivation, and capacity for joint action. She then used linear mixed-effects models to test the influence of collaboration dynamics on various outcomes. In general, her findings show that greater levels of collaboration dynamics influence several potentially desirable outcomes, such as participant satisfaction and learning, higher-quality outputs (in this case, hydropower licenses), and predicted improvements in the environment and economy.

In addition to assessing the individual components of collaboration dynamics, it is important to examine the interactions between them. As noted in chapter 3, the three components of collaboration dynamics interact and reinforce one another in what—when successful—can be thought of as a "virtuous cycle" (Ansell and Gash 2008; Huxham 2003; Imperial 2005). Simply put, each individual component contributes to and reinforces the other two components in collaboration dynamics. Researchers may want to parse out the relationships between the components to confirm their direction and influence, assess the degree to which they reinforce one another, and determine whether these interactions are consistent with the integrative framework.

One way of doing this parsing out would be through structural equation modeling. For example, in their innovative study using agent-based modeling in computer simulations, Choi and Robertson (2013) focused on the interaction between deliberation and decision making (both elements of principled engagement). Their process performance outcomes include three measures relating to group agreements—the percentage of groups that reached agreement, after simulated runs; the mean acceptability of those decisions across the agents/participants; and the equity of the decisions, measured as the standard deviation of individual acceptability measures. Based on their results, they concluded that given time for deliberation, better agreements emerge regardless of the decision rule chosen.

Beyond examining the individual components of collaboration dynamics and the relationships between them, several other research trajectories could also be explored. In particular, assessing process performance across CGR types, over time, and at different units of analysis could yield interesting insights and generate important understandings about collaboration dynamics and process performance. Here, we briefly discuss each of these.

First, it would be useful to compare collaboration dynamics across the three different types of CGRs. Specifically, if data were collected at only one point in time but across several cases, then different levels of process performance could be compared; and, with information on the varying system contexts and drivers, hypotheses that relate to process performance could be tested. For example, in chapter 8 we noted that each formative type of CGR is likely to have varying initial levels of the three components in collaboration dynamics: Self-initiated CGRs are likely to have high initial levels of shared motivation, but low capacity for joint action; independently convened CGRS are likely to have high initial levels of principled engagement, but low levels of shared motivation; and externally directed CGRs are likely to have high initial levels of capacity for joint action, but low levels of principled engagement. Comparative data could be used to test these assertions more rigorously.

Second, another useful research direction would be to explore process performance over time. Collaboration dynamics are not static; they evolve as a CGR forms, grows, and adapts. Thus, assessments of process performance could look at collaboration dynamics at various stages in a CGR's development—for example, during formation, stabilization, routinization, extension, and adaptation (cf. Mandell and Keast 2008). One area in which we have a particular interest is adaptation. Specifically, we noted in chapter 4 that the outcomes from collaborative actions might lead to adaptation in collaboration dynamics (and elsewhere). Although we believe this to be true, and though there are claims that CGRs are more adaptive and resilient than hierarchical bureaucracies, there is little empirical evidence supporting these assumptions (Emerson and Gerlak 2014). Thus, examining the process performance of CGRs over time and how it changes as a result of subsequent actions, outcomes, and adaptations would significantly advance our understanding of collaborative governance regimes.

Third and finally, and consistent with our overall approach to assessment, it is important to be clear about and consider multiple units of analysis in process performance. Two units of analysis stand out to us as being most relevant here: (1) the participant level, which represents an individual unit of analysis; and (2) the CGR level, which represents a group, or system, unit of analysis.

At the participant level, it would be useful to learn from individual CGR participants about their collaborative behaviors, attitudes toward the CGR and collaboration dynamics, and views of and relationships with others. Such data could be collected using surveys, interviews, or perhaps even focus groups. It would be particularly useful if such data were coupled with information about the different attributes of these participants—for example, the sector from which they come; whether they joined the CGR voluntarily or by mandate; their alternatives to collaboration; and their perceived (and perhaps actual) degree of power, authority, and resources. Such information would go a long way toward uncovering and understanding the roles of individuals in helping or hindering collaboration dynamics and process performance.

At the CGR level, one must either aggregate observations from individual participants and accept the limitations of these indirect data or seek additional information about the group as a whole. If the group approach is taken, the most likely sources of information on collaboration dynamics would be proxy measures from archival data and direct observation. For example, meeting minutes may reveal the degree of consensus reached on group determinations; attendance records could be used to assess the degree of participant commitment; or the percentage of participants contributing to CGR budget or providing other assets could be used to assess the resources element of capacity for joint action. Although perhaps more challenging and requiring a greater degree of creativity, such group-level data can be found or collected, and they would again contribute to our understanding of collaboration dynamics and process performance.

In sum, there are many approaches to assessing process performance. It is important that researchers work to identify and employ relevant indicators for each component of collaboration dynamics, as well as for the elements embedded in each component. Examining collaboration dynamics within a single case, across multiple cases, and over time, as well as with individual and group-level units of analysis, will undoubtedly reveal important information about process performance and advance our understanding of CGRs.

Measuring the Productivity Performance of Collaborative Governance Regimes

We now turn to the production side of the integrative framework, where we take an instrumental approach to CGR productivity performance. What CGRs produce directly and indirectly through their actions (outputs), outcomes, and adaptation needs to be well conceptualized and measured. Of course, this is complicated because productivity is multidimensional and dependent on the perspective or unit of analysis that one is valuing or studying.

To address these complications, we construct a productivity performance matrix consisting of three production levels and three units of analysis (see Emerson and Nabatchi 2015). Specifically, we identify three levels of productivity derived from the "production" chain of actions, which include intermediate and end outputs; outcomes, which include intermediate and end results from the preceding outputs; and adaptation, which includes responses to those outcomes. This production chain is described in chapter 4 and is illustrated in the case study chapters. To capture the fact that CGRs involve multiple autonomous organizations working across boundaries to jointly address a public problem, we build on Provan and Milward's (2001) work, and specify three units of analysis for assessing CGR productivity performance: the participant organizations, the CGR itself, and the target goals.

In assessing the productivity performance of CGRs, one could evaluate any of the three performance levels—outputs, outcomes, adaptation—at any of the three units of analysis—participant organizations, CGR, target goals. However, the integration of the three performance levels and three units of analysis provides the analytical space to assess specific dimensions of collaborative productivity. Although many possible productivity dimensions exist, we focus on the nine presented in table 9.5. In the following discussion, we explain each of the nine dimensions by performance level.

Performance Level One: Actions/Outputs

In the language of logic models, collaborative actions are comparable to intermediate or end outputs (cf. Thomas and Koontz 2011). Such collaborative outputs could be generated by the actions of a CGR itself, its participating organizations, or other agents in furtherance of the CGR's collective purpose. Intermediate outputs would include completed plans or delivered services, whereas end outputs would include more final products, such as project implementation or collaborative monitoring.

When assessing performance at the participant organization unit of analysis, the efficiency of collaborative outputs matters. Efficiency here refers to any reduced internal costs or net gains attributable to participation in the CGR. Each participant organization is likely to ask: Are we attaining any efficiencies in our own operating realm, by sharing or delegating collective

Table 9.5   Dimensions of Collaborative Governance Productivity

	Unit of Analysis		
Performance Level	*Participant Organization*	*Collaborative Governance Regime*	*Target Goals*
Level one: actions/outputs (intermediate and end outputs)	Efficiency	Efficacy	Equity
Level two: outcomes (intermediate or end outcomes)	Effectiveness	External Legitimacy	Effectiveness
Level three: adaptation (responses to outcomes)	Equilibrium	Viability	Sustainability

action? In some cases, efficiencies can be measured with hard data; but in other cases, perceptions about efficiency gains may need to suffice.

At the CGR unit of analysis, the efficacy of these outputs is key. By efficacy, we mean the extent to which outputs are aligned with the CGR's collective purpose and shared theory of change. Specifically, the CGR is likely to ask: Are we taking actions (i.e., generating outputs) that are consistent with what we set out to achieve and how we planned to achieve it? One way to measure efficacy is to rate the fit or consonance between the CGR's previously reported goals and theory of change and the outputs actually produced by the CGR.

In the target goals unit of analysis, equity is particularly salient; generally, it is defined as the allocation of attention, effort levels, and resources to collaborative outputs, and specifically as the distribution of benefits, costs, and risks of actions among beneficiaries. The beneficiaries may be the participating organizations themselves, but they can also be the public at large or specific communities, as well as the public resource or public service conditions targeted for improvement. The performance question here is: Do the CGR outputs equitably address the multiple interests and needs of beneficiaries? To assess equity, one could employ comparative measures for the distribution of net benefits, or one could determine the extent to which CGR participants and/or beneficiaries are satisfied with the distribution of benefits, costs, and risks.

Performance Level Two: Outcomes

The outcomes that result from CGR outputs include changes in conditions necessary to reach target goals (intermediate outcomes), as well as the final accomplishment of those goals (end outcomes) (cf. Thomas and Koontz 2011). As noted above, outcomes can (and often should) be measured over time; but as outcomes become more distant from actions or outputs, the harder it becomes to determine causation.

When assessing performance at the participant organization unit of analysis, a salient dimension is the effectiveness of outcomes in generating internal benefits or improvements. In essence, effectiveness captures the added value for the CGR participants generated by the outcomes of collaborative actions. Thus, organizations are likely to ask: Have the CGR outcomes contributed to the capacity of our organization to accomplish its individual mission and goals? One way to measure effectiveness is through participants' perceptions of the extent to which the outcomes have contributed to their organizations.

The primary dimension of interest in the CGR unit of analysis is the external legitimacy of the outcomes—that is, whether the outcomes have contributed to positive perceptions or the improved status of the CGR among external stakeholders. Thus, as a whole, the CGR will ask: Do the outcomes generate positive perceptions of our collective efforts among the external organizations whose acceptance is essential for future funding or public support? In addition to using data that capture internal perceptions of reputational benefits, one could measure external legitimacy by examining statements from external constituents or press coverage.

With respect to the target goal unit of analysis, effectiveness is the central and most familiar performance dimension. Here, we employ the common and straightforward meaning of effectiveness: the extent to which collaborative outputs produce their intended outcomes. The relevant performance question is: To what extent are CGR actions producing outcomes that are meeting the CGR's target goals? Although easily understood, effectiveness is often far more difficult to measure; direct or indirect evidence of desired changes in targeted conditions, goods, services, or product can be collected, but the timing and distribution of these changes can make data collection challenging. This can be expedited by early identification of agreed-upon indicators of outcome success.

Performance Level Three: Adaptation

The long-term productivity of CGRs may be viewed through the lens of adaptation, that is, the adaptive responses to outcomes. Adaptation has long been important for policy implementation and performance management, where an iterative or incremental policy change is being sought (e.g., Koliba, Meek, and Zia 2010; Lindblom 1959; Moynihan 2008; Poister 2008; Pressman and Wildavsky 1973).

In the participant organization unit of analysis, equilibrium—that is, the balance between stability and change—is the most important dimension of adaptation. Organizations are constantly seeking the right balance between stability and change, asserting continuity in mission and identity while responding to changing demands, opportunities, and exigencies. Thus, participant organizations are likely to ask: Do adaptations to outcomes enable us to find this dynamic equilibrium and strengthen organizational resilience? CGR participants' perceptions about resilience will probably be the best indicators of this dimension. The specific indicators will be context specific; and in some settings, transformational responses to outcomes that lead to radical shifts in participant organizations may well be anticipated or welcomed.

In the CGR unit of analysis, viability—that is, the capacity to continue generating outputs, outcomes, and other CGR-related work in light of changing conditions—is an important performance dimension to assess. For CGRs, the relevant performance question is: Does adaptation increase the operational and financial capacity of the CGR in ways that will continue to support collective action? Ways to measure viability could include the maintenance or growth in the number of CGR participants or in the available CGR capacity.

Finally, in the target goal unit of analysis, sustainability—that is, the longevity of outcomes—is a key dimension for assessing productivity. Here the performance question is: Are the demonstrated effects robust, resilient, and lasting over time? Measures of sustainability are, of course, time dependent and would require assessing the enduring nature of the adaptive responses to outcomes over the appropriate time period.

Whether one is researching causal relations within the integrative framework or evaluating the performance of a specific CGR, some or all of these nine dimensions of productivity performance may be useful. However, measuring performance for all the units of analysis and across all the performance levels would arguably provide the most comprehensive understanding of CGR productivity. Numerous data sources for measuring the nine dimensions exist, including a wide variety of archival records and documentation, surveys, interviews, and direct observation. In table 9.6 we summarize the nine dimensions of productivity performance and provide sample indicators and sources of data for each. Emerson and Nabatchi (2015) used these dimensions to assess the productivity of an interagency partnership between the US Border Patrol and the Coronado National Forest along the United States–Mexico border. The authors found that the productivity of this partnership was observable and positive for most of the nine dimensions. However, the indicators for measuring equity of the partnership's actions or outputs were negative, as was one of the indicators for the perceived legitimacy of the CGR and its outcomes.

Connecting Process and Productivity Performance

Implicit in the integrative framework for collaborative governance is the proposition that to improve actions, outcomes, and adaptation (productivity performance), one needs to improve collaboration dynamics (process performance). Although both process and productivity performance are each important in their own right, they are also causally linked. Though more research is needed, a growing number of scholars are working to empirically confirm these linkages.

For example, in the context of marine and freshwater ecosystem restoration in the Puget Sound, Scott and Thomas (2015) studied the connections between participation in CGRs and membership in associated organizational networks. They surveyed participants in fifty-seven collaborative groups,

Table 9.6 Indicators and Data Sources for Productivity Performance Dimensions

Performance Level	Unit of Analysis	Dimension	Defined	Sample Indicators	Potential Data Sources
Actions	Participating organizations	Efficiency	Gains in internal efficiencies of the CGR participants	Measures/perception of net efficiency gains for the CGR participants	Organizational records; reported gains (surveys/interviews)
	CGR	Efficacy	Alignment of actions with stated CGR intentions and theory of change	Consistency of actions with shared theory of change	Meeting minutes and work plans; external confirmation of implemented actions
	Target goals	Equity	Fairness in distribution of benefits, costs, and risks among beneficiaries of actions	Comparative measures of distribution of net benefits Satisfaction with the distribution of benefits across beneficiaries and/or the CGR participants	Monetized values and distribution of actions or investments; perceptions of beneficiaries and the CGR participants (surveys/interviews); shared criteria set by the CGR participants for equitable distribution
Outcomes	Participating organizations	Effectiveness	Added value to the CGR participants from outcomes	Benefits/improvements to the CGR participants attributable to the CGR outputs	Organizational records; reported benefits/improvements (surveys/interviews)
	CGR	External Legitimacy	Acknowledged status of the CGR and effects of outputs	Observations by leaders/media of the CGR Reputational benefits	Organizational records; media and social media attention; repeat and new funding
	Target goals	Effectiveness	Extent to which outputs produce intended effects	Evidence of desired change in targeted conditions, goods, services, or products	Criteria set for target goals; objective measurements of attainment; judgments of third-party observers; perceptions of the CGR participants

Table 9.6 (continued)

Performance Level	Unit of Analysis	Dimension	Defined	Sample Indicators	Potential Data Sources
Adaptation	Participating organizations	Equilibrium	Balance achieved between stability and change (resilience)	Evidence of resilience attributed to the CGR	Organizational records; reported resilience (surveys/interviews)
	CGR	Viability	Capacity to continue to carry out actions and adapt to changing conditions	Maintenance/growth in number of the CGR participants Maintenance/growth of available CGR capacity	Organizational records; strategic plans and financial reports
	Target goals	Sustainability	Ability for targeted effects to be sustained through adaptive responses	Extent to which adaptive responses to impacts are sustained over time	Criteria set for sustainability of target goal attainment; judgments of third-party observers; perceptions of the CGR participants

thirty-four of which were externally directed CGRs launched with funding from the Puget Sound Partnership. The remaining twenty-three CGRs were either self-initiated or independently convened. Their results suggest that when a CGR fosters principled engagement and cultivates the capacity for joint action, the likelihood of reported consultation, planning, or implementation increases both among CGR participant organizations and within larger networks. They also found that increases in three particular measures of principled engagement—awareness of other organizations' interests and values, increased face-to-face communication, and the use of common language—are associated with increases in network ties (with the first two measures being significant). Moreover, they found that increased access to information, human resources, and financial resources (measures of capacity for joint action) are related to increases in network ties. They did not measure shared motivation. Based on their findings, Scott and Thomas (2015) proposed that collaboration dynamics reduce transaction costs, which in turn helps form and strengthen ties between organizations in the CGR and those in other networks. They further suggested that this effect on network ties diminishes with the presence of more overlapping CGRs. These findings support investment in a CGR when collaborators are seeking to cultivate and sustain organizational networks and suggest that the creation of multiple CGRs may be less likely to increase network ties.

In perhaps the most comprehensive empirical research to date of our integrative framework, Ulibarri (2015a) studied the effect of collaboration dynamics and its individual components on specific outcomes across twenty-four hydropower relicensing cases under the Federal Energy Regulatory Commission's alternative or integrated licensing processes. Based on survey research with 270 participants, Ulibarri employed measures for principled engagement, shared motivation, and the capacity for joint action, as well as for outcome variables including perceptions about the decision-making process, the quality of the issued licenses, and predictions by the participants of subsequent effects on the local environment and economy. She found evidence not only of reinforcing relationships between the three components of collaboration dynamics but also of their effect on process performance in terms of decision making and participant satisfaction, and on productivity performance in terms of the perceived quality of the license and predicted environmental and economic changes.

In an extension of her research on Federal Energy Regulatory Commission relicensing, Ulibarri (2015b) compared three different cases with high, medium, and low ratings on collaboration dynamics and found significant differences in the quality of the resulting environmental decisions. For example, she found that high-quality collaboration led to jointly developed and highly implementable operating regimes designed to improve numerous resources, whereas lesser-quality collaboration resulted in operating requirements that ignored environmental concerns raised by stakeholders and lacked implementation provisions. Again, she found that different components and elements of collaboration dynamics have differential effects on process and productivity performance.

In sum, assessing productivity performance is as important as assessing process performance. Indeed, CGRs are created to overcome the limitations of individual action and have meaningful effects on some problematic condition. Without an assessment of productivity performance, it is impossible to ascertain the extent to which CGRs are effective in meeting their goals. We have identified nine dimensions that are likely to be useful for assessing productivity performance, although scholars and practitioners could certainly identify other dimensions that are relevant to the particular CGR of interest. Examining productivity performance at multiple levels and with multiple units of analysis will undoubtedly advance our understanding of collaborative governance regimes. Future empirical research that draws on the entire framework and tests the interactions between process and productivity performance will be especially important.

Summary

In this chapter we reviewed some of the most salient challenges to measuring CGR performance and outlined our approach to assessment. We examined assessment issues related to CGR antecedents and formation, process performance, and productivity performance, each of which captures a set of constituent components and elements in our framework. For each assessment area, we provided definitions, sample indicators, and potential data sources. We concluded with a brief discussion about linking CGR process and productivity performance that synthesizes our argument, uncovers and rethinks underlying assumptions about collaborative governance, and offers specific suggestions for future directions in both practice and research.

Note

1. Some of the material in this chapter was first presented by Emerson and Nabatchi (2015).

Conclusion

Stepping Back, Stepping Up, and Stepping Forward: Summary Observations and Recommendations

Knowledge comes by taking things apart: analysis.
But wisdom comes by putting things together.
—John A. Morrison

We began this book by inviting people to step into the world of collaborative governance and collaborative governance regimes (CGRs). Throughout the chapters, we provided a broad overview of our integrative framework for collaborative governance, and examined and illustrated its individual components in more detail. We also offered a typology of CGRs and a framework for assessing their performance. In this conclusion, we first step back and review our efforts, offering summary observations on collaborative governance and CGRs. We then step up and offer recommendations for improving the design and management of CGRs. Finally, we make recommendations that invite scholars, students, and practitioners to step out into future research on CGRs.

Stepping Back: Summary Observations about Collaborative Governance

As we noted in the introduction, our intention in writing this book was to assist in improving the study and practice of collaborative governance by

1. Helping to make sense of the numerous terms and concepts associated with collaborative governance by offering a broader, more integrated definition and perspective on collaborative governance and its applications;
2. Encouraging more systematic study of collaborative governance through the development of an integrated framework on collaborative governance and the concept of CGRs;
3. Exploring the variations across collaborative arrangements and developing a typology of CGRs; and
4. Contributing to the empirical study of the performance of CGRs.

To do this, we first reviewed the complex provenance of collaborative governance, offered a broader, more integrative definition of collaborative governance, established and developed the concept of a collaborative governance regime, and introduced the integrative framework for collaborative governance (see chapter 1). To help systematize the study of CGRs, we unpacked and explored the constituent dimensions, components, and elements of the integrative framework. Specifically, we identified many conditions in the system context that give rise to CGRs, as well as the essential drivers that propel the formation of CGRs (see chapter 2). We also examined principled engagement, shared motivation, and the capacity for joint action as, respectively, the behavioral, relational, and functional aspects of collaboration dynamics; and we explored how these dynamics contribute to the development of a shared theory of change (see chapter 3). Likewise, we explained the CGR production chain of collaborative actions, outcomes, and adaptation (see chapter 4). Our contributors illustrated the entire integrative framework in a series of case studies (see chapters 5, 6, and 7). To help make sense of CGR variations, we introduced and developed a typology based on formative type, which can be used not only to distinguish between CGR "species" but also to better explain their strengths and weaknesses (see chapter 8). Finally, we presented a framework for thinking about the process and productivity performance of CGRs that can be used to advance empirical study (see chapter 9).

By necessity, we followed a rather linear path in this book, although we repeatedly acknowledged that collaborative governance and CGRs work in interactive and cyclical (nonlinear) ways. Lest we leave readers with any doubt about the complexity of collaborative governance, we offer four additional general observations. First, collaborative governance is not a cure-all; it is neither always feasible nor always desirable—and even when it is feasible and desirable, it will not always work to address the policy issues or circumstances at hand. Second, CGRs are not themselves separate institutional forms, but rather are often embedded within hierarchies and may use market-based approaches to conduct their work. Third, CGRs are different from networks, although we acknowledge that CGRs are embedded within multiple social, organizational, and policy networks and may themselves function as networks. Fourth and finally, not all CGRs are created equal; collaboration is hard work, and success is not guaranteed. We further discuss each of these observations here.

Collaborative Governance Is Not a Cure-All

In this book we have presented several cases to demonstrate how collaborative governance works; but collaborative governance is not always appropriate or successful. Even a cursory examination of the rapidly growing literature on collaborative governance would suggest that scholars are either overtly or cautiously optimistic about its prowess to solve complex problems. And though "cross-sector collaboration is increasingly assumed to be both necessary and desirable as a strategy for addressing many of society's most difficult public challenges" (Bryson, Crosby, and Stone 2006, 44), it is not now—and will never be—a panacea.

Espoused in the notion of collaborative governance are numerous values that many of us hold dear: diversity and inclusion, transparency and shared information, democratic engagement and power sharing. However, as shown in the Comités Técnicas de Aguas Subterraneas (COTAS) Guadalupe case (see chapter 7), these values are not always realized in collaboration, and, in some cases, they may even be undermined. It is important to reiterate that collaborative governance in and of itself is neither inherently good nor inherently bad; its merit lies in the intentions and principles it puts in place. We presented several cases (and can point to several others) where collaborative governance was used to good effect. However, we also provided cases that were less successful, and we can point to other examples where collaborative governance intentionally or inadvertently led to delays or diversions that were not productive.

Further, though cross-sector collaboration is increasingly believed to be necessary and desirable, it is rarely easy. Indeed, collaborative governance is difficult, even under the best of circumstances. It is born out of complex challenges—the decline of a valued ecosystem, the threatened demise of a remote coastal community, the fragmentation of authority in a complex metropolis—that influence and are influenced by myriad issues and that cannot be solved by any one organization or group. It requires the presence of several essential drivers just to get off the ground (see chapter 2), and then it depends on the integration of collaboration dynamics—including the social behavioral processes of principled engagement, the interpersonal relationships built through shared motivation, and the functional structures of the capacity for joint action—to operate and evolve in a timely and effective manner (see chapter 3). It requires the coordination of complex actions that have meaningful outcomes for the CGR, its participants, and, perhaps most important, the target goals, as well as the ability to adapt in light of these outcomes (see chapter 4). When one considers all the pieces that need to come together and interact in some reasonable progression, it is extraordinary that any CGR succeeds and that so many people want to continue collaborative efforts!

That said, and as others have observed, when not managed well, collaborative governance can actually harm individual and organizational relationships and can set back the potential for needed solutions for years to come, as we saw in the COTAS Guadalupe case. And yet the risk of collaborative failure may not be as great as the risk of leaving a troubling public problem unaddressed, as is clear in the Newtok Planning Group case (see chapter 6). Given the seriousness of so many cross-boundary problems, it is worth the effort to seek to better understand CGRs and improve the odds of collaborative success.

CGRs Are Not Distinct Institutional Forms

It can be analytically useful to distinguish collaborative governance and CGRs from other institutional arrangements, such as the command-and-control hierarchy of government bureaucracy and the competitive exchange properties of free markets (e.g., Ansell and Gash 2008; Tang and Mazmanian 2010). Such distinctions help us parse structural differences, identify the challenges specific to each arrangement, and consider which arrangements and related policy instruments are most suitable for specific issues and contexts. Although useful, these institutional differentiations are only simplified heuristics that intentionally overstate these distinctions (see chapter 1).

Indeed, CGRs are more than institutional arrangements. Although CGRs certainly develop (or should develop) procedural and institutional arrangements, they are also fluid, dynamic systems of processes, relationships, capacities, and functions. Furthermore, the participants in CGRs represent public, private, and nonprofit organizations, as well as less formal groups and associations, and must be accountable both to these organizations and to the CGR. The Military Community Compatibility Committee (MC3), for example, was composed of multisectoral representatives who had to attend to their individual missions, motivations, and incentive structures (see chapter 4). In this way, CGRs accommodate and integrate other institutional arrangements through the common drivers that enable CGR formation and through the collaboration dynamics between the participants who work in or represent an array of different organizations and associations.

Moreover, CGRs are not isolated, bounded entities. They can exist within other institutional arrangements, such as when government induces or mandates CGRs, as occurred with the Everglades Restoration Task Force (see chapter 3). Similarly, self-initiated and independently convened CGRs can necessitate or incentivize government involvement, as was the case with MC3, which essentially required the air force base to engage in its deliberations. CGRs can also use markets (to better or worse effect) to accomplish their goals—as, for example, COTAS Guadalupe could have done with water. This interconnectedness makes the distinctions between hierarchy, markets, and collaborative governance even more problematic. In short, CGRs cannot be functionally contrasted with and separated from the hierarchies that sanction or authorize collaborative efforts, especially when CGRs are helping to implement a public program or service. Therefore, CGRs are not orthogonal to hierarchy, but rather are often nested within vertical bureaucracies, if not co-ordinated by them.

CGRs within and beyond Networks

Likewise, CGRs can exist both within and across a variety of formal and informal networks that characterize their larger system context. Numerous overlapping networks influence and are influenced by CGRs: the social networks of the individual participants, the interorganizational networks of participating organizations, and the policy networks operating at different scales. For example, the National Collaborative for Higher Education Policy was embedded in a system context of overlapping state and federal education policy networks (see chapter 2). These myriad networks play a role in interpreting and intervening in the system context in ways that can temper the workings of CGRs and enhance or detract from collaboration dynamics, actions, outcomes, and adaptation.

CGRs themselves may be considered goal-oriented, heterogeneous public networks—as described by Provan, Fish, and Sydow (2007)—a point that we noted in chapter 1. The Greater Toronto Civic Action Alliance is a particularly good representation of this point (see chapter 5). Admittedly, the network literature can contribute much more to our understanding of CGRs. Through our integrated framework, however, we have attempted to explore not only the structures and relational variables prominent in network analysis but also the dynamic processes involved, as well as additional dimensions of agency, leadership, context, and function. We understand CGRs as including multidimensional systems of behavioral processes, interpersonal relationships, and functional capacities. Nonetheless, there remains a direct kinship between CGRs and goal-directed, heterogeneous public networks.

Not All CGRs Are Created Equal

Finally, collaboration across institutional and sectoral boundaries does not come naturally or easily. It is a lot to ask people to engage in the work of CGRs; they face many challenges and complexities along the way. For many, collaboration with others outside their own organization is beyond the scope of their job responsibilities; often, participation in such collaborations is voluntary and uncompensated. Regardless, all the CGR participants need to commit time and energy, and work hard to broaden their perspectives, to pursue multiple goals, and to face conflicts rather than avoid them. The high initial transaction costs can be followed by frustrating efforts to garner the necessary resources to move forward. In efforts to gain some efficiencies, tasks may be prematurely routinized, the time needed for relationship building or repair may not be provided, and process corners may be cut short for expediency. The participants' expectations may often be too high at the outset, and early collective ambitions may be easily dashed. After the low-hanging fruit of those first collaborative actions is harvested, the reach to tougher and more taxing issues can often be too high. The hoped-for cooperative spirit and egalitarian process may be easily tarnished by the inevitable power imbalances that may well go unaddressed. Process fatigue, burnout, and turnover are also all too common occurrences. However, as some of the cases in this book illustrate, many CGRs persist despite these challenges, and sometimes the participants are justly rewarded.

Nevertheless, the cases in this book make clear that all CGRs are neither created equal nor perform equally well. Moreover—given CGRs' multidimensional, dynamic, and complex natures—no single factor can predict their success. The practice literature offers sound guidance and suggestions for how to convene and facilitate collaborative processes based on valuable first-hand professional experience. But less guidance is available on how to design and manage complex governance systems like CGRs over time. In the next section, we draw on the ideas and cases presented in this book to identify several avenues through which the design and management of CGRs can be improved.

Stepping Up: Strengthening Collaborative Governance Regimes

CGRs may be convened, designed, led, and managed by many different individuals in different positions with different degrees of formal authority. Some groups may fully self-manage (as appears to be the case in the National Collaborative for Higher Education), others may rotate that role (as was done in the Everglades Restoration Task Force), and still others may seek assistance from professional third-party facilitators or be coordinated by external agencies (as was the case with MC3). Depending on the CGR type, the actors who are instrumental in guiding it may be initiating leaders, independent conveners, external agents, professional facilitators, participants, stakeholders, or others. Thus, our suggestions for improving CGR design and management are intended for any and all CGR players who can help assess, design, direct, or manage the operation and performance of CGRs. For purposes of simplicity, in this section we sometimes use the general term "collaborators" to refer to the relevant persons who play various influential roles in different types of

CGRs.[1] We use this term instead of "participants" when referring specifically to core actors, who may or may not include the initiating leaders, but whose collective and proactive responsibility are required to make CGRs work—and work better.

Improving CGR Design

The appropriateness and feasibility of collaborative governance are often simply assumed. However, rather than jumping into designing and planning for a CGR, time should be taken to assess whether collaborative governance is needed and practical in the given situation. Conducting a situation assessment can help the potential collaborators answer these questions, and can also inform the design, formation, and management of a CGR.

Conducting Situation Assessments

Situation (or conflict) assessments have been recommended as a best practice for decades in the fields of alternative dispute resolution and consensus building. This guidance is also warranted for CGRs; and, based on our framework, we emphasize the importance of carefully assessing both the system context and the essential drivers *before* recommending, let alone designing, any CGR. In chapter 2, we identified several conditions in the broader system context that are useful to explore. Initiating leaders should carefully analyze these contextual conditions—in terms of both the opportunities and constraints they create—before attempting to launch a collaborative effort. Some of these conditions may pose risks to or discourage CGR formation, whereas others might derail collaborative efforts down the line; therefore, current, prior, and potential future conditions in the system context should be considered. Moreover, leaders should pay particular attention to public resource or service conditions, because these often provide the rationale and target goal for embarking on a collaborative effort. CGRs are generally created to address a public problem, and doing so requires understanding the surrounding set of conditions that create, aggravate, or sustain that problem. Changing the conditions in the system context is an inherently long-term and complex endeavor; the clearer the collaborators are at the start about the conditions targeted for change, the more likely the CGR is to be successful in setting actionable target goals. Thorough situation assessments were conducted in the National Collaborative for Higher Education and MC3 cases, but not in the COTAS Guadalupe case.

From the system context emerge several drivers for collaboration (see chapter 2). As is evident in the cases, all these drivers—uncertainty, interdependence, consequential incentives, and initiating leadership—will be present to some degree and level of salience to bring the collaborators together and activate the initial cycle of collaboration dynamics. A situation assessment can gauge the sufficiency of these drivers and test the timeliness and appropriateness of undertaking a collaborative effort. Numerous questions can guide such an assessment: What underlying uncertainties inhibit progress? Is there interdependence between the actors, and how well is it recognized? Are there sufficient incentives for collaboration, and what are the consequences of not collaborating? Who are (or should be) the initiating leaders? Are these drivers likely to remain stable enough to warrant an extended collaborative commitment?

If the combination of drivers is insufficient or unstable, then further consideration needs to be given before launching a CGR. For example, if uncertainty or interdependence is not recognized, then the collaborators might need to convince the key stakeholders of their existence. If consequential incentives are absent or unacknowledged, then perhaps it is premature to launch such an undertaking. Key actors may first need to be made aware of and come to appreciate the consequences of inaction or alternative courses of action. Moreover, in contemplating these drivers, the initiating leaders must also pay attention to framing the central issue(s) in a broad and inclusive manner, to articulating a strategic vision for collaboration, and to creating the climate and opportunity necessary for a successful first convening of the potential participants. These points are well demonstrated in the Toronto Civic Action case, where David Pecaut gave a meaningful and impactful keynote address at the 2002 summit that galvanized support for the formation of the CGR.

Creating a CGR

Once the collaborators have completed the initial assessment of the system context and have considered whether there are sufficient drivers, they can then make more informed decisions about whether and why a CGR is needed. If their analyses suggest that a CGR is feasible and desirable, then comes the task of creating and designing it. Here, people must nimbly move back and forth between inviting the potential participants, designing initial meetings, and continuing assessments. These invitation, design, and assessment steps are not linear, but rather cyclical and integrative. For example, assessments may yield insights about CGR design and membership, but as the participants come to the table, more assessments must be done and additional design considerations are likely to emerge.

As we noted in chapter 2, these steps can be made easier if the collaborators do their homework—not only in terms of conducting initial assessments of the system context and drivers but also in terms of identifying the appropriate participants, understanding why they will (or will not) want to come together, and creating an attractive forum for collaboration. To do so, the collaborators should consider the incentives for collaboration, as well as the costs and benefits of participation, in terms of transaction costs, power sharing, resources, time, and effort. They should seek to involve those with credibility and legitimacy, talents and resources, and collaborative attitudes and dispositions. They should issue direct and personal invitations that articulate shared concerns and values and speak to the importance of collaboration—as was done, for example, in the MC3 case.

In addition, representation and diversity among the participants are important factors to consider at the design stage. Representation and diversity convey critical normative values, such as equality and inclusion. Thus, having a purposefully broad range of participants at the table signifies to all that these values matter to the CGR and its work. Beyond their intrinsic value, however, representation and diversity also have instrumental value. When individuals are confronted by a greater diversity of people, they are also inevitably confronted by a greater diversity of views and ideas. In certain circumstances, this exposure could easily lead to confrontation and conflict; but when tolerance and an appreciation of differences are cultivated through principled engagement, people are more likely to understand and empathize with others, become more open-minded, learn more, and engage in a deeper consideration of issues. Cultivating this tolerance and appreciation can be made easier if the norms of reciprocity and trust are developed up front—in part, by engaging the participants in the design of the CGR and in further situation assessments.

Of course, how and by whom such assessments are conducted will vary, particularly by CGR type (see chapter 8), as will the attention paid to CGR design and participant invitations. These differences can easily be seen by contrasting CGR formation in the MC3 case to that in the COTAS Guadalupe case. Regardless of whether a CGR is self-initiated, independently convened, or externally directed, the collaborators should keep in mind that to the extent the participants can design the CGR system together, revisit that design periodically in response to internal and external changes, and engage in assessments of the broader system context and issues at hand, the more invested the participants will be in their CGR.

Self-initiated CGRs, such as Toronto's Civic Action and the Newtok Planning Group, arise organically at the grassroots level and involve people who are directly affected by the situation at hand, and thus are likely to be the least intentionally designed as they are being formed. Situation assessments are likely to be a matter of self-discovery, and at least initially narrowly focused, with the participants working through immediate differences and issues. In self-initiated CGRs, the collaborators need to help ensure that the participants take a broader perspective. The participants should be cognizant not only of the full system context and all the drivers, but also of the influence the system context and drivers can and will have on their efforts. Doing so may lessen concerns about engaging those with authority and influence and can help ensure diversity and representation among the CGR participants and perspectives.

Independently convened CGRs, such as the National Collaborative for Higher Education and MC3, are led by a neutral, boundary-spanning organization or professional facilitator, and thus are the most likely to be designed intentionally in a way that is consistent with best practices. However, although the conveners may bring process knowledge to the table, they may lack in-depth contextual knowledge about the specific situation and the players on the ground. Thus, though the conveners may assist in the assessment process and may recommend appropriate first steps, the collaborators must be sure that both the conveners and the participants are fully engaged in a comprehensive examination of the system context and drivers.

Externally directed CGRs, such as the Everglades Restoration Task Force and COTAS Guadalupe cases, are encouraged or induced from above, at the grasstops level, and may pay the least attention to CGR design, given that mandates may already spell out many specifics. As both cases demonstrate, however, no mandate can speak to all the issues that need to be addressed, and the collaborators will have many opportunities to exercise design discretion. Thus, in externally directed CGRs, the collaborators would be well served by providing support and an appropriate time frame to underwrite a grounded assessment and design process that involve all the participants.

Improving CGR Management

We have discussed numerous implications for managing CGRs throughout the chapters of this book. Here, we draw on our framework and the cases in this book to touch on some of the most salient recommendations, including the strengthening of collaboration dynamics, making explicit the shared theory of change, cultivating leaders and leadership, improving the participants' accountability, thinking toward implementation, and measuring performance.

Strengthening Collaboration Dynamics

In our framework, we deconstruct and delineate the basic components that enable the collaborators to forge effective cross-boundary CGRs (see chapter

3). It falls to the collaborators to guide the collaboration dynamics in the field—and, as the cases show, this is done more successfully in some cases (e.g., MC3, Civic Action, and the Newtok Planning Group) than in others (e.g., COTAS Guadalupe). Thus, understanding the evolving interplay between principled engagement, shared motivation, and the capacity for joint action, as well as recognizing overall variations in collaboration dynamics as a function of CGR type, are useful tasks for all involved with a CGR. The collaborators may consider drawing on some of the indicators we suggest in chapter 9 to appraise the various components and elements of collaboration dynamics.

Particular attention should be paid to the extent to which the engagement between the participants is indeed "principled." In chapter 3, we explained the meaning of principled engagement, and in chapter 8, we suggested that principled engagement may be easier in some types of CGRs than in others— for example, in self-initiated or independently convened CGRs as opposed to externally directed CGRs. Regardless, the collaborators should recognize principled engagement as more than simple mechanics; it entails the active cultivation and realization of behavioral standards and ideals. Operating norms—such as transparency, inclusion, civility, integration, fair dealing, good faith participation, and similar values—can be elicited from the participants and incorporated into a group charter or serve to guide more concrete process ground rules. Breaches in conduct should be addressed early on as the group sets expectations for participation. To jump-start or accelerate principled engagement, it may be useful to conduct process training, rotate the manager role, or bring in an outside facilitator or coach to advise the group during its formation or at critical junctures.

Much could be said about how to initiate and improve the cycling of discovery, definition, deliberation, and determination. But here, suffice it to say that one can think about process at the micro level (e.g., when working through a single agenda item in the Everglades Restoration Task Force), at the meso level (e.g., when developing an initial shared theory of change in the initial MC3 meetings), or at the macro level (e.g., when contemplating the longer temporal scale for the relocation of the entire Newtok community through collaborative actions, likely outcomes, and potential consequent adaptations). Regardless of the decision-making level (or the type of CGR), the collaborators will be well served by noting the sequence of the principled engagement cycle: discovery through information exchange and research, definitional work involving clear framing and shared language, full deliberative discourse, and reasoned determinations based on objective criteria.

The dynamic linkage between principled engagement and shared motivation evolves over time and takes shape in different ways, depending, in part, on the CGR type. All CGRs, however, require longer-term dedication from the participants for success, and dedication requires ongoing trust, mutual understanding, internal legitimacy, and commitment. The collaborators can be instrumental in cultivating and monitoring shared motivation within CGRs. They can create opportunities to build relationships before and after regular meetings, through formal and informal exchanges, in special workshops or at retreats, and by scheduling one-to-one and small group conversations. They can track levels of shared motivation through the direct observation of group interactions and through short surveys or informal check-ins with the group as a whole, or on an individual basis. Moreover, they can increase shared motivation by modeling open, trustworthy, and reliable behavior. Their consistency and dependability will also assist in sustaining shared motivation over the life of a CGR.

The value and timing for generating specific capacities for joint action depends on many factors. Some level of procedural and institutional arrangements, leadership, knowledge, and resources will be required at the outset, and to varying degrees throughout the life of a CGR. We noted in chapter 8 that different types of CGRs are likely to lead with different capacities for joint action. If the collaborators understand the strengths and weaknesses of their CGR capacity, then they can build on assets, address deficiencies, and anticipate needs over time. Moreover, the participants can be engaged in pinpointing the needs and identifying resources and opportunities for building the capacity for joint action. The more all the CGR participants understand and appreciate the importance of capacities for joint action, the more they will be able to assess whether and when to take specific collaborative actions.

Making Explicit the Shared Theory of Change

The field of collaborative problem solving has given much attention to framing. For framing, it is critical to get people to focus on and understand the problem or issue at hand through a common lens. Although principled engagement, with its focus on creating a shared language and shared perspective on the nature and scope of the target condition, speaks to the concept of framing, this alone is insufficient. The collaborators must also help the CGR and all its participants articulate a shared theory of change, or a collective strategy to guide the CGR's actions.

The shared theory of change should be derived from the group's collective understanding of the problem and its careful deliberation about what is needed to address it. This may seem an unnecessary specification to some, but just as people bring their own frames about the problem to the table, so too do they bring their own assumptions about how to solve it. In some cases, strategies may be obvious (as they were in MC3), though in others they may be obscured or constrained by ideologies, resources, or opportunities that direct CGR action from the outset (as they were in COTAS Guadalupe). Before jumping to strategies, however, we encourage all involved with a CGR to spend time deliberating about their assumptions (a feature that helped improve the work of the Everglades Restoration Task Force). Careful and creative thinking at the initial stages of work might produce more effective or efficient paths forward, or lead back to entirely different ways of framing the problem.

Ideally, a CGR will articulate a shared theory of change in the early stages of its work; however, in some cases, the theory of change cannot be specified until after several rounds of collaboration dynamics. In most cases, a CGR will need to periodically adjust its theory of change so as to respond or adapt to its actions and their outcomes, as happened with Civic Action. To improve a CGR's processes and productivity, we recommend making this shared theory of change explicit so that everyone understands and agrees not only on the CGR's collective purposes and target goals but also on its chosen means for achieving them.

Cultivating Leaders and Leadership

We have mentioned several times the importance of leaders in collaborative governance, and the cases in this book bear this out (for a summary of leadership roles, see box 3.1 in chapter 3). Leaders are critical for driving the formation of a CGR, are important as facilitators of collaboration dynamics, and are significant as an element of a CGR's capacity for joint action. The participants themselves must be leaders at the table advocating for their interests, as well as in their home organization representing the CGR's progress and requirements. And a CGR fosters strong collaborative leadership as an intermediate outcome of collaboration dynamics. Simply put, CGRs demand more leadership, not less.

To meet this important and ever-present demand for leaders and leadership, the collaborators should have a clear understanding of the attributes and skills that leaders need in their various positions and roles. In this regard, there has been fruitful empirical research on collaborative leadership competencies that can inform those who are managing CGRs (e.g., see Emerson and Smutko 2011; Getha-Taylor 2006, 2008; Linden 2010; O'Leary, Choi, and Gerard 2012; O'Leary and Gerard 2012).

When there are leadership voids or barriers, CGRs will face tougher internal challenges, along with greater threats to external legitimacy. Therefore, the collaborators will be more likely to strengthen the CGR and its activities if they look for these qualities and competencies when identifying initiating leaders and selecting participants, and if they cultivate these skills and abilities among CGR participants during collaboration dynamics. Again, this speaks to the need for diversity and representation among participants. Although there has been considerable case study research confirming the importance of such leadership (e.g., see the case on Civic Action), further comparative research on the extent to which shared and multiple leadership roles contribute to the collaborative process and productivity performance would be very useful, a point that Allison Bramwell makes in chapter 5.

Improving the Participants' Accountability

For CGR participants to become collaborative leaders, they must carefully manage the multiple accountabilities expected in collaboration. The participants must reconcile at least four levels of accountability: (1) to the organization or constituency they represent, (2) to their own values and their professional training and ethics, (3) to the CGR itself, and (4) to the broader public interest. As seen in the Newtok Planning Group case, when these four accountabilities are generally in sync, the participants are better able to advocate clearly and consistently for their interests and values within the CGR. But when these accountabilities are in tension, as they were in the Everglades Restoration Task Force, the participants may experience internal conflict and cognitive dissonance, and may struggle to be effective players. These accountability tensions are especially amplified when the represented organizations or constituencies are diverse and are divided over how to pursue various positions and strategies, and even over whether participation in a CGR is appropriate.

The collaborators should not only be mindful of these potential tensions but also look for ways to reduce them. During principled engagement, the collaborators can help the participants articulate their multiple accountabilities, acknowledge that perfect alignment is unlikely to occur at the outset (and indeed may never occur in some instances), and encourage all the participants to appreciate others' challenges. In some collaborative settings, it may be possible for the group to work through some of these tensions together, as occurred in MC3 with the assistance of an independent facilitator. In turn, this can strengthen process performance, particularly in terms of building trust, mutual understanding, internal legitimacy, and commitment through the cycle of shared motivation.

The collaborators can also help the group set explicit expectations for the participants with respect to representation and communication with their organizations or constituents. This may be more automatic for those CGRs whose participants are from more formal, grasstops organizations, such as the Everglades Restoration Task Force and the National Higher Education Collaborative, but less automatic for grassroots CGRs, whose participants may be less familiar with such responsibilities. This can later become problematic as the CGR starts making group determinations and committing to joint actions. Many initial misalignments in accountability are likely to be discovered at this juncture. Encouraging the participants to communicate regularly with their home organizations, and to report back to the CGR, can help identify emergent tensions and potential steps for reducing them. Perhaps most important, clarifying the participant organizations' expectations and abilities can contribute to the institutional arrangements and procedures that strengthen the capacity for joint action.

Thinking toward Implementation

One of the important definitional properties of CGRs is their collaborative decision-making function. In chapter 3, we described decision making as determinations, an element of principled engagement. Collaborative decisions are also a significant intermediate output of CGRs. In some cases, single decisions are used by researchers as the final benchmark for successful collaborative performance. On occasion, researchers will attempt to assess the degree to which these decisions were consensus based. In our view, whether the group reached a decision and the degree to which that decision was consensual are important but incomplete measures of productivity performance. Such measures sidestep the more critical performance measures of outcomes and ignore the full range of productivity dimensions discussed in chapter 9.

The collaborators can strengthen their CGR's performance by prompting the full group to consider how well decisions align with the shared theory of change, along with the degree to which such decisions are representative of what is expected from its effective implementation. In short, the collaborators should consider whether the decision is actionable, whether such actions are likely to result in outcomes that meet the target goal, and whether the anticipated outcomes may lead to adaptations in the system context or in the CGR itself.

Of course, the degree to which CGRs have implementation authority can vary by formative type, as well as by collective purpose and shared goals. However, even when CGRs do not have the formal authority to act (e.g., as would be the case for CGRs that are established in an advisory capacity, much like MC3 or COTAS Guadalupe), they can still influence action directly and indirectly, by activating the CGR participants, their surrounding networks, and other agents. Thus, those involved in CGRs should consider not only what can be doable immediately through direct action but also what might be possible through indirect means.

Measuring Performance

As we discussed in chapter 9, it is important to measure process performance in terms of collaboration dynamics and to measure productivity performance in terms of actions, outcomes, and adaptation. For the collaborators, performance measurement can be used to improve the operation of CGRs and to demonstrate their successes. For researchers, performance measurement can help determine what works when, where, why, how, and to what effect. We encourage everyone to use the indicators and units of analysis we identified in chapter 9 to aid in measuring collaborative performance.

Throughout this book, we have articulated several aspects of what goes into the "doing" of collaboration. Given the centrality of collaboration dynamics in our framework and growing research on the importance of process performance, we encourage collaborators to periodically set aside time for group reflection, appraisal, and feedback. Strengthening collaboration entails reflective practice and thus thoughtful consideration not just of "what we have done" but also of "how we are doing." By understanding the components and elements of collaboration dynamics, collaborators can better determine appropriate strategies and interventions and gauge group progress within CGRs. And the ultimate collaborative achievement may well be enlisting the CGR participants in assessing the condition of their own principled engagement, shared motivation, and capacity for joint action, and encouraging them to consider how to best strengthen their own collaboration dynamics.

Measuring performance should not be limited to CGR collaboration dynamics; productivity performance is also critically important. We encourage collaborators to have explicit discussions about what success looks like with respect to achieving target goals, meeting participating organizations' needs, and strengthening the CGR as a whole. Using these different perspectives (or units of analysis, as we refer to them in chapter 9), collaborators can consider how best to measure productivity performance at the levels of CGR actions, outcomes, and adaptation. Some measures may be well within the capacity of the CGR to evaluate. Others may require identifying available resources to support external evaluations. It may be possible to reduce the costs of independent evaluations by documenting CGR activities and by keeping meeting minutes, writing reports, making internal assessments, conducting participant surveys, taking notes, and maintaining other records about CGR pursuits, target goals, and expectations of progress toward their achievement.

Stepping Forward: Researching Collaborative Governance Regimes

Scholars and researchers from a variety of disciplines and from countries around the world have been studying collaborative governance for years, and in some cases, decades. They have developed (and continue to develop) a rich and robust literature on the topic—ranging from conceptual frameworks to theoretical propositions to empirical and meta-analyses. We have stood on their broad shoulders while writing this book. Many of these scholars have offered excellent research agendas on collaboration and collaborative governance (e.g., Ansell and Gash 2008; Bingham and O'Leary 2008; O'Leary and Bingham 2009). We do not wish to duplicate those efforts; here, we simply offer suggestions that pertain specifically to future research on our integrative framework for collaborative governance and CGRs. We are particularly interested in research that tests, critiques, and expands this framework. Depending on their disciplines, perspectives, and interests, some scholars may study the individual components and/or elements of CGRs (as we demonstrated in the case illustrations in chapters 2, 3, and 4), whereas others may study CGRs as a whole (as our contributing authors demonstrated with their case studies in chapters 5, 6, and 7).

Examining the Parts of Collaborative Governance Regimes

The integrative framework for collaborative governance distinguishes between numerous components and elements—from system context and external drivers through collaboration dynamics to actions, outcomes, and adaptation. Each component and its subsidiary elements are worthy of further investigation. In what follows, we focus on the research questions we find to be particularly interesting, though one could identify dozens more.

Getting Started: The System Context and Drivers

We believe that closer attention to the system context and drivers could generate a better understanding of how various conditions influence CGRs at the outset and affect them over time. Do certain conditions matter more or less depending on CGR variations? How do changing conditions or stochastic events in the system context affect the evolution of a CGR? With respect to drivers, does our argument hold that all four exist to some degree and configuration when CGRs are initiated? How do these drivers function together and work over time? Do certain drivers matter more in certain cases? If so, why and how? How might variations in the presence and strength of the drivers, or in the combinations of drivers, affect the initial nature of CGRs, their evolution over time, and their staying power? It would also be helpful to explore the interplay between the system context and drivers: What is the relationship between the system context, the drivers, and the formative CGR type?

Becoming Operational: Collaboration Dynamics

Four sets of important research questions about collaboration dynamics deserve attention. First, it would be helpful to know more about each of the components of collaboration dynamics—principled engagement, shared motivation, and the capacity for joint action—as well as their respective subsidiary elements. How, for example, does the cycling of the elements in each component evolve over time? Can we characterize different modes or phases of component development?

Second, it would be useful for scholars to look at the development of the components (and the relationships between the components) in light of collaboration dynamics as a whole. What factors help or hinder the functioning of collaboration dynamics? How do the components contribute to and reinforce collaboration dynamics? If one component breaks down, can other components be used to rebuild it? Such questions are particularly important, given that collaboration dynamics are not linear, with easily separate components and elements, a point raised by the authors of both the Everglades Restoration Task Force and the Newtok Planning Group cases (see chapters 3 and 6).

Third, we would like to see research that gives more attention to the development of a CGR's shared theory of change. How important is it to make a CGR's theory of change explicit? Can a CGR succeed with implicit or tacit assumptions about its course of action? How do collaboration dynamics feed into the development of a shared theory of change?

Fourth and finally, issues of power are inherent throughout our framework; power is implicitly embedded in every component and weaves throughout the whole framework, much like leadership. However, we have not treated it sufficiently in our work, a point Chantelise Pells makes in chapter 7. More critical examinations of power in CGRs, and particularly in collaboration dynamics, would be useful. For example, how do power and differential power relations affect principled engagement, contribute to or detract from shared motivation, and enhance or damage the capacity for joint action?

Doing Implementation: Actions, Outcomes, and Adaptation

Issues of implementation and performance are particularly fertile, albeit challenging, areas for future research, because the empirical study of actions and outcomes is often confined to indirect measures based on post hoc participant perceptions, and very little work has been done on adaptation. It will be important to connect the rich literature on policy implementation to the productivity performance of collaborative governance.

To help draw these connections, it would be useful for scholars to address several questions: Does effective implementation depend on who is executing the actions? How does implementation change when actions are taken by the CGR itself, its agents, one or more of its participants, or external authorities or jurisdictions? What types of actions and outcomes are most likely to lead to adaptation? And how is adaptation within a CGR different from organizational change within a single institution?

Examining Collaborative Governance Regimes as a Whole

The integrative framework not only enables scholars to examine CGRs' individual components and elements but also facilitates research on CGRs as a whole. More interdisciplinary research from this macro perspective would be useful for theory building on complex, multilevel systems. We have identified four macro-level research areas of particular interest: CGR types and variations, process and productivity performance, building data sets for comparative case analyses, and building theory and models.

First, we need additional research on CGR types and variations. In chapter 8, we laid out a typology of CGRs. Specifically, we identified three overarching types of regimes—self-initiated, independently convened, and externally directed—each of which is distinguished by a set of prevailing conditions and characteristics and patterns of collaboration dynamics. We would like to see researchers explore and test this typology. Are these three formative types useful, and do they capture the essential differences among CGR variations? Are the assumptions and implicit propositions in the typology accurate? With respect to productivity, do different CGR types perform differently? For example, do self-initiated CGRs produce actions more closely aligned with their shared intentions and theory of change, given the engagement of the leaders and participants most directly affected by the targeted conditions? Do independently convened CGRs produce actions that are more equitably distributed among beneficiaries, given that the interests of all the contending participants must be negotiated and balanced? Do externally directed CGRs produce actions with greater efficiency for the participating organizations, depending on how well the CGR is designed and resourced?

Along with others, and particularly Ansell and Gash (2008), we have asserted that the advancement of research on collaborative governance requires moving from the species to the genus; however, we also believe that more work needs to be done to better understand the species of CGRs. Examining multiple CGR applications, particularly in light of the typology, would help to advance theory and also our ability to systematically and empirically assess CGRs.

Second, we believe that our understanding of collaborative governance and CGRs can be improved by paying more attention to process and productivity performance. In chapter 9, we demonstrated how the integrative framework translates easily from a visual and conceptual representation of CGRs to a logic model that can be used to assess CGR process and productivity performance. In that chapter, we also identified numerous research questions worthy of investigation. We believe that better assessing the performance of CGRs will lead to a clearer understanding of what works (and does not) when, where, why, and how.

Of course, better performance assessment also requires better measurement and better instruments, and developing these tools would be invaluable. Moreover, it will be useful for researchers to approach performance measurement using different methods. Numerous research approaches can contribute to our knowledge—including, for example, network analysis, narrative analysis, process tracing, and statistical testing. It should be clear that multiple methodologies are needed to capture the multidimensional nature of collaborative governance and CGRs.

Third, not only does the integrative framework provide a tool for better understanding CGR types, variations, and performance, but it also enables the possibility for large-n, comparative studies. If researchers were to use the framework consistently and over time, it would be possible to create data sets of cases for comparative analyses. For example, data from multiple cases could be compared or aggregated to assess the influence of an array of factors or conditions on individual outcomes.

Fourth and finally, we made clear at the start of this book that our integrative framework is just that—a framework. We have specified a general set of variables and the relationships between them so as to guide further inquiry about collaborative governance and CGRs. Now, we look to others to refine this framework by building and using theory to explain and predict how the variables interact, and by developing models to test hypotheses (for more on the difference between frameworks, theories, and models, see box 1.1 in chapter 1). However, just as CGRs traverse sectoral, organizational, and jurisdictional boundaries, so too should scholars traverse research boundaries—both disciplinary and methodological.

Stepping Out

Our search for integration and synthesis has helped give shape and meaning to our understanding of collaborative governance and CGRs. We have tried to assemble what we see as the critical pieces of the collaborative governance puzzle into a coherent whole. In doing so, we have stepped across many conceptual and disciplinary boundaries (but hopefully not stepped on too many toes). We hope this book inspires scholars and practitioners alike to take similar risks in striving to integrate and expand the boundaries of theoretical and practical knowledge to advance creative work in collaborative governance.

Scholars in all research fields, not just public administration and management, tend to compartmentalize knowledge into different schools of thought, concepts, and approaches. We intentionally place disciplinary blinders on our research. In practice, however, we need to synthesize and integrate our knowledge into informed action. Because our framework draws on and applies knowledge and concepts from a wide range of fields, we hope it will be relevant to those studying and working in several diverse applications and settings. We encourage scholars to explore this rich complexity more fully and to search for integrative theories, research designs, and methods that are more agile at handling multiple variables and interactions.

The need to explore and explain collaborative governance is not likely to fade away any time soon. The conditions that have given rise to its practice will be with us for decades to come. Moreover, as we improve both our understanding and practice of collaborative governance, it is more likely to gain increasing traction and prominence over time. Within the fields of public administration and public management, we face the complex task of preparing the next generation of scholars and practitioners to work in an increasingly complex network of interdependent organizations and sectors. We hope this book contributes to this important work and encourages scholars, practitioners, and students to step out of their silos and into the world of collaborative governance.

Note

1. As noted in chapter 1, we recognize that the term "collaborators" has negative historical connotations; however, in this chapter, we use this word not in a pejorative sense but rather in its original, literal sense, to refer to those who choose to collaborate, to co-labor, to work together to get things done.

Glossary

adaptation refers to the transformative changes, or to the small but significant adjustments, that are made in response to the outcomes of collaborative actions. Adaptation can occur within the collaborative governance regime, between the participant organizations, and in the target goals.

capacity for joint action is a component of collaboration dynamics. It refers to the functional assets available to the collaborative governance regime (CGR), and it consists of four elements:

- *procedural/institutional arrangements:* the protocols and structures for managing a CGR over time;
- *leadership:* the variety of roles taken on by CGR participants to carry out various functions;
- *knowledge:* the generation, sharing, and analysis of information, data, and expertise; and
- *resources:* the acquisition of human, technological, financial, and other assets needed to achieve the CGR's collective purpose.

collaboration dynamics is a dimension of the integrative framework for collaborative governance. It refers to the progressive and iterative cycling of three components—principled engagement, shared motivation, and the capacity for joint action—which takes place over time between collaborative governance regime participants and between participants and their parent organizations. Collaboration dynamics, along with collaborative actions, constitute collaborative governance regimes.

collaborative actions refer to the intentional efforts taken as a consequence of the shared theory of change developed by the collaborative governance regime during collaboration dynamics to achieve its collective purpose and target goals. Collaborative actions (along with collaboration dynamics) constitute collaborative governance regimes.

collaborative governance refers to the processes and structures of public policy decision making and management that engage people across the boundaries of public agencies, levels of government, and/or the public, private for-profit, and civic spheres to carry out a public purpose that could not otherwise be accomplished.

collaborative governance regime (CGR) denotes a particular mode of, or system for, public decision making in which cross-boundary collaboration represents the prevailing pattern of behavior and activity between autonomous participants who have come together to achieve some collective purpose defined by one or more target goals. CGRs are constituted by both collaboration dynamics and collaborative actions.

consequential incentives, one of the four drivers of collaborative governance regime formation, include internal issues, resource needs, interests, or opportunities and external situational or institutional crises, threats, or opportunities that must be addressed to mitigate salient risk or advance desired conditions for key stakeholders and the broader public.

cross-boundary collaboration refers to the need for, or the activity of, collaboration between people from different organizations, sectors, or jurisdictions.

drivers refer to the combination of four specific factors—uncertainty, interdependence, consequential incentives, and initiating leadership—that help propel the creation of a collaborative governance regime.

externally directed collaborative governance regimes (CGRs) are one type of CGR. They are formed by initiating leaders with a more removed or indirect stake in addressing extensive, recurring policy challenges, and who are situated in agencies or organizations with explicit, concentrated authority in the subject policy area. These CGRs develop through a formally structured approach that creates incentives or mandates for participants whose collective autonomy is constrained or directed to some extent by the authorized collaborative structure.

governance refers to the act of governing, or how actors use processes and make decisions to exercise authority and control, grant power, take action, and ensure performance—all of which are guided by the sets of principles, norms, roles, and procedures around which actors converge.

independently convened collaborative governance regimes (CGRs) are one type of CGR. They are formed by initiating leaders who can bridge differences to address complex policy challenges where multiple, often overlapping authorities are involved. These CGRs are intentionally designed to provide a process and structure attractive to the disparate stakeholders who are encouraged or induced to participate. The group's autonomy is assisted by the impartial facilitation and guidance of the third-party convener.

initiating leadership, one of the four drivers of collaborative governance regime formation, refers to the presence and actions of a person or core group that stimulates interest in and instigates preliminary discussions about creating a collaborative endeavor.

interdependence, one of the four drivers of collaborative governance regime formation, refers to the acknowledged necessity of mutual reliance between groups and organizations to accomplish desired goals.

outcomes refer to the intermediate changes in conditions necessary to reach target goals and the end effects of accomplishing these goals. Outcomes are a consequence of collaborative actions.

principled engagement is a component of collaboration dynamics. It refers to the behavioral interactions between collaborative governance regime (CGR) participants and consists of four elements:

- *discovery:* the identification and analysis of relevant information, interests, and values;
- *definition:* the effort to build shared meaning around concepts, terms, and issues relevant to a CGR;
- *deliberation:* the use of candid and reasoned discussion to address issues; and
- *determinations:* the procedural and substantive decisions reached by a CGR.

process performance refers to the level of functioning of collaboration dynamics that emerges from the combined interactions of principled engagement, shared motivation, and the capacity for joint action.

productivity performance refers to the actions (or outputs) of the collaborative governance regime and the resulting outcomes and adaptation they generate.

public governance describes the processes and institutions for public decision making and action that include actors from the governmental, private for-profit, and nonprofit sectors. It consists of legal frameworks that regulate the production and delivery of publicly supported goods and services and guide collective decision making.

self-initiated collaborative governance regimes (CGRs) are one type of CGR. They are formed by initiating leaders with a direct stake in addressing acute policy challenges where responsible authorities are diffuse and fragmented. These CGRs develop in an ad hoc, emergent manner, and engage stakeholders who participate voluntarily and have a high level of group autonomy.

shared motivation is a component of collaboration dynamics. It refers to the interpersonal relations between collaborative governance regime (CGR) participants, and consists of four elements:

- *trust:* confidence in the reliability, truthfulness, and abilities of others;
- *mutual understanding:* appreciation and tolerance of differences;
- *internal legitimacy:* beliefs about the worthiness and credibility of the CGR and its participants; and
- *commitment:* dedication and responsibility to CGR, its collective purpose, target goals, and theory of change.

shared theory of change refers to the strategy developed during collaboration dynamics for achieving the collective purpose and target goals of the collaborative governance regime.

system context is a dimension in the integrative framework for collaborative governance. It refers to the broad and dynamic set of surrounding conditions that create opportunities and constraints for initiating and sustaining collaborative governance regimes. Included among the many important conditions in the system context are public resource or service conditions, policy and legal frameworks, socioeconomic and cultural characteristics, network characteristics, political dynamics and power relations, and the history of conflict.

uncertainty, one of the four drivers of collaborative governance regime formation, describes situations of doubt and limited information about future conditions, events, availability of resources, or decisions by other actors.

References

ACE (US Army Corps of Engineers). 2006. *Alaska Village Erosion Technical Assistance Program: An Examination of Erosion Issues in the Communities of Bethel, Dillingham, Kaktovik, Kivalina, Newtok, Shishmaref, and Unalakleet.* Anchorage: ACE.

————. 2008a. *Revised Environmental Assessment: Finding of No Significant Impact—Newtok Evacuation Center, Mertarvik, Nelson Island, Alaska.* Anchorage: ACE.

————. 2008b. *Section 117 Project Fact Sheet.* Anchorage: ACE.

————. 2009. *Study Findings and Technical Report: Alaska Baseline Erosion Assessment.* Anchorage: ACE.

ACE and SFWMD (US Army Corps of Engineers and South Florida Water Management District). 2013. "Central Everglades Planning Project: Facts and Information." www.evergladesrestoration.gov/content/cepp/cepp.html.

Acheson, James M. 2006. "Institutional Failure in Resource Management." *Annual Review of Anthropology* 35 (1): 117–34.

ACIA. 2004. *Arctic Climate Impact Assessment.* Cambridge: Cambridge University Press.

Agassiz, Louis. 1857. *Contributions to the Natural History of the United States of America, Volume I.* Boston: Little, Brown.

Agranoff, Robert. 2006. "Inside Collaborative Networks: Ten Lessons for Public Managers." *Public Administration Review* 66 (s1): 56–65.

————. 2007. *Managing within Networks: Adding Value to Public Organizations.* Washington, DC: Georgetown University Press.

————. 2008. "Collaboration for Knowledge: Learning from Public Management Networks." In *Big Ideas in Collaborative Public Management*, edited by L. B. Bingham and R. O'Leary. Armonk, NY: M. E. Sharpe.

————. 2012. *Collaborating to Manage: A Primer for the Public Sector.* Washington, DC: Georgetown University Press.

Agranoff, Robert, and Michael McGuire. 2001a. "American Federalism and the Search for Models of Management." *Public Administration Review* 61 (6): 671–81.

————. 2001b. "Big Questions in Public Network Management Research." *Journal of Public Administration Research and Theory* 11 (3): 295–326.

————. 2003. *Collaborative Public Management: New Strategies for Local Governments.* Washington, DC: Georgetown University Press.

Agranoff, Robert, and Valerie Lindsay Rinkle. 1986. *Intergovernmental Management: Human Services Problem-Solving in Six Metropolitan Areas.* Albany: State University of New York Press.

Agrawal, Arun. 2003. "Sustainable Governance of Common-Pool Resources: Context, Methods, and Politics." *Annual Review of Anthropology* 32 (1): 243–62.

Agrawal, Arun, and Clark C. Gibson. 1999. "Enchantment and Disenchantment: The Role of Community in Natural Resource Conservation." *World Development* 27 (4): 629–49.

Agrawal, Arun, and Maria Carmen Lemos. 2007. "A Greener Revolution in the Making? Environmental Governance in the 21st Century." *Environment: Science and Policy for Sustainable Development* 49 (5): 36–45.

Agrawal, Arun, and Elinor Ostrom. 2001. "Collective Action, Property Rights, and Decentralization in Resource Use in India and Nepal." *Politics and Society* 29 (4): 485–514.

Agrawal, Arun, and Jesse C. Ribot. 1999. "Accountability in Decentralization: A Framework with South Asian and West African Cases." *Journal of Developing Areas* 33 (4): 473–502.

Andersson, Krister. 2006. "Understanding Decentralized Forest Governance: An Application of the Institutional Analysis and Development Framework." *Sustainability: Science Practice and Policy* 2 (1): 25–35.

Andrews, Rhys, and Tom Entwistle. 2010. "Does Cross-Sectoral Partnership Deliver? An Empirical Exploration of Public Service Effectiveness, Efficiency, and Equity." *Journal of Public Administration Research and Theory* 20 (3): 679–701.

Ansell, Chris, and Alison Gash. 2008. "Collaborative Governance in Theory and Practice." *Journal of Public Administration Research and Theory* 18 (4): 543–71.

———. 2012. "Stewards, Mediators, and Catalysts: Toward a Model of Collaborative Leadership." *The Innovation Journal: The Public Sector Innovation Journal* 17 (1): article 7.

ASCG. 2008. *Village of Newtok, Local Hazards Mitigation Plan.* Newtok, AK: ASCG Inc. of Alaska, Bethel Planning and Development.

Bandura, Albert. 1977. *Social Learning Theory.* Englewood Cliffs, NJ: Prentice Hall.

Bardach, Eugene. 1998. *Getting Agencies to Work Together: The Practice and Theory of Managerial Craftsmanship.* Washington, DC: Brookings Institution Press.

Beck, Tony, and Madan G. Ghosh. 2000. "Common Property Resources and the Poor: Findings from West Bengal." *Economic and Political Weekly* 35 (3): 147–53.

Benner, Chris, and Manuel Pastor. 2011. "Moving On Up? Regions, Megaregions, and the Changing Geography of Social Equity Organizing." *Urban Affairs Review* 47 (3): 315–48.

Bentley, Arthur. 1949. *The Process of Government.* Evanston, IL: Principia Press.

Bentrup, Gary. 2001. "Evaluation of a Collaborative Mode: A Case Study Analysis of Watershed Planning in the Intermountain West." *Environmental Management* 27 (5): 739–48.

Berardo, Ramiro, Tanya Heikkila, and Andrea K. Gerlak. 2014. "Interorganizational Engagement in Collaborative Environmental Management: Evidence from the South Florida Ecosystem Restoration Task Force." *Journal of Public Administration Research and Theory* 24 (3): 697–719.

Berkes, Fikrit, Johan Colding, and Carl Folke, eds. 2002. *Navigating Social-Ecological Systems: Building Resilience for Complexity and Change.* Cambridge: Cambridge University Press.

Berkes, Fikret, and Nancy J. Turner. 2006. "Knowledge, Learning and the Evolution of Conservation Practice for Social-Ecological System Resilience." *Human Ecology* 34 (4): 479–94.

Bianchi, Carmine, and William C. Riverbank. 2012. "A Comparative Analysis of Performance Management Systems: The Cases of Sicily and North Carolina." *Public Performance & Management Review* 35 (3): 509–26.

Bingham, Lisa Blomgren. 2008. "Legal Frameworks for Collaboration in Governance and Public Management." In *Big Ideas in Collaborative Public Management*, edited by L. B. Bingham and R. O'Leary. Armonk, NY: M. E. Sharpe.

———. 2009. "Designing Justice: Legal Institutions and Other Systems for Managing Conflict." *Ohio State Journal on Dispute Resolution* 24 (1): 1–50.

———. 2010. "The Next Generation of Administrative Law: Building the Legal Infrastructure for Collaborative Governance." *Wisconsin Law Review* 10:297–356.

Bingham, Lisa Blomgren, Tina Nabatchi, and Rosemary O'Leary. 2005. "The New Governance: Practices and Processes for Stakeholder and Citizen Participation in the Work of Government." *Public Administration Review* 65 (5): 547–58.

Bingham, Lisa Blomgren, and Rosemary O'Leary, eds. 2008. *Big Ideas in Collaborative Public Management*. Armonk, NY: M. E. Sharpe.

Borrini-Feyerabend, Grazia. 1996. *Collaborative Management of Protected Areas: Tailoring the Approach to the Context*. Gland, Switzerland: IUCN.

Boswell, Michael R. 2005. "Everglades Restoration and the South Florida Ecosystem." In *Adaptive Governance and Water Conflict: New Institutions for Collaborative Planning*, edited by J. T. Scholz and B. Stiftel. Washington, DC: Resources for the Future Press.

Boudreau, Julie-Anne, Roger Keil, and Douglas Young. 2009. *Changing Toronto: Governing Urban Neoliberalism*. Toronto: University of Toronto Press.

Bourne, Larry, John Britton, and Deborah Leslie. 2011. "The Greater Toronto Region: The Challenges of Economic Restructuring, Social Diversity, and Globalization." In *Canadian Urban Regions: Trajectories of Growth and Change*, edited by L. S. Bourne, T. Hutton, R. Shearmur, and J. Simmons. Toronto: Oxford University Press.

Bradford, Neil, and Allison Bramwell, eds. 2014. *Governing Urban Economies: Innovation and Inclusion in Canadian City-Regions*. Toronto: University of Toronto Press.

Bramwell, Allison, and David Wolfe. 2014. "Dimensions of Governance in a Mega-City: Scale, Scope and Coalitions in Toronto." In *Governing Urban Economies: Innovation and Inclusion in Canadian City-Regions*, edited by N. Bradford and A. Bramwell. Toronto: University of Toronto Press.

Brass, Daniel J., Joseph Galaskiewicz, Henrich R. Greve, and Wenpin Tsai. 2004. "Taking Stock of Networks and Organizations: A Multilevel Perspective." *Academy of Management Journal* 47 (6): 795–817.

Bronen, Robin. 2011. "Climate-Induced Community Relocations: Creating an Adaptive Governance Framework Based in Human Rights Doctrine." *New York University Review of Law and Social Change* 35 (2): 356–406.

Bronen, Robin, and F. Stuart Chapin III. 2013. "Adaptive Governance and Institutional Strategies for Climate-Induced Village Relocations in Alaska." *Proceedings of the National Academy of Sciences USA* 110 (23): 9320–25.

Bryant, Raymond L. 1998. "Power, Knowledge and Political Ecology in the Third World: A Review." *Progress in Physical Geography* 22 (1): 79–94.

Bryson, John M., Barbara C. Crosby, and Melissa Middleton Stone. 2006. "The Design and Implementation of Cross-Sector Collaborations: Propositions from the Literature." *Public Administration Review* 66 (s1): 44–55.

Bryson, John M., Kathryn S. Quick, Carissa Schively Slotterback, and Barbara C. Crosby. 2013. "Designing Public Participation Processes." *Public Administration Review* 73 (1): 23–34.

Cahn, Dudley D., ed. 1994. *Conflict in Personal Relationships*. Hillsdale, NJ: Lawrence Erlbaum Associates.

Callan, Patrick M., William Doyle, and Joni E. Finney. 2001. "State Higher Education Performance: Measuring Up 2000." *Change* 33 (2): 10–19.

Carlson, Christine. 2007. *A Practical Guide to Collaborative Governance*. Portland, OR: Policy Consensus Initiative.

Carlson, Christine, and Jim Arthur. 1999. *A Practical Guide to Consensus*. Portland, OR: Policy Consensus Initiative.

CFRP (Collaborative Forest Restoration Program). 2014. "Collaborative Forest Restoration: Program Information." Forest Service, US Department of Agriculture. *Catalog of Federal Domestic Assistance*. www.cfda.gov/?s=program&mode=form&tab=step1& id=01faaa5cf35045781405337cbd6fc8be.

Chaskin, Robert J., and Harold A. Richman. 1992. "Concerns about School-Linked Services: Institution-Based versus Community-based Models." *The Future of Children* 2 (1): 107–17.

Cheng, Antony S., and Steven E. Daniels. 2003. "Examining the Interaction between Geographic Scale and Ways of Knowing in Ecosystem Management: A Case Study of Place-Based Collaborative Planning." *Forest Science* 49 (6): 841–54.

———. 2005. "Getting to the We: Examining the Relationship between Geographic Scale and Ingroup Emergence in Collaborative Watershed Planning." *Human Ecology Review* 12 (1): 30–43.

Cheng, Antony S., Linda E. Kruger, and Steven E. Daniels. 2003. "Place as an Integrating Concept in Natural Resource Politics: Propositions for a Social Science Research Agenda." *Society & Natural Resources* 16 (2): 87–104.

Cheng, Antony S., and Victoria E. Sturtevant. 2012. "A Framework for Assessing Collaborative Capacity in Community-Based Public Forest Management." *Environmental Management* 49 (3): 675–89.

Choi, Taehyon, and Peter J. Robertson. 2013. "Deliberation and Decision in Collaborative Governance: A Simulation of Approaches to Mitigate Power Imbalance." *Journal of Public Administration Research and Theory* 24 (2): 495–518.

Clarke, Susan, and Gary L. Gaile. 1998. *The Work of Cities.* Minneapolis: University of Minnesota Press.

Cleveland, Harlan. 1972. *The Future Executive: A Guide for Tomorrow's Managers.* New York: Harper & Row.

Coleman, James S. 1988. "Social Capital in the Creation of Human Capital." *American Journal of Sociology* 94 (Supplement): S95–S120.

CONAGUA (Comisión Nacional del Agua). 2007. *Plan de Manejo Integrado de las Aguas Subterraneas en el Acuífero de Guadalupe.* Mexico City: CONAGUA.

———. 2009. *Actualización de la Disponibilidad Media Anual de Agua Subterránea Acuífero.* Mexico City: CONAGUA.

CONAPO (Consejo Nacional de Población). 2005. *Proyecciónes de la Población de México 2005–2030.* Mexico City: CONAPO. www.portal.conapo.gob.mx/00cifras/proy/Proy05-50.pdf

Cooper, Terry L., Thomas A. Bryer, and Jack W. Meek. 2006. Citizen-Centered Collaborative Public Management. *Public Administration Review* 66 (s1): 76–88.

Cox, Sally. 2007. *An Overview of Erosion, Flooding, and Relocation Efforts in the Native Village of Newtok.* Anchorage: Alaska Department of Commerce, Community, and Economic Development.

Cross, Rob, and Andrew Parker. 2004. *The Hidden Power of Social Networks: Understanding How Work Really Gets Done in Organizations.* Boston: Harvard Business School Press.

Culpepper, Pepper D. 2004. *Institutional Rules, Social Capacity, and the Stuff of Politics: Experiments in Collaborative Governance in France and Italy.* EUI Working Papers, RSCAS No 2004/06. Florence: Robert Schuman Centre for Advanced Studies of European University Institute.

Cupach, William R., and Daniel J. Canary. 1997. *Competence in Interpersonal Conflict.* New York: McGraw-Hill.

Daesslé, Luis W., Leopoldo G. Mendoza-Espinosa, Victor F. Camacho-Ibar, W. Rozier, Ofelia Morton, L. Van Dorst, Karina Carmen Lugo-Ibarra, Ana Luz Quintanilla-Montoya, and A. Rodríguez-Pinal. 2006. "The Hydrogeochemistry of a Heavily Used Aquifer in the Mexican Wine-Producing Guadalupe Valley, Baja California." *Environmental Geology* 51 (1): 151–59.

Daniels, Steven E., and Gregg Walker. 2001. *Working Through Environmental Conflict: The Collaborative Approach*. Westport, CT: Praeger.

Davies, Gordon K. 2006. *Setting a Public Agenda for Higher Education in the States: Lessons Learned from the National Collaborative for Higher Education Policy*. San Jose: National Collaborative for Higher Education Policy.

DiGaetano, Alan, and Elizabeth Strom. 2003. "Comparative Urban Governance: An Integrated Approach." *Urban Affairs Review* 38 (3): 356–95.

DiMaggio, Paul J., and Walter W. Powell. 1983. "The Iron Cage Revisited: Institutional Isomorphism and Collective Rationality in Organizational Fields." *American Sociological Review* 48 (2): 147–60.

DMAFB (Davis-Monthan Air Force Base). 2007. "D-M Stands Up Military Community Relations Committee." Davis-Monthan Air Force Base, Tucson. www.dm.af.mil/news /story.asp?id=123070359.

Donahue, John. 2004. *On Collaborative Governance*, Working Paper 2. Cambridge, MA: Corporate Social Responsibility Initiative at Harvard University. www.hks.harvard.edu/mr cbg/CSRI/publications/workingpaper_2_donahue.pdf.

Donahue, John D., and Richard J. Zeckhauser. 2011. *Collaborative Governance: Private Roles for Public Goals in Turbulent Times*. Princeton, NJ: Princeton University Press.

Dreier, Peter, John Mollenkopf, and Todd Swanstrom. 2004. *Place Matters: Metropolitics for the Twenty-First Century*. Lawrence: University Press of Kansas.

Dukes, E. Franklin. 2001. *Collaboration: A Guide for Environmental Advocates*. Charlottesville: University of Virginia Press.

———. 2004. "What We Know about Environmental Conflict Resolution: An Analysis Based on Research." *Conflict Resolution Quarterly* 22 (1–2): 191–220.

Ehrmann, John R., and Barbara Stinson. 1999. "Joint Fact-Finding and the Use of Technical Experts." In *The Consensus Building Handbook: A Comprehensive Guide to Reaching Agreement*, edited by L. Susskind, S. McKearnan, and J. Thomas-Larmer. Thousand Oaks, CA: Sage.

Elazar, Daniel J. 1962. *The American Partnership: Intergovernmental Cooperation in the Nineteenth Century United States*. Chicago: University of Chicago Press.

———. 1984. *American Federalism: A View from the States*, 3rd edition. New York: Harper & Row.

Emerson, Kirk, and Andrea K. Gerlak. 2014. "Adaptation in Collaborative Governance Regimes." *Environmental Management* 54 (4): 768–81.

Emerson, Kirk, and Tina Nabatchi. 2015. "Evaluating the Productivity of Collaborative Governance Regimes: A Performance Matrix." *Public Performance & Management Review*. 38(4): 717.

Emerson, Kirk, Tina Nabatchi, and Stephen Balogh. 2012. "An Integrative Framework for Collaborative Governance." *Journal of Public Administration Research and Theory* 22 (1): 1–29.

Emerson, Kirk, Tina Nabatchi, Rosemary O'Leary, and John Stephens. 2003. "The Challenges of Environmental Conflict Resolution." In *The Promise and Performance for Environmental Conflict Resolution*, edited by R. O'Leary and L. B. Bingham. Washington, DC: Resources for the Future Press.

Emerson, Kirk, Patricia J. Orr, Dale L. Keyes, and Katherine M. McKnight. 2009. "Environmental Conflict Resolution: Evaluating Performance Outcomes and Contributing Factors." *Conflict Resolution Quarterly* 27 (1): 27–64.

Emerson, Kirk, and Steve Smutko. 2011. *UNCG Guide to Collaborative Competencies*. Portland,

OR: University Network for Collaborative Governance of National Center for Policy Consensus.

Emery, Fred, and Eric Trist. 1965. "The Causal Texture of Organizational Environments." *Human Relations* 18:21–32.

Fienup-Riordan, Ann. 1983. *The Nelson Island Eskimo: Social Structure and Ritual Distribution.* Anchorage: Alaska Pacific University Press.

Finn-Stevenson, Matia, and Barbara M. Stern. 1997. "Integrating Early-Childhood and Family-Support Services with a School Improvement Process: The Comer-Zigler Initiative." *Elementary School Journal* 98 (1): 51–66.

Fisher, Robert, and William Ury. 1981. *Getting to Yes: Negotiating Agreement without Giving In.* New York: Penguin Books.

Fisher, Roger, and Scott Brown. 1989. *Getting Together: Building Relationships As We Negotiate.* New York: Penguin Books.

Foster, Stephen, Hector Garduno, and Karin Kemper. 2004. *The "COTAS": Progress with Stakeholder Participation in Guanajuato.* Washington, DC: Global Water Partnership Associate Program of the World Bank.

Foucault, Michel. 1978. "On Governmentality, Lecture at the College de France." In *The Foucault Effect: Studies in Governmentality*, edited by G. Burchell, C. Gordon, and P. Miller. Hemel Hempstead, UK: Harvester Wheatsheaf.

Frederickson, H. George. 1991. "Toward a Theory of the Public for Public Administration." *Administration and Society* 22 (4): 395–417.

———. 1999. "The Repositioning of American Public Administration." *PS: Political Science and Politics* 32 (4): 701–12.

———. 2007. "Whatever Happened to Public Administration? Governance, Governance Everywhere." In *The Oxford Handbook of Public Management*, edited by C. Pollitt, L. E. Lynn Jr., and E. Ferlie. New York: Oxford University Press.

Frederickson, David G., and H. George Frederickson. 2006. *Measuring the Performance of the Hollow State.* Washington, DC: Georgetown University Press.

Fukuyama, Francis. 2011. *The Origins of Political Order: From Prehuman Times to the French Revolution.* New York: Farrar, Straus & Giroux.

———. 2014. *Political Order and Political Decay: From the Industrial Revolution to the Globalization of Democracy.* New York: Farrar, Straus & Giroux.

Fung, Archon. 2003. "Recipes for Public Spheres: Eight Institutional Design Choices and Their Consequences." *Journal of Political Philosophy* 11 (3): 338–67.

———. 2006. "Varieties of Participation in Complex Governance." *Public Administration Review* 66 (s1): 66–75.

Fung, Archon, and Erik O. Wright. 2001. *Deepening Democracy: Institutional Innovations in Empowered Participatory Governance.* New York: Verso.

GAO (US Government Accountability Office). 2003. *Alaska Native Villages: Most Are Affected by Flooding and Erosion, but Few Qualify for Federal Assistance.* Washington, DC: GAO.

———. 2007. *Some Restoration Progress Has Been Made, but the Effort Faces Significant Delays, Implementation Challenges and Rising Costs.* Washington, DC: GAO.

———. 2009. *Alaska Native Villages: Limited Progress Has Been Made on Relocating Villages Threatened by Flooding and Erosion.* Washington, DC: GAO.

Gastil, John. 2005. "Deliberation." In *Communication as . . . Perspectives on Theory*, edited by G. J. Shepherd, J. St. John, and T. Striphas. Thousand Oaks, CA: Sage.

———. 2008. *Political Communication and Deliberation.* Thousand Oaks, CA: Sage.

GCRP (US Global Change Research Program). 2009. *Global Climate Change Impacts in the United States.* Washington, DC: GCRP.

Geddes, Mike. 2006. "Partnership and the Limits to Local Governance in England: Institutionalist Analysis and Neoliberalism." *International Journal of Urban and Regional Research* 30 (1): 76–97.

Gerlak, Andrea K., and Tanya Heikkila. 2011. "Building a Theory of Learning in Collaboratives: Evidence from the Everglades Restoration Program." *Journal of Public Administration Research and Theory* 21 (4): 619–44.

Getha-Taylor, Heather. 2006. "Preparing Leaders for High-Stakes Collaborative Action: Darrell Darnel and the Department of Homeland Security." *Public Administration Review* 66 (s1): 159–60.

———. 2008. "Identifying Collaborative Competencies." *Review of Public Personnel Administration* 28 (2): 103–19.

Giloth, Robert P., ed. 2004. *Workforce Development Politics: Civic Capacity and Performance.* Philadelphia: Temple University Press.

Global Water Partnership. 2000. *Integrated Water Resources Management.* Technical Advisory Committee Background Paper 4. Stockholm: Global Water Partnership.

Goldsmith, Stephen, and William Eggers. 2004. *Governing by Network: The New Shape of the Public Sector.* Washington, DC: Brookings Institution Press.

Gormley, William T., Jr., and Seven J. Balla. 2004. *Bureaucracy and Democracy: Accountability and Performance.* Washington, DC: CQ Press.

Granovetter, Mark S. 1973. "The Strength of Weak Ties." *American Journal of Sociology* 78 (6): 1360–80.

Gray, Barbara. 1985. "Conditions Facilitating Interorganizational Collaboration." *Human Relations* 38 (10): 911–36.

———. 1989. *Collaborating: Finding Common Ground for Multiparty Problems.* San Francisco: Jossey-Bass.

———. 2000. "Assessing Inter-Organizational Collaboration: Multiple Conceptions and Multiple Methods." In *Cooperative Strategy: Economic, Business, and Organizational Issues,* edited by D. Faulkner and M. de Rond. New York: Oxford University Press.

Green, Gary P., and Anna Haines. 2012. *Asset Building and Community Development,* 3rd edition. Los Angeles: Sage.

Groff, Todd R., and Thomas P. Jones. 2003. *Introduction to Knowledge Management: KM in Business.* Burlington, MA: Elsevier Science.

Grunwald, Michael. 2006. *The Swamp: The Everglades, Florida, and the Politics of Paradise.* New York: Simon & Schuster.

Guarneros-Meza, Valeria, and Mike Geddes. 2010. "Local Governance and Participation under Neoliberalism: Comparative Perspectives." *International Journal of Urban and Regional Research* 34 (1): 115–29.

Gunton, Thomas I., and John C. Day. 2003. "The Theory and Practice of Collaborative Planning in Resource and Environmental Management." *Environments* 31 (2): 5–19.

Hambleton, Robin. 2003. "The New City Management." In *Globalism and Local Democracy: Challenge and Change in Europe and North America,* edited by R. Hambleton, H. V. Savitch, and M. Stewart. New York: Palgrave Macmillan.

Hardin, Garrett. 1968. "The Tragedy of the Commons." *Science* 162 (3859): 1243–248. Harvey, David. 2005. *A Brief History of Neoliberalism.* New York: Oxford University Press.

Head, Brian W. 2008. "Wicked Problems in Public Policy." *Public Policy* 3 (2): 101–18.

Heikkila, Tanya, and Andrea K. Gerlak. 2005. "The Formation of Large-Scale Collaborative Resource Management Institutions: Clarifying the Roles of Stakeholders, Science, and Institutions." *Policy Studies Journal* 33 (4): 583–612.

———. 2014. "Investigating Collaborative Processes over Time: A 10-Year Study of the South Florida Ecosystem Restoration Task Force." *American Review of Public Administration.* DOI: 10.1177/0275074014544196.

Heikkila, Tanya, Andrea A. Gerlack, and Mark W. Davis. 2012. "Structuring Public Engagement in Collaborative Environmental Management: A 10-Year Analysis of the South Florida Ecosystem Restoration Program." Paper presented at American Political Science Association Annual Meeting, New Orleans, August 30–September 2.

Heinrich, Carolyn J. 2002. "Outcomes-Based Performance Management in the Public Sector: Implications for Government Accountability and Effectiveness." *Public Administration Review* 62 (6): 712–25.

Henton, Doug, John Melville, Terry Amsler, and Malka Kopell. 2005. *Collaborative Governance: A Guide for Grantmakers.* Menlo Park, CA: William and Flora Hewlett Foundation.

Himmelman, Arthur T. 1994. "Communities Working Collaboratively for a Change." In *Resolving Conflict: Strategies for Local Government,* edited by M. Herrman. Washington, DC: International City/County Management Association.

Holling, Crawford Stanley. 1978. *Adaptive Environmental Assessment and Management.* New York: John Wiley & Sons.

Howey, Kenneth, and Bruce Joyce. 1978. "A Data Base for Future Directions in Inservice Education." *Theory into Practice* 17 (3): 206–11.

Hufford, Gary, and James Partain. 2005. *Climate Change and Short-Term Forecasting for Alaskan Northern Coasts.* Anchorage: National Weather Service.

Hulchanski, David. 2007. *The Three Cities within Toronto: Income Polarization among Toronto's Neighbourhoods 1970–2005.* Toronto: Centre for Urban and Community Studies.

Huxham, Chris. 2003. "Theorizing Collaboration Practice." *Public Management Review* 5 (3): 401–23.

Huxham, Chris, and Siv Vangen. 2005. *Managing to Collaborate: The Theory and Practice of Collaborative Advantage.* New York: Routledge.

Huxham, Chris, Siv Vangen, Christine Huxham, and Colin Eden. 2000. "The Challenge of Collaborative Governance." *Public Management Review* 2 (3): 337–58.

IAWG (Immediate Action Workgroup). 2008. *Recommendations Report to the Governor's Subcabinet on Climate Change.* Juneau, AK: Alaska SubCabinet on Climate Change of IAWG.

———. 2009. *Recommendations Report to the Governor's Subcabinet on Climate Change.* Juneau: Alaska SubCabinet on Climate Change of IAWG.

———. 2011a. *Meeting Summary, February 17, 2011.* Anchorage: Alaska SubCabinet on Climate Change of IAWG.

———. 2011b. *Meeting Summary, March 3, 2011.* Anchorage: Alaska SubCabinet on Climate Change of IAWG.

Imperial, Mark. 2005. "Using Collaboration as a Governance Strategy: Lessons from Six Watershed Management Programs." *Administration & Society* 37 (3): 281–320.

Ingraham, Patricia W., Philip G. Joyce, and Amy K. Donahue. 2003. *Government Performance: Why Management Matters.* Baltimore: Johns Hopkins University Press.

Innes, Judith E., and David E. Booher. 1999. "Consensus Building and Complex Adaptive Systems: A Framework for Evaluating Collaborative Planning." *Journal of the American Planning Association* 65 (4): 412–23.

Institute for Patient Care Services and Massachusetts General Hospital. 2002. *Patient Care Services Operating Plan 2002*. Boston: Massachusetts General Hospital.

IPCC (Intergovernmental Panel on Climate Change). 2007. "Summary for Policymakers." In *Climate Change 2007: Impacts, Adaptation and Vulnerability*, edited by M. L. Parry, O. F. Canziani, J. P. Palutikof, P. J. van der Linden, and C. E. Hanson. Cambridge: Cambridge University Press.

Jochim, Ashley E., and Peter J. May. 2010. "Beyond Subsystems: Policy Regimes and Governance." *Policy Studies Journal* 38 (2): 303–27.

Jones, Candace, William Hesterly, and Stephen Borgatti. 1997. "A General Theory of Network Governance: Exchange Conditions and Social Mechanisms." *Academy of Management Review* 22 (4): 911–45.

Jun, Jong S., ed. 2002. *Rethinking Administrative Theory: The Challenge of the New Century*. Westport, CT: Praeger.

Karkkainen, Bradley C. 2002. "Collaborative Ecosystem Governance: Scale, Complexity, and Dynamism." *Virginia Environmental Law Journal* 21 (2): 189–243.

Kellogg Foundation. 2005. *Logic Model Development Guide*. Battle Creek, MI: W. K. Kellogg Foundation.

Kelman, Steven, Sounman Hong, and Irwin Turbitt. 2013. "Are There Managerial Practices Associated with the Outcomes of an Interagency Service Delivery Collaboration? Evidence from British Crime and Disorder Reduction Partnerships." *Journal of Public Administration Research and Theory* 23 (3): 609–30.

Kemper, Karin Erica. 2007. "Instruments and Institutions for Groundwater Management." In *The Agricultural Groundwater Revolution: Opportunities and Threats to Development*, edited by M. Giodano and K. G. Villholth. Wallingford, UK: CABI.

Kettl, Donald F. 2002. *The Transformation of Governance: Public Administration for Twenty-First Century America*. Baltimore: Johns Hopkins University Press.

———. 2005. *The Next Government of the United States: Challenges for Performance in the 21st Century*. Washington, DC: IBM Center for the Business of Government.

———. 2006. "Managing Boundaries in American Administration: The Collaborative Imperative." *Public Administration Review* 66 (s1): 10–19.

Kim, Yushom, Erik W. Johnston, and H.S. Kang. 2011. "A Computational Approach to Managing Performance Dynamics in Networked Governance Systems." *Public Performance & Management Review* 34 (4): 580–97.

Knoke, David, and Song Yang. 2008. *Social Network Analysis*, 2nd edition. Thousand Oaks, CA: Sage.

Koliba, Christopher, Jack W. Meek, and Asim Zia. 2010. *Governance Networks in Public Administration and Public Policy*. Boca Raton, FL: CRC Press.

Koontz, Tomas M., Toddi A. Steelman, JoAnn Carmin, Katrina Smith Korfmacher, Cassandra Moseley, and Craig W. Thomas. 2004. *Collaborative Environmental Management: What Roles for Government?* Washington, DC: Resources for the Future Press.

Koontz, Tomas M., and Craig W. Thomas. 2006. "What Do We Know and Need to Know about the Environmental Outcomes of Collaborative Management?" *Public Administration Review* 66 (s1): 111–21.

———. 2012. "Measuring the Performance of Public–Private Partnerships: A Systematic Method for Distinguishing Outputs from Outcomes." *Public Performance & Management Review* 35 (4): 769–86.

Koppenjan, Joop, and Erik-Hans Klijn. 2004. *Managing Uncertainty in Networks: A Network Approach to Problem Solving and Decision Making*. New York: Routledge.

Krasner, Stephen D. 1983. "Structural Causes and Regime Consequences: Regimes as Intervening Variables." In *International Regimes*, edited by S. D. Krasner. Ithaca, NY: Cornell University Press.

Kvammen, Lorna J. 1976. *A Study of the Relationship between Population Growth and the Development of Agriculture in the Guadalupe Valley Baja California Mexico*. Los Angeles: California State University Press.

Lax, David A., and James K. Sebenius. 1986. *The Manager as Negotiator*. New York: Free Press.

Leach, William D. 2006a. "Collaborative Public Management and Democracy: Evidence from Western Watershed Partnerships." *Public Administration Review* 66 (s1): 100–110.

———. 2006b. "Public Involvement in USDA Forest Service Policymaking: A Literature Review." *Journal of Forestry* 104 (1): 43–49.

Leach, William D., and Neil W. Pelkey. 2001. "Making Watershed Partnerships Work: A Review of the Empirical Literature." *Journal of Water Resources Planning and Management* 127 (6): 378–85.

Leach, William D., and Paul A. Sabatier. 2005. "To Trust an Adversary: Integrating Rational and Psychological Models of Collaborative Policy Making." *American Political Science Review* 99 (4): 491–503.

Lemke, Peter, Jiawen Ren, Richard B. Alley, Ian Allison, Jorge Carrasco, Gregory Flato, Yoshiyuki Fujii, Georg Kaser, Philip Mote, Robert H. Thomas, and Tingjun Zhang. 2007. *Observations: Changes in Snow, Ice and Frozen Ground, in Climate Change 2007—The Physical Science Basis*. Cambridge: Cambridge University Press.

Lichbach, Mark Irving. 1996. *The Cooperator's Dilemma*. Ann Arbor: University of Michigan Press.

Light, Paul. 2002. *The True Size of Government*. Washington, DC: Brookings Institution Press.

Lindblom, Charles E. 1959. "The Science of Muddling Through." *Public Administration Review* 19 (2): 79–88.

Linden, Russell M. 2010. *Leading across Boundaries:Creating Collaborative Agencies in a Networked World*. San Francisco: Jossey-Bass.

Lindley, Dennis V. 2006. *Understanding Uncertainty*. Hoboken, NJ: John Wiley & Sons.

Lubell, Mark. 2005. "Do Watershed Partnerships Enhance Beliefs Conducive to Collective Action?" In *Swimming Upstream: Collaborative Approaches to Watershed Management*, edited by P. A. Sabatier, W. Focht, M. Lubell, Z. Trachtenberg, A. Vedlitz and M. Matloc. Cambridge, MA: MIT Press.

Lubell, Mark, and Edelenbos, Jurian. 2013. "Integrated Water Resources Management: A Comparative Laboratory for Water Governance." *International Journal of Water Governance* 1 (3): 177–96.

Lubell, Mark, Mark Schneider, John Scholz, and Mihriye Mete. 2002. "Watershed Partnerships and the Emergence of Collective Action Institutions." *American Journal of Political Science* 46 (1): 148–63.

Lulofs, Roxane S., and Dudley D. Cahn. 2000. *Conflict: From Theory to Action*. Boston: Allyn and Bacon.

Lynn, Laurence E., Carolyn J. Heinrich, and Carolyn J. Hill. 2000. "Studying Governance and Public Management: Challenges and Prospects." *Journal of Public Administration Research and Theory* 10 (2): 233–62.

Mandell, Myrna P., and Robyn Keast. 2008. "Evaluating the Effectiveness of Interorganizational Relations through Networks: Developing a Framework for Revised Performance Measures." *Public Management Review* 10 (6): 715–31.

March, James G., and Johan P. Olsen. 1983. "The New Institutionalism: Organizational Factors in Political Life." *American Political Science Review* 78 (3): 734–49.

Margerum, Richard D. 2011. *Beyond Consensus: Improving Collaborative Planning and Management*. Cambridge, MA: MIT Press.

Markon, Carl J., Sarah F. Trainor, and F. Stuart Chapin III, eds. 2012. *The United States National Climate Assessment: Alaska Technical Report*. Reston, VA: US Geological Survey.

Mayeske, George W., and Michael T. Lambur. 2001. *How to Design Better Programs: A Staff Centered Stakeholder Aprroach to Program Logic Modeling*. Crofton, MD: Program Design Institute.

McGinnis, Michael D. 2011. "An Introduction to IAD and the Language of the Ostrom Workshop: A Simple Guide to a Complex Framework for the Analysis of Institutions and Their Development." *Policy Studies Journal* 39 (1): 169–82.

McGuire, Michael. 2006. "Collaborative Public Management: Assessing What We Know and How We Know It." *Public Administration Review* 66 (s1): 33–43.

MCRC (Military Community Relations Committee). 2014. "Current Bylaws," revised July 18, 2012. https://sites.google.com/site/mcrctucson/-mcrc-subcommittees/-mcrc-bylaws-subcommittee.

MC3 (Military Community Compatibility Committee). 2006. "Final Report: Consensus Recommendations." https://docs.google.com/uc?id=0B7CFqGiTlGYmM2UyNGFlZmYtODhiNy00YTA0LTliYjYjYtOTgwMjhmMmQ5ZTE5.

Milward, H. Brinton, and Keith G. Provan. 2000. "How Networks Are Governed." In *Governance and Performance: New Perspectives*, edited by C. J. Heinrich and L. E. Lynn Jr. Washington, DC: Georgetown University Press.

———. 2006. *A Manager's Guide to Choosing and Using Collaborative Networks*. Washington DC: IBM Center for the Business of Government.

Moe, Terry M. 2005. "Power and Political Institutions." *Perspectives on Politics* 3 (2): 215–33.

Moore, Elizabeth A., and Tomas M. Koontz. 2003. "Research Note: A Typology of Collaborative Watershed Groups: Citizen-Based, Agency-Based, and Mixed Partnerships." *Society & Natural Resources* 16 (5): 451–60.

Moore, Mark H. 2002. *Some Alternative Conceptions of Governance as an Idea*. Working Paper. Cambridge, MA: Weil Program on Collaborative Governance of John F. Kennedy School of Government at Harvard University.

Morse, Ricardo S., and John B. Stephens. 2012. "Teaching Collaborative Governance: Phases, Competencies, and Case-Based Learning." *Journal of Public Affairs Education* 18 (3): 565–83.

Morse, Ricardo S., Terry F. Buss, and C. Morgan Kinghorn. 2007. *Transforming Public Leadership for the 21st Century*. Armonk, NY: M. E. Sharpe.

Mostert, Erik, Marc Craps, and Claudia Pahl-Wostl. 2008. "Social Learning: The Key to Integrated Water Resources Management?" *Water International* 33 (3): 293–304.

Moynihan, Donald P. 2008. *The Dynamics of Performance Management: Constructing Information and Reform*. Washington, DC: Georgetown University Press.

Nabatchi, Tina. 2010. "Addressing the Citizenship and Democratic Deficits: Exploring the Potential of Deliberative Democracy for Public Administration." *American Review of Public Administration* 40 (4): 376–99.

———. 2012. *A Manager's Guide to Evaluating Citizen Participation*. Washington, DC: IBM Center for the Business of Government.

Nabatchi, Tina, Holly T. Goerdel, and Shelly Peffer. 2011. "Public Administration in Dark

Times: Some Questions for the Future of the Field." *Journal of Public Administration Research and Theory* 21 (s1): i29–i43.

Nabatchi, Tina, and Matt Leighninger. 2015. *Public Participation for 21st Century Democracy*. San Francisco: Jossey-Bass.

National Research Council. 2009. *Informing Decisions in a Changing Climate*. Washington, DC: National Academies Press.

Nelles, Jennifer. 2012. *Comparative Metropolitan Policy: Governing Beyond Local Boundaries in the Imagined Metropolis*. London: Routledge.

Nelson, Donald R., W. Neil Adger, and Katrina Brown. 2007. "Adaptation to Environmental Change: Contributions of a Resilience Framework." *Annual Review of Environment and Resources* 32:395–419.

North, Douglass C. 1991. "Institutions." *Journal of Economic Perspectives* 5 (1): 97–112.

NSIDC (National Snow and Ice Data Center). 2012. "Arctic Sea Ice Extent Settles at Record Seasonal Minimum." National Snow and Ice Data Center, Boulder, CO, September 19. http://nsidc.org/arcticseaicenews/2012/09/arctic-sea-ice-extent-settles-at-record-seasonal-minimum/.

———. 2015. "Arctic Sea Ice Maximum Reaches Lowest Extent on Record." National Snow and Ice Data Center, Boulder, CO, March 19. http://nsidc.org/news/newsroom/arctic-sea-ice-maximum-reaches-lowest-extent-record.

OECD (Organization for Economic Cooperation and Development). 2013. *Making Water Reform Happen in Mexico: Assessment and Recommendations*. Paris: OECD Publishing.

Office of Public Affairs of 162nd Fighter Wing. 2012. "US Air Force Releases Final EIA for Proposed F-35A Training at Tucson International Airport." Office of Public Affairs of 162nd Fighter Wing, Tucson. www.162wing.ang.af.mil/news/story.asp?id=123305561.

O'Leary, Rosemary, and Lisa Blomgren Bingham. 2007. *A Manager's Guide to Resolving Conflicts in Collaborative Networks*. Washington, DC: IBM Center for the Business of Government.

———, eds. 2009. *The Collaborative Public Manager*. Washington, DC: Georgetown University Press.

O'Leary, Rosemary, Yujin Choi, and Catherine M. Gerard. 2012. "The Skill Set of the Successful Collaborator." *Public Administration Review* 72 (s1): S70–S83.

O'Leary, Rosemary, Beth Gazeley, Michael McGuire, and Lisa Blomgren Bingham. 2009. "Public Managers in Collaboration." In *The Collaborative Public Manager*, edited by Rosemary O'Leary and Lisa Blomgren Bingham. Washington, DC: Georgetown University Press.

O'Leary, Rosemary, and Catherine Gerard. 2012. *Collaboration across Boundaries: Insights and Tips for Federal Senior Executives*. Washington, DC: IBM Center for the Business of Government.

O'Leary, Rosemary, Catherine Gerard, and Lisa Blomgren Bingham. 2006. "Introduction to the Symposium of Collaborative Public Management." *Public Administration Review* 66 (s1): 6–9.

O'Leary, Rosemary, and Nidhi Vij. 2012. "Collaborative Public Management: Where Have We Been and Where Are We Going?" *American Review of Public Administration* 42 (5): 507–22.

Olsen, Mancur. 1965. *The Logic of Collective Action: Public Goods and the Theory of Groups*. Cambridge, MA: Harvard University Press.

Opp, Susan M., and Kyle L. Saunders. 2013. "Pillar Talk: Local Sustainability Initiatives and Policies in the United States." *Urban Affairs Review* 49 (5): 678–717.

Orr, Patricia J., Kirk Emerson, and Dale L. Keyes. 2008. "Environmental Conflict Resolution Practice and Performance: An Evaluation Framework." *Conflict Resolution Quarterly* 25 (3): 283–301.

Osborne, David, and Ted Gaebler. 1992. *Reinventing Government: How the Entrepreneurial Spirit Is Transforming the Public Sector*. Reading, MA: Addison-Wesley.

Ostrom, Elinor. 1990. *Governing the Commons: The Evolution of Institutions for Collective Action*. Cambridge: Cambridge University Press.

———. 1998. "A Behavioral Approach to the Rational Choice Theory of Collective Action." *American Political Science Review* 92 (1): 1–22.

———. 2005. *Understanding Institutional Diversity*. Princeton, NJ: Princeton University Press.

———. 2007. "A Diagnostic Approach for Going beyond Panaceas." *Proceedings of the National Academy of Sciences* 104 (39): 15181–87.

———. 2009. "A General Framework for Analyzing Sustainability of Social-Ecological Systems." *Science* 325 (5939): 419–22.

———. 2011. "Background on the Institutional Analysis and Development Framework." *Policy Studies Journal* 39 (1): 7–27.

O'Toole, Laurence J., Jr. 1997. "Implementing Public Innovations in Network Settings." *Administration and Society* 29 (2): 115–38.

Ozawa, Connie. 1991. *Recasting Science: Consensual Procedures in Public Policy Making*. Boulder, CO: Westview Press.

Pahl-Wostl, Claudia. 2007. "Transitions toward Adaptive Management of Water Facing Climate and Global Change." *Water Resources Management* 21:49–62.

Pahl-Wostl, Claudia, Marc Craps, Art Dewulf, Erik Mostert, David Tàbara, and Tharsi Taillieu. 2007. "Social Learning and Water Resources Management." *Ecology and Society* 12 (2): article 5.

Phillips, Rhonda, and Robert H. Pittman. 2009. *An Introduction to Community Development*. New York: Routledge.

Pierre, Jon. 1999. "Models of Urban Governance: The Institutional Dimension of Urban Politics." *Urban Affairs Review* 34 (3): 372–96.

———. 2005. "Comparative Urban Governance: Uncovering Complex Causalities." *Urban Affairs Review* 40 (4): 446–62.

———. 2011. *The Politics of Urban Governance*. New York: Palgrave Macmillan.

Pierre, Jon, and B. Guy Peters. 2012. "Urban Governance." In *The Oxford Handbook of Urban Governance*, edited by K. Mossberger, S. E. Clarke, and P. John. New York: Oxford University Press.

Poister, Theodore H. 2008. *Measuring Performance in Public and Nonprofit Organizations*. San Fransisco: John Wiley & Sons.

Popp, Janise K., H. Brinton Milward, Gail MacKean, Anne Casebeer, and Ronald Lindstrohm. 2014. *Interorganizational Networks: A Review of the Literature to Inform Practice*. Washington, DC: IBM Center for the Business of Government.

Powell, Walter W. 1990. "Neither Market nor Hierarchy: Network Forms of Organization." In *Research in Organizational Behavior*, edited by B. M. Staw and L. L. Cummings. Greenwich, CT: JAI Press.

Powell, Walter W., and Paul J. DiMaggio, eds. 2012. *The New Institutionalism in Organizational Analysis*. Chicago: University of Chicago Press.

Pressman, Jeffrey L., and Aaron Wildavsky. 1973. *Implementation*. Berkeley: University of California Press.

Provan, Keith G, Amy Fish, and Joerg Sydow. 2007. "Interorganizational Networks at the Network Level: A Review of the Empirical Literature on Whole Networks." *Journal of Management* 33 (3): 479–516.

Provan, Keith G., Patrick Kenis, and Sherrie E. Human. 2008. "Legitimacy Building in Organizational Networks." In *Big Ideas in Collaborative Public Management*, edited by L. B. Bingham and R. O'Leary. Amonk, NY: M. E. Sharpe.

Provan, Keith G., and Robin H. Lemaire. 2012. "Core Concepts and Key Ideas for Understanding Public Sector Organizational Networks: Using Research to Inform Scholarship and Practice." *Public Administration Review* 72 (5): 638–48.

Provan, Keith G., and H. Brinton Milward. 1995. "A Preliminary Theory of Interorganizational Effectiveness: A Comparative Study of Four Community Mental Health Systems." *Administrative Science Quarterly* 40 (1): 1–33.

———. 2001. "Do Networks Really Work? A Framework for Evaluating Public-Sector Organizational Networks." *Public Administration Review* 61 (4): 414–23.

Purdy, Jill M., 2012. "A Framework for Assessing Power in Collaborative Governance Processes." *Public Administration Review* 72 (3): 409–17.

Putnam, Robert. 1995. "Bowling Alone: America's Declining Social Capital." *Journal of Democracy* 6 (1): 65–78.

———. 2000. *Bowling Alone: The Collapse and Revival of American Community*. New York: Simon & Schuster.

Putnam, Robert, Robert Leonardi, and Raffaella Y. Nanetti. 1993. *Making Democracy Work: Civic Traditions in Modern Italy*. Princeton, NJ: Princeton University Press.

Raadschelders, Jos C. N., Eran Vigoda-Gadot, and Mirit Kisner. 2015. *Global Dimensions of Public Administration and Governance: A Comparative Voyage*. San Francisco: Jossey-Bass.

Radin, Beryl A. 1996. "Managing across Boundaries." In *The State of Public Management*, edited by D. F. Kettl and H. B. Milward. Baltimore: Johns Hopkins University Press.

———. 2000. "The Government Performance and Results Act and the Tradition of Federal Management Reform: Square Pegs in Round Holes?" *Journal of Public Administration Research and Theory* 10 (1): 111–35.

———. 2006. *Challenging the Performance Movement: Accountability, Complexity, and Democratic Values*. Washington, DC: Georgetown University Press.

Raiffa, Howard. 1982. *The Art and Science of Negotiation: How to Resolve Conflicts and Get the Best Out of Negotiation*. Cambridge, MA: Harvard University Press.

Randall, L., ed. 1996. *Reforming Mexico's Agrarian Reform*. Armonk, NY: M. E. Sharpe.

Reid, Andy. 2010. "Florida Supreme Court Endorses Everglades Restoration Land Buy, but Throws Out $50 Million 'Option' Once Planned for U.S. Sugar." *Sun Sentinel*, November 18. http://articles.sun-sentinel.com/2010-11-18/news/fl-supreme-court-everglades-deal-20101118_1_everglades-restoration-land-long-stalled-everglades-projects-land-deal.

Ribot, Jesse C., Arun Agrawal, and Anne M. Larson. 2006. "Recentralizing While Decentralizing: How National Governments Reappropriate Forest Resources." *World Development* 34 (11): 1864–86.

Ribot, Jesse C., and Nancy Lee Peluso. 2003. "A Theory of Access." *Rural Sociology* 68 (2): 153–81.

Ring, Peter Smith, and Andrew H. Van de Ven. 1994. "Development Processes of Cooperative Interorganizational Relationships." *Academy of Management Review* 19 (1): 90–118.

Rittel, Horst, and Melvin Webber. 1973. "Dilemmas in a General Theory of Planning." *Policy Sciences* 4 (2): 155–69.

Roberts, Nancy. 2004. "Public Deliberation in the Age of Direct Citizen Participation." *American Review of Public Administration* 34 (4): 315–53.

Romzek, Barbara S., Kelly LeRoux, and Jeannette M. Blackmar. 2012. "A Preliminary Theory of Informal Accountability among Network Organizational Actors." *Public Administration Review* 72 (3): 442–53.

Sabatier, Paul A. 1988. "An Advocacy Coalition Framework of Policy Change and the Role of Policy-Oriented Learning Therein." *Policy Sciences* 21 (2–3): 139–68.

Sabatier, Paul A., Will Focht, Mark Lubell, Zev Trachtenberg, Arnold Vedlitz, and Marty Matlock, eds. 2005. *Swimming Upstream: Collaborative Approaches to Watershed Management.* Cambridge, MA: MIT Press.

Sabatier, Paul A., and Hank Jenkins-Smith, eds. 1993. *Policy Change and Learning: An Advocacy Coalition Approach.* Boulder, CO: Westview Press.

Sabatier, Paul A., and Hank C. Jenkins-Smith. 1999. "The Advocacy Coalition Framework: An Assessment." In *Theories of the Policy Process,* edited by P. A. Sabatier. Boulder, CO: Westview Press.

Safford, Sean. 2009. *Why the Garden Club Couldn't Save Youngstown: The Transformation of the Rust Belt.* Cambridge, MA: Harvard University Press.

Saint-Onge, Hubert, and Charles Armstrong. 2004. *The Conductive Organization Building beyond Sustainability.* New York: Elsevier.

Salamon, Lester, ed. 2002. *The Tools of Government: A Guide to the New Governance.* New York: Oxford University Press.

Sancton, Andrew. 2005. "The Governance of Metropolitan Areas in Canada." *Public Administration and Development* 25 (4): 317–27.

———. 2008. *The Limits of Boundaries: Why City-Regions Cannot Be Self-Governing.* Montreal and Kingston: McGill–Queen's University Press.

Saravanan, V. S., Geoffrey T. McDonald, and Peter P. Mollinga. 2009. "Critical Review of Integrated Water Resources Management: Moving beyond Polarised Discourse." *Natural Resources Forum* 33 (1): 76–86.

Schlager, Edella. 1995. "Policy Making and Collective Action: Defining Coalitions within the Advocacy Coalition Framework." *Policy Sciences* 28 (3): 243–70.

———. 1999. "A Comparison of Frameworks, Theories, and Models of Policy Processes." In *Theories of the Policy Process,* edited by P. A. Sabatier. Boulder, CO: Westview Press.

———. 2007. "Community Management of Groundwater." In *The Agricultural Groundwater Revolution: Opportunities and Threats to Development,* edited by M. Giodano and K. G. Villholth. Wallingford, UK: CABI.

Schlosberg, David. 2003. "The Justice of Environmental Justice: Reconciling Equity, Recognition, and Participation in a Political Movement." In *Moral and Political Reasoning in Environmental Practice,* edited by A. Light and A. De-Shalit. Cambridge, MA: MIT Press.

Schmieder, Oscar. 1928. *Lower California Studies II: The Russian Colony of Guadalupe Valley.* Berkeley: University of California Press.

Schneider, Aaron. 2003. "Decentralization: Conceptualization and Measurement." *Studies in Comparative International Development* 38 (3): 32–56.

Schneider, Mark, John Scholz, Mark Lubell, Denisa Mindruta, and Mathew Edwardsen. 2003. "Building Consensual Institutions: Networks and the National Estuary Program." *American Journal of Political Science* 47 (1): 143–58.

Schwarz, Roger M. 1995. *Ground Rules for Effective Groups.* Chapel Hill: Institute of Government of University of North Carolina at Chapel Hill.

Scott, Christopher A., and Jeff M. Banister. 2008. "The Dilemma of Water Management

'Regionalization' in Mexico under Centralized Resource Allocation." *Water Resources* 24 (1): 61–74.

Scott, Tyler, and Craig W. Thomas. 2015. "Do Collaborative Groups Enhance Interorganizational Networks?" *Public Performance & Management Review* 38(4): 654–68.

Scott, W. Richard, and John W. Meyer. 1991. "The Organization of Societal Sectors: Propositions and Early Evidence." In *The New Institutionalism in Organizational Analysis*, edited by W. W. Powell and P. J. DiMaggio. Chicago: University of Chicago Press.

Selin, Steve, and Deborah Chavez. 1995. "Developing a Collaborative Model for Environmental Planning and Management." *Environmental Management* 19 (2): 189–95.

Sellers, Jeffery. 2002. *Governing from Below: Urban Regions and the Global Economy*. Cambridge: Cambridge University Press.

Serreze, Mark C., 2008. "Arctic Climate Change: Where Reality Exceeds Expectations." *Witness the Arctic* 13 (1): 1–4.

SFERTF (South Florida Ecosystem Restoration Task Force). 1997. *Charter, South Florida Ecosystem Restoration Task Force*. Davie, FL: Office of Everglades Restoration Initiatives of US Department of the Interior. www.evergladesrestoration.gov/content/tf.html.

———. 2002. *Task Force Protocol Regarding Consensus and Voting*. Davie, FL: Office of Everglades Restoration Initiatives of US Department of the Interior. www.evergladesrestoration.gov/content/tf.html.

———. 2011. *Enhanced Public and Stakeholder Engagement Protocol*. Davie, FL: Office of Everglades Restoration Initiatives of US Department of the Interior. www.evergladesrestoration.gov/content/cepp/cepp.html. [Accessed January 11, 2015].

Shah, Tushaar. 2008. *Taming the Anarchy: Groundwater Governance in South Asia*. Washington, DC: Resources for the Future Press.

Shah, Tushaar, Christopher Scott, and Stephanie Buechler. 2004. "Water Sector Reforms in Mexico: Lessons for India's New Water Policy." *Economic and Political Weekly* 39 (4): 361–70.

Shulski, Martha, and Gerd Wendler. 2007. *The Climate of Alaska*. Fairbanks: University of Alaska Press.

Sipe, Neil G., and Bruce Stiftel. 1995. "Mediating Environmental Enforcement Disputes: How Well Does It Work?" *Environmental Impact Assessment Review* 15 (2): 139–56.

Sirianni, Carmen. 2009. *Investing in Democracy: Engaging Citizens in Collaborative Governance*. Washington, DC: Brookings Institution Press.

Steinhauser, Paul. 2014. "CNN Poll: Trust in Government at All-Time Low." *CNN Politics*. http://politicalticker.blogs.cnn.com/2014/08/08/cnn-poll-trust-in-government-at-all-time-low-2/.

Stoker, Gerry. 2004. *Designing Institutions for Governance in Complex Environments: Normative Rational Choice and Cultural Institutional Theories Explored and Contrasted*. ESRC Fellowship Paper 1. London: Economic and Social Research Council.

Stone, Clarence.1989. *Regime Politics: Governing Atlanta 1946–1988*. Lawrence: University Press of Kansas.

———. 2004. "It's More than the Economy After All: Continuing the Debate about Urban Regimes." *Journal of Urban Affairs* 26 (1): 1–19.

———. 2005. "Looking Back to Look Forward: Reflections on Urban Regime Analysis." *Urban Affairs Review* 40 (3): 309–41.

Storper, Michael. 2013. *Keys to the City: How Economics, Institutions, Social Interaction, and Politics Shape Development*. Princeton, NJ: Princeton University Press.

Stren, Richard., Eleanor Rae, Frank Cunningham, Lionel Feldman, Gabriel Eidelman,

Aaron Moore, Andrew Sancton, Andre Sorenson, and Mariana Valverde. 2010. *The Governance of Toronto: Challenges of Size and Complexity.* Toronto: Cities Centre.

Susskind, Lawrence, and Jeffrey Cruikshank. 1987. *Breaking the Impasse: Consensual Approaches to Resolving Public Disputes.* New York: Basic Books.

Susskind, Larry, Sarah McKearnan, and Jennifer Thomas-Larmer, eds. 1999. *The Consensus-Building Handbook: A Comprehensive Guide to Reaching Agreement.* Thousand Oaks, CA: Sage.

Swyngedouw, Erik. 2005. "Governance Innovation and the Citizen: The Janus Face of Governance-beyond-the-State." *Urban Studies* 42 (11): 1991–2006.

Tang, Shui Yan, and Daniel A. Mazmanian. 2010. *Understanding Collaborative Governance from the Structural Choice Politics, IAD, and Transaction Cost Perspectives.* http://ssrn.com/abstract=1516851 or http://dx.doi.org/10.2139/ssrn.1516851.

Thomas, Craig W. 2003. *Bureaucratic Landscapes: Interagency Cooperation and the Preservation of Biodiversity.* Cambridge, MA: MIT Press.

Thomas, Craig W., and Tomas M. Koontz. 2011. "Research Designs for Evaluating the Impact of Community-Based Management on Natural Resource Conservation." *Journal of Natural Resources Policy Research* 3 (2): 97–111.

Thomas, John C. 1995. *Public Participation in Public Decisions: New Skills and Strategies for Public Managers.* San Francisco: Jossey-Bass.

———. 2012. *Citizen, Customer, Partner: Engaging the Public in Public Management.* Armonk, NY: M. E. Sharpe.

Thomson, Ann Marie, and James L. Perry. 2006. "Collaboration Processes: Inside the Black Box." *Public Administration Review* 66 (s1): 20–32.

Toronto City Summit Alliance. 2003. *Enough Talk: An Action Plan for the Toronto Region.* Toronto: Toronto City Summit Alliance. http://civicaction.ca/wp-content/uploads/2010/12/TCSA_report.pdf.

Torres, Lars H. 2003. *Deliberative Democracy: A Survey of the Field.* Washington, DC: AmericaSpeaks.

Turrini, Alex, Daniele Cristofoli, Francesca Frosini, and Greta Nasi. 2010. "Networking Literature about Determinants of Network Effectiveness." *Public Administration* 88 (2): 528–50.

Ulibarri, Nicola. 2015a. "Collaboration in Federal Hydropower Licensing: Impacts on Process, Outputs, and Outcomes." *Public Performance & Management Review* 38(4): 578–606.

———. 2015b. "Tracing Process to Performance of Collaborative Governance: A Comparative Case Study of Federal Hydropower Licensing." *Policy Studies Journal* 43(2): 283–308.

United Way of Greater Toronto. 2004. *Poverty by Postal Code: The Geography of Neighbourhood Poverty, 1981–2001.* Toronto: United Way of Greater Toronto and Canadian Council on Social Development.

US Institute for Environmental Conflict Resolution. 2014. "Project Case Summary: Military Community Compatibility Committee (MC3)." www.udall.gov/OurPrograms/Institute/ProjectCaseSummary.aspx?Project=877.

Wagner, Cheryl L., and Maria E. Fernandez-Gimenez. 2009. "Effects of Community-Based Collaborative Group Characteristics on Social Capital." *Environmental Management* 44 (4): 632–45.

Weber, Edward P. 2003. *Bringing Society Back In: Grassroots Ecosystem Management: Accountability and Sustainable Communities.* Cambridge, MA: MIT Press.

Weible, Christopher, Paul A. Sabatier, Hank C. Jenkins-Smith, Danial Nohrstedt, Adam

Douglas Henry, and Peter de Leon. 2011. "A Quarter Century of the Advocacy Coalition Framework: Special Issue." *Policy Studies Journal* 39 (3): 349–60.

Wester, Philippus, Ricardo Sandoval Minero, and Jaime Hoogesteger. 2011. "Assessment of the Development of Aquifer Management Councils (COTAS) for Sustainable Groundwater Management in Guanajuato, Mexico." *Hydrogeology Journal* 19 (4): 889–99.

Wester, Philippus, Christopher A. Scott, and Martin Burton. 2005. "River Basin Closure and Institutional Change in Mexico's Lerma-Chapala Basin." In *Irrigation and River Basin Management: Options for Governance and Institutions*, edited by M. Svendsen. Wallingford, UK: CABI.

Wilder, Margaret. 2005. "Water, Power and Social Transformation: Neoliberal Reforms in Mexico." *VertigO: La Revue en Sciences de l'environnement* 6 (2): 1–5.

Wilder, Margaret, and Patricia Romero Lankao. 2006. "Paradoxes of Decentralization: Water Reform and Social Implications in Mexico." *World Development* 34 (11): 1977–95.

Wilder, Margaret, and Scott Whiteford. 2006. "Flowing Uphill toward Money: Groundwater Management and Ejidal Producers in Mexico's Free Trade Environment." In *Changing Structure of Mexico: Political, Social, and Economic Prospects*, edited by L. Randall. Armonk, NY: M. E. Sharpe.

Wolfe, David A., and Allison Bramwell. 2008. "Innovation, Creativity and Governance: Social Dynamics of Economic Performance in City-Regions." *Innovation: Management Policy & Practice* 10 (2–3): 170–82.

Wood, Donna J., and Barbara Gray. 1991. "Toward a Comprehensive Theory of Collaboration." *Journal of Applied Behavioral Science* 27 (2): 139–62.

Wright, Deil S. 1988. *Understanding Intergovernmental Relations*. Belmont, CA: Duxbury Press.

Yang, Kaifeng. 2011. "The Sisyphean Fate of Government-Wide Performance Accountability Reforms: Federal Performance Management Efforts and Employees' Daily Work 2002–2008." *Public Performance & Management Review* 35 (1): 149–76.

Yarger, Sam T., and Gwendolynne P. Yarger. 1978. "And So We Asked Ourselves: About Teacher Centers." *Theory into Practice* 17 (3): 248–57.

About the Authors and Contributors

The Authors

Kirk Emerson is a professor of practice in collaborative governance at the University of Arizona School of Government and Public Policy, with joint appointments in the School of Planning and School of Public Health. She is also a faculty associate of the University of Arizona's Udall Center for Studies in Public Policy and of Syracuse University's Program for Advancement of Research on Conflict and Collaboration in the Maxwell School of Citizenship and Public Affairs. Her research focuses on collaborative governance, interagency cooperation, and conflict management, particularly related to climate change, public lands management, and border security. Her recent research has been published in the *Journal of Public Administration Research and Theory*, *Public Performance and Management Review*, *Conflict Resolution Quarterly*, *Environmental Management*, and in several book chapters. She has had a long-standing career in environmental conflict resolution and collaborative problem solving as a practitioner, trainer, researcher, and administrator. She currently serves on the working board of the National Institute for Civil Discourse, and from 1998 to 2008 was the founding director of the US Institute for Environmental Conflict Resolution of the Morris K. Udall Foundation. She received her PhD in political science and public policy from Indiana University–Bloomington.

Tina Nabatchi is an associate professor of public administration and international affairs at the Maxwell School of Citizenship and Public Affairs of Syracuse University, where she also co-directs the Collaborative Governance Initiative for the Program for the Advancement of Research on Conflict and Collaboration. Her research focuses on collaborative governance, citizen participation, and conflict resolution. She has published articles in numerous journals, including the *Journal of Public Administration Research and Theory*, *Public Administration Review*, *Public Performance and Management Review*, *American Review of Public Administration*, *National Civic Review*, and *Conflict Resolution Quarterly*. She has also published several book chapters, monographs, research reports, and white papers. She is the lead editor of *Democracy in Motion: Evaluating the Practice and Impact of Deliberative Civic Engagement* (Oxford University Press, 2012); and coauthor of *Public Participation for 21st-Century*

Democracy (with Matt Leighninger; Jossey-Bass, 2015). She received her PhD in public affairs from Indiana University–Bloomington.

The Contributors

Allison Bramwell—the author of chapter 5, a case study of Civic Action in Toronto—is an assistant professor in the Department of Political Science at the University of North Carolina at Greensboro, where she teaches urban politics, public administration, and community and economic development. Consistent with her overarching interest in the social dynamics of community resilience and economic performance, her current research focuses on collaborative urban governance, regional economic development, and workforce development, with an empirical emphasis on the emerging digital economy and renewable energy industries in restructuring city-regions in Canada and the United States. Her recent research has been published by *Urban Affairs Review* and *Research Policy*, and she recently coedited the book *Governing Urban Economies: Innovation and Inclusion in Canadian City-Regions* (with Neil Bradford; University of Toronto Press, 2014).

Robin Bronen—the author of chapter 6, a case study of the Newtok Planning Group in Alaska—is a human rights attorney and has been researching the climate-induced relocation of Native Alaska communities since 2007. She is a senior research scientist at the University of Alaska's Fairbanks Institute of Arctic Biology. She is also the executive director of the Alaska Institute for Justice, which in 2012 was awarded the Federal Bureau of Investigation's Director's Community Service Award. The Alaska Bar Association awarded her the 2007 Robert Hickerson Public Service award and the 2012 International Human Rights Award, and Soroptimist International awarded her the 2012 Advancing the Rights of Women Award.

Andrea K. Gerlak—the coauthor of chapter 3's case illustration on the Everglades Restoration Task Force—is the director of academic development at the International Studies Association and a senior policy associate with the Udall Center for Studies in Public Policy at the University of Arizona. Her research interests are in the fields of public policy, institutional theory, collaborative governance, natural resource management, and water governance. She studies the conditions supporting collective action, the interface between science and policy, and institutional change and adaptability. She received a BA and MA from the University of Nevada, Las Vegas, and a PhD in political science from the University of Arizona.

Tanya Heikkila—the coauthor of chapter 3's case illustration on the Everglades Restoration Task Force—is an associate professor and doctoral program director in the School of Public Affairs at the University of Colorado Denver. Her research interests are in the fields of environmental policy and governance, and comparative institutional analysis. She has examined interstate water conflicts and cooperation in the United States, conflicts and cooperation related to hydraulic fracturing, the organization and performance of large-scale ecosystem restoration programs, and the institutions for coordinating groundwater and surface water management. She received an MPA and a PhD from the University of Arizona.

Chantelise Pells—the author of chapter 7, a case study of the Comité Técnicas de Aguas Subterraneas Guadalupe—received her PhD in geography from the University of California, Davis, in 2014. Her research interests focus broadly on community-based environmental resource governance, water governance, and socioenvironmental sustainability. Her dissertation research is a case study of participation dynamics of the local groundwater user association in Northern Baja California. Her work specifically focuses on power relations in local governance and the related socioenvironmental effects. Her recent publications related to her dissertation research include a feasibility report for a water fund for the Nature Conservancy. As a University of California, Davis, postdoctoral researcher, she is conducting research for a project funded by the US Department of Agriculture that focuses on the institutional analysis of agriculture pest management.

Index

CPSIA information can be obtained
at www.ICGtesting.com
Printed in the USA
BVHW07s0516170818
524653BV00003B/154/P